D0205857

THE FEDERAL BUDGET AND FINANCIAL SYSTEM

Recent Titles from QUORUM BOOKS

Utilizing Consultants Successfully: A Guide for Management in Business,
Government, the Arts and Professions
Herman Holtz

International Broadcasting by Satellite: Issues of Regulation, Barriers to
Communication
Jon T. Powell

Corporate and Commercial Free Speech: First Amendment Protection of
Expression in Business
Edwin P. Rome and William H. Roberts

The Impact of Office Automation on Clerical Employment, 1985–2000:
Forecasting Techniques and Plausible Futures in Banking and Insurance
*J. David Roessner, Robert M. Mason, Alan L. Porter, Frederick A. Rossini, A. Perry
Schwartz, and Keith R. Nelms*

The Learning Curve: A Management Accounting Tool
Ahmed Belkaoui

Willing Workers: The Work Ethics in Japan, England, and the United States
Tamotsu Sengoku, translated by Koichi Ezaki and Yuko Ezaki

University-Industry Research Partnerships: The Major Legal Issues in Research and
Development Agreements
Bernard D. Reams, Jr.

Managing the Corporate Image: The Key to Public Trust
James G. Gray, Jr.

Interstate Banking: Strategies for a New Era: Conference Proceedings
Federal Reserve Bank of Atlanta, sponsor

Marketing with Seminars and Newsletters
Herman Holtz

Corporate PACs and Federal Campaign Financing Laws: Use or Abuse of Power?
Ann B. Matasar

A Practitioner's Guide to Financial Statement Disclosures
Paul Munter and Thomas A. Ratcliffe

THE FEDERAL BUDGET AND FINANCIAL SYSTEM

A Management Perspective

JOSEPH F. MORAGLIO
AND
HARRY D. KERRIGAN

QUORUM BOOKS
NEW YORK • WESTPORT, CONNECTICUT • LONDON

Library of Congress Cataloging-in-Publication Data

Moraglio, Joseph F.
    The federal budget and financial system.

    Bibliography: p.
    Includes index.
    1. Budget—United States. 2. United States—
Appropriations and expenditures. I. Kerrigan,
Harry D. II. Title.
HJ2051.M65 1986   353.0072'2   85-12303
ISBN 0-89930-127-4 (lib. bdg. : alk. paper)

Library of Congress Catalog Card Number: 85-12303
ISBN: 0-89930-127-4

First published in 1986 by Quorum Books

Greenwood Press, Inc.
88 Post Road West, Westport, Connecticut 06881

Printed in the United States of America

∞™

The paper used in this book complies with the
Permanent Paper Standard issued by the National
Information Standards Organization (Z39.48-1984).

10 9 8 7 6 5 4 3 2 1

Copyright Acknowledgments
Selections from *The Wall Street Journal* are reprinted by permission of *The Wall
Street Journal* © Dow Jones and Company, Inc. 1984. All rights reserved.

Exhibit 5 is excerpted from Gail Makinen and Craig Simmons, "Perspectives on the
Federal Budget Deficit," *GAO Review*, Spring 1984.

CONTENTS

EXHIBITS

FINANCIAL STATEMENTS ————————————

PREFACE

Currently, our federal government must collect, invest, and pay nearly two trillion dollars each year. The federal budget and financial systems employed to account for and control those receipts and disbursements are complex and unique. Most federal agencies have their own financial systems and specialists, but the Department of the Treasury's Financial Management Service oversees the federal government's overall financial operations. It receives periodic financial reports from individual agencies and prepares consolidated financial summaries for the use of the Congress, the President, and the American people. The Office of Management and Budget (OMB) annually reviews, analyzes, and evaluates the agencies' budget requests and puts together the President's budget which is sent to the Congress. The General Accounting Office (GAO) formulates basic accounting principles and standards to be observed by the federal agencies. In such an environment, timely, accurate, and accessible information can be created and disseminated only by a combination of competent financial managers, coordination among directing authorities, and sophisticated budget and financial systems.

Much is being done to improve the present accounting systems and procedures used by the federal government. OMB has developed and is implementing several programs and has published relevant guidelines. Several departments and agencies are installing advanced accounting systems. Appendix B is a digest of the accounting principles and standards for federal agencies recently issued by the GAO. The authors hope that this book will play a small role in the overall process of improvement and understanding by providing the reader with an indepth analysis and explanation of the current process.

A follow-up of this effort is the work of the President's Private

Sector Survey on Cost Control (the Grace Commission) with Peter J. Grace serving as chairman. President Reagan established it on June 30, 1982. The commission produced 36 task force reports, all addressed to related aspects of federal management principles and practices and how they can be developed further to improve the government's effectiveness and efficiency.

This book describes and illustrates the structure and process of the federal budget and financial system in a meaningful manner. It discusses and presents government-wide combined financial statements and the budgeting, accounting, and reporting process of a federal agency.

The illustrative financial statements are customized in the sense that they are prepared especially for this book for discussion, analysis, and interpretation. Such exhibits provide the best means to present and discuss the financial effects of policies and practices followed by the federal government. The cumulative effect is a clear and meaningful presentation of how the system is structured and how it works. Only with a good understanding of how the system works, can efficient and effective improvements be made.

The sequence of the topics is from the macro to the micro, that is, from a government-wide basis to an operating unit or agency basis. The order of the book can be easily reversed. The dollar amounts used throughout the book are used for illustrative purposes and are not the latest actual amounts for the federal government. Such amounts can be readily obtained from the Treasury Department if the reader so desires.

Mr. Moraglio is an employee of the American Institute of CPAs, and his views, as expressed in this book, do not necessarily reflect the views of the AICPA. Official positions of the AICPA are determined through certain specific committee procedures, due process, and deliberation.

A preface is a good occasion for authors to acknowledge their debt to others. First, a special tribute is due to the following, unsung all, who in their years of service in government welcomed, encouraged, and supported progressive ideas for advancing the quality of the federal financial system. We have in mind the past and present Comptrollers General of the United States; the past and present Secretaries of the Treasury; and the past and present Directors of the Office of Management and Budget. We are also in debt to the growing number, still too few, of researchers and writers in this field. A note of appreciation is due to the following members of the present administration, who kindly read parts of the book before publication and offered helpful commentaries that are reflected in every chapter: Assistant Secretary of the Navy R. H. Conn and members of his staff, especially Mr. John Rush; Mr. Marcus W. Page, Deputy Commissioner Financial Management Service, Department of the Treasury, and members of his staff, especially Mr. Michael T. Smokovich and Mr. Alan Evans.

Finally, the authors would like to thank their families for their patience and understanding during the writing of this book. Special thanks go to Carol and Beth Moraglio for their hours spent proofreading the manuscript.

THE FEDERAL BUDGET AND FINANCIAL SYSTEM

1.

ORGANIZATIONAL STRUCTURE OF THE FEDERAL GOVERNMENT

INTRODUCTION

The budgeting, accounting, and reporting concepts and procedures discussed and illustrated in this book are unique to the federal government. They have evolved over time and reflect the social, economic, and political forces that have shaped the government's financial organization and management. Three outstanding characteristics set the federal structure apart from state and local governments and explain the way it is organized and managed:

1. *Wide Dispersion of Activities.* A wide dispersion of activities exists in relatively independent agencies or organizational units in which budgetary and accounting functions are primarily attuned to the needs and concerns at activity level.

2. *Decentralization of Management.* Dispersal of activities has created a large degree of decentralized management, including financial management, within each agency or organizational unit, especially the larger ones.

3. *Influence of National Politics and Legislation.* National politics and legislation lie behind much of the formulations of the government's financial policies and practices.[1]

Those conditions and circumstances have shaped the federal government's financial and accounting model to date. Affected are programs and activities administered and conducted everywhere—within the country and overseas. Consistent with this phenomenon, management authority is delegated extensively, although the reins of government are held centrally. Control of decentralized activities is achieved the only way possible: through systems or channels of communication carrying information flows back and forth. The network of communications spans continents, the seas between them, and the air and space above them. The flows of information feed forward downstream to units wherever located and, in the other direction, feed back upstream to national headquarters in Washington. A very large part of these flows includes financial information in the nature of budgetary and accounting data.

The role and process of this country's government begins with Congress, which initiates, directs, finances, and evaluates federal activities and operations. Organizationally, the President and the vast executive branch under the presidency carry out congressional mandates. For political reasons, Congress and the President prefer to act as co-partners, but constitutionally they are separate and coordinated branches. They constitute, along with the judicial branch, the system of checks and balances that the founding fathers built into the national government structure. Congress asserts its will and policies by passing legislation. The President can either sign or veto a bill as passed by the Congress. If he vetoes it, the bill is sent back to the Congress where it can override the President's veto by a two-thirds majority. If the President signs the bill, or the Congress overrides his veto, it becomes law. At this point the separation of powers is evident, since the implementation of the laws is left to the executive branch, including reporting the results of actual experience. At the same time, the judicial branch is expected to monitor the actions of the other two branches to see that they meet the tests of fairness and equity in response to people who may challenge their actions.

HOW THE GOVERNMENT IS ORGANIZED

A visual glimpse of the major elements of organization of the federal government is provided in Exhibit 1. Highlighted are the three principal branches: the legislative, the executive, and the judicial. In fact, the three branches are as separate and independent as they appear visually in the chart and as they are required to be by the provisions of the Constitution. This approach prevents the same branch from enacting the laws, then putting the laws into effect, and, as necessary, interpreting the laws. (The essentials of this model have been adopted by state and local governments.)

The chart also accurately conveys the dominance of the executive branch in terms of resources received and used and the sheer size and complexity of the organization in place to carry out its functions and missions. Following are the major components of this branch:

Executive Office of the President. Immediate staff of the presidency.

Executive Departments. The principal conduits of organization and action of the government, as established by long tradition, though modified and ex-

The Government of the United States

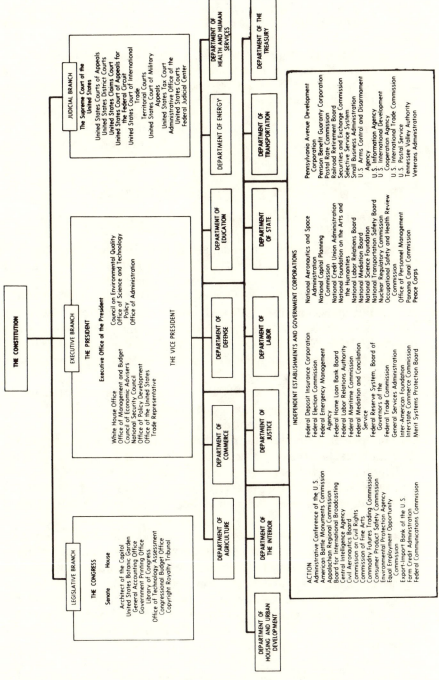

THE CONSTITUTION

LEGISLATIVE BRANCH

THE CONGRESS

Senate   House

Architect of the Capitol
United States Botanic Garden
General Accounting Office
Government Printing Office
Library of Congress
Office of Technology Assessment
Congressional Budget Office
Copyright Royalty Tribunal

EXECUTIVE BRANCH

THE PRESIDENT

Executive Office of the President

White House Office
Office of Management and Budget
Council of Economic Advisers
National Security Council
Office of Policy Development
Office of the United States
Trade Representative

Council on Environmental Quality
Office of Science and Technology
Policy
Office of Administration

THE VICE PRESIDENT

JUDICIAL BRANCH

**The Supreme Court of the
United States**

United States Courts of Appeals
United States District Courts
United States Claims Court
United States Court of Appeals for
the Federal Circuit
United States Court of International
Trade
Territorial Courts
United States Court of Military
Appeals
United States Tax Court
Administrative Office of the
United States Courts
Federal Judicial Center

DEPARTMENT OF
HOUSING AND URBAN
DEVELOPMENT

DEPARTMENT OF
AGRICULTURE

DEPARTMENT OF
COMMERCE

DEPARTMENT OF
DEFENSE

DEPARTMENT OF
EDUCATION

DEPARTMENT OF
ENERGY

DEPARTMENT OF
HEALTH AND HUMAN
SERVICES

DEPARTMENT OF
THE INTERIOR

DEPARTMENT OF
JUSTICE

DEPARTMENT OF
LABOR

DEPARTMENT
OF STATE

DEPARTMENT OF
TRANSPORTATION

DEPARTMENT OF THE
TREASURY

INDEPENDENT ESTABLISHMENTS AND GOVERNMENT CORPORATIONS

ACTION
Administrative Conference of the U.S.
American Battle Monuments Commission
Appalachian Regional Commission
Board for International Broadcasting
Central Intelligence Agency
Civil Aeronautics Board
Commission on Civil Rights
Commission of Fine Arts
Commodity Futures Trading Commission
Consumer Product Safety Commission
Environmental Protection Agency
Equal Employment Opportunity
Commission
Export-Import Bank of the U.S.
Farm Credit Administration
Federal Communications Commission

Federal Deposit Insurance Corporation
Federal Election Commission
Federal Emergency Management
Agency
Federal Home Loan Bank Board
Federal Labor Relations Authority
Federal Maritime Commission
Federal Mediation and Conciliation
Service
Federal Reserve System, Board of
Governors of the
Federal Trade Commission
General Services Administration
Inter-American Foundation
Interstate Commerce Commission
Merit Systems Protection Board

National Aeronautics and Space
Administration
National Capital Planning
Commission
National Credit Union Administration
National Foundation on the Arts and
the Humanities
National Labor Relations Board
National Mediation Board
National Science Foundation
National Transportation Safety Board
Nuclear Regulatory Commission
Occupational Safety and Health Review
Commission
Office of Personnel Management
Panama Canal Commission
Peace Corps

Pennsylvania Avenue Development
Corporation
Pension Benefit Guaranty Corporation
Postal Rate Commission
Railroad Retirement Board
Securities and Exchange Commission
Selective Service System
Small Business Administration
U.S. Arms Control and Disarmament
Agency
U.S. Information Agency
U.S. International Development
Cooperation Agency
U.S. International Trade Commission
U.S. Postal Service
Tennessee Valley Authority
Veterans Administration

panded from time to time to adjust to the contemporary needs of the country, as indicated by the 13 segments shown in the latest chart. (The heads, or Secretaries as they are called, of the executive departments make up the President's Cabinet.)

Independent Agencies, Boards, Commissions, Authorities, and Federal Corporations. Currently, some 57 individual organizational elements are identified and listed in the chart. They are intended to cope with problem areas best suited to their responsibilities. Some of the organizations are transitory and cease to exist when their mandates expire, but most of them are specialist organizations. A number of the latter are huge in size, and form the group from which new executive departments are chosen when political advocacy is strong enough to counter political opposition.

THE PRESIDENT AND THE EXECUTIVE BRANCH

The executive branch of the federal government is made up of large and small departments and agencies. As used in this book, the term *agency* includes any executive department or independent agency or both. They are relatively free of central governance in keeping with the dispersed activities and the multiplicity and size of the functions assigned to them. The agencies range from tiny single offices to immense national and international enterprises managing huge resources and conducting their affairs through multi-layered and far-flung activities. Nevertheless, each agency is subject to the direction, coordination, and control of the President, no matter how broadly its mandates may be stated.

Since the President obviously cannot give much attention to the internal operation of each agency, he assigns responsibility for running the agencies to presidential appointees. This enables the President to apportion his time to the more urgent matters facing him and the nation in the areas of international, domestic, and political issues. Although his staff has grown substantially over the years, it is still relatively small, and he generally tries to prevent it from actually coming between himself and agency heads, including members of the Cabinet.

Certain problems (especially those dealing with international security) cross the lines of two or more agencies. This requires the President's coordination to the extent necessary to avoid differences, as well as his decisions on major high-level policies. Although the Cabinet would appear to be the President's top board of planning and control, it is too unwieldly a group and generally tends to push the viewpoints of the respective agencies represented. Thus, some Presidents are inclined to use the Cabinet in a very limited degree for consultation and coordination of problems in formal meetings. A much more effective instrument for top planning and control are a few small committees of agency heads that personally assist the President. The most notable of these are the National Security Council and the Council of Economic Advisors.

DEPARTMENTS AND AGENCIES

A department or agency is one that is separately budgeted and funded pursuant to an explicit public law authorizing its program(s). It receives a separate annual appropriation from the Congress but only after the agency's officials appear before the designated committees of Congress to explain, defend, and propose the financing for an upcoming year. In the larger agencies, the appearance of an agency head in congressional hearings on its budget is followed by his or her top assistants, each concentrating the data in hand to the affairs of the immediate segment for which the assistant is responsible.

The heads of each federal department or agency are primarily and directly responsible to the President for the management of their agencies. Since they are appointed by the President (and confirmed by the Senate), the President can remove them for cause, such as for unsatisfactory performance.

But agency heads are also accountable to the Congress for the satisfactory performance of their agency, including observance of the many laws affecting administration of their agency's affairs.[2] Presidential appointments of agency heads (and many lesser agency officials) are subject to review and confirmation of the Senate in a time-honored proceeding known as getting the Senate's advice and consent. Later, after the officials are in office, they can be impeached by the Senate and tried for malfeasance (misconduct).

Agency heads and other officials and employees are also subject to criminal and civil punishment in the event of violation of laws affecting the administration of each agency. In practice, these legal punishments are seldom inflicted because agency officials not only obey laws they are sworn to uphold, but they generally respect even the wishes of the Congress and its committees. Such respect is no doubt due to Congress's broad powers, especially its power over each agency's budget.

Statutory Prerogatives of a Federal Agency

The head of an agency and his or her management staff operate as a fully accountable entity, with rights and privileges commensurate with such accountability. Each entity designs its own financial management system that is capable of planning and controlling the agency's budget and activities. The design must provide for adequate internal controls and periodic financial statements.

EXHIBIT 2
Consumer Product Safety Commission

The Consumer Product Safety Commission is an independent Federal regulatory agency established by the Consumer Product Safety Act, approved October 27, 1972 (86 Stat. 1207; 15 U.S.C. 2051). In addition to the authority created by the Consumer Product Safety Act, the Commission has responsibility for implementing provisions of the Flammable Fabrics Act (67 Stat. 111; 15 U.S.C. 1191), the Poison Prevention Packaging Act of 1970 (84 Stat. 1670; 15 U.S.C. 1471), the Federal Hazardous Substances Act (74 Stat. 372; 15 U.S.C. 1261), and the act of August 2, 1956 (70 Stat. 953; 15 U.S.C. 1211) which prohibits the transportation of refrigerators without door safety devices. **Functions and Activities** To help protect the public from unreasonable risks of injury associated with consumer products, the Commission:	Requires manufacturers to report products that could create substantial product hazards; Requires, where appropriate, corrective action with respect to specific substantially hazardous consumer products already in commerce; Collects information on consumer product-related injuries and maintains a comprehensive Injury Information Clearinghouse. Conducts research on consumer product hazards; Encourages and assists in the development of voluntary standards related to the safety of consumer products; Establishes, where appropriate, mandatory consumer product standards; Bans, where appropriate, hazardous consumer products; and Conducts outreach programs for consumers, industry, and local governments.

These prerogatives are rooted in the laws and amendments that created the agency and defined its mission. The statutory prerogatives give an agency its authority, identity, and responsibility. The law states what an agency may and may not do. The President and his aides cannot interfere with this mandate and neither can Congress, except by changing the governing law. To illustrate how an agency's prerogatives are derived from statutory law, consider the facts relating to the Consumer Product Safety Commission presented in Exhibit 2.

CENTRAL DIRECTING AUTHORITIES

The work of federal agencies, though scattered far and wide, is nevertheless subject to the coordinating and controlling directives of three central directing authorities. Two of these, the Treasury Department

(Treasury) and the Office of Management and Budget (OMB), are in the executive branch, and are primarily responsible to the President. The third, the General Accounting Office (GAO), is an independent authority that is primarily responsible to the Congress, and is part of the legislative branch of the government.

Treasury Department

By law, the Treasury Department is the government's banker, collector of federal revenues, and manager of the federal debt, popularly known as the national or public debt. In addition, Treasury is responsible directly for government-wide financial reporting. The responsibility is fulfilled mainly in terms of reporting cash receipts and disbursements in relation to appropriations of Congress, but the flow of published data is enormous. It is this function of Treasury that traditionally gives it the authority to prescribe forms, formats, and content of periodic financial reports to be prepared and submitted by federal agencies to Treasury.

Treasury's Fiscal Roles

Treasury fills a number of specific fiscal roles which include the following:

- Prepares financial reports for the government as a whole;
- Maintains central records (accounts) for the government;
- Manages central depository accounts in Federal Reserve Banks and in other banks designated by Treasury for receiving federal tax collections and other receipts;
- Operates regional disbursing offices that serve most of the government's civilian agencies in issuing checks and receiving collections; and
- Exercises technical control of collecting and disbursing offices located in certain agencies from whom periodic reports are required covering cash transactions and balances (for use in maintaining Treasury's central records).

Other divisions within the Treasury Department having important responsibilities for carrying out Treasury's financial functions include:

Internal Revenue Service; U.S. Customs Service. Administers the tax laws, collects taxes and duties.

Bureau of the Public Debt. Manages the issuance of new debt obligations and redemptions of matured debt obligations; maintains internal control for management of the public debt.

Bureau of Engraving and Printing. Manages the printing, storage, and distribution of Federal Reserve Currency (that is, Federal Reserve Notes issued by Federal Reserve Banks through their member banks to the public, by charging their bank accounts) and U.S. postage stamps.

Bureau of the Mint. Manages the manufacture, storage, and distribution of U.S. coins or metal currency issued by Federal Reserve Banks to whom the coins are sold by Treasury; the acquisition, storage, and sale of gold and silver bullion; and the acquisition and storage of coinage metals (for manufacture into coins).

Relationships with the Federal Reserve System. Manages the government's relationships with the Federal Reserve Banks and their central Board of Governors, the Federal Reserve Board, as further discussed at the end of this chapter.

Office of Management and Budget

The functions of OMB are to review, analyze, and evaluate annually the budget requests of all federal agencies. After reviewing, analyzing, and evaluating, including reducing or expanding the agencies' budget requests, OMB then puts together the President's budget. Thus formulated, the President's budget is sent to Congress to support the President's appropriation proposals. However, and most significantly, the agencies themselves actually explain and justify the details of their respective budgets in budget hearings before the designated committees of Congress, namely, the Appropriation Committee of the House and the Appropriation Committee of the Senate. By-plays of the parties are to be expected. Thus, an agency has the opportunity to present justifications of certain program proposals that OMB may have reduced or eliminated, hoping for adjustments that restore, in whole or in part, cuts made by OMB. However, since agency heads are presidential appointees, as is the director of OMB, they usually support the President's budget.

Appropriations made by Congress are directly for the use of the respective agencies. This is subject, however, to OMB's legal authority to govern the rate at which expenditures are made; that is, the timing of expenditures. OMB also may withhold altogether amounts appropriated that it does not think should be made available for the present to agencies, keeping congressional committees informed of the actions taken.

OMB also is increasing its involvement in the ongoing business of day-to-day government. Thus, it has the authority to prescribe the accounting basis for budget and budget-related reports. The authority is quite comprehensive: it extends over the form, basis, scope, and content of such reports, as required to be submitted to it by the agencies. Following are some additional oversight roles, all bearing on ways and means of raising the quality of government operation by increasing efficiency of performance and through tighter internal controls, reducing (if not eliminating) incidents of fraud and waste of federal resources:

1. Improving and expediting communication and information flow, including computerized information systems;
2. Improving the productivity of organizational resources, in terms of both human and physical elements; and
3. Closer monitoring of internal controls in agency organizations by regular reviews and evaluations against standards of control criteria as set by expertise outside an agency organization, namely, the General Accounting Office (GAO) in consultation with OMB.[3]

A practical question is: Should agency budgets be increased to finance the cost of designing and installing tighter systems of internal controls? The authors believe the answer is yes, because the savings of costs resulting from improved internal controls should be more than adequate to finance the cost of making the system changes. There are presently a number of initiatives under way in OMB, the agencies, and GAO to improve the federal financial management systems.

Organizationally, OMB is part of the Executive Office of the President and is directly under the President. OMB advises the President almost on a daily basis on the business of government. The director of OMB is the President's director of the federal budget. A summary of the work of OMB is presented below.

- Develops and researches the organizational structure and management procedures of the executive branch of the government;
- Develops and researches the executive branch's coordinating mechanisms and interagency cooperation;
- Oversees the preparation of the President's budget and formulates the government's fiscal program on behalf of the President;
- Clears and coordinates proposed legislation and recommends related action on the part of the President;
- Develops and researches government regulatory reforms and reduction of government paperwork;
- Considers and clears proposed Executive Orders signed by the President;
- Develops and researches ways and means of improving the government's communication and information systems;
- Provides the President with data on program performance throughout the executive branch;

- Provides the President with data on productivity of federal workers;
- Develops and researches, through a special Office of Federal Procurement Policy, ways and means of improving the economy, efficiency, and effectiveness of the federal procurement process.

OMB Directives

Periodically, OMB issues directives that provide guidelines to accountants, auditors, financial managers, and others in the form of circulars. The following are representative of the subject matter of these circulars:

A-21   Cost principles for contracts with educational institutions

A-87   Cost principles applicable to contracts with state and local governments

A-122   Cost principles for contracts with nonprofit organizations

A-123   Policies and standards in establishing and maintaining internal controls over the government's revenues, expenses, receipts, disbursements, liabilities, and property.

General Accounting Office

A traditional prerogative of each federal agency is to design and operate its own information system, including its accounting system and the related financial reporting, internal auditing, and other procedures for internal control. However, all aspects of operating a federal agency, including the financial management of the agency, are subject to the oversight of the General Accounting Office, either as legally required under standing federal statutes or as a result of specific requests by Congress. GAO is headed by the Comptroller General of the United States. The oversight responsibility of the GAO for the financial management of federal agencies is of particular importance in two respects:

1. GAO formulates basic accounting principles and standards for observance by federal agencies. (Appendix A gives GAO's glossary of federal terms and definitions, which is the only such aid published, and Appendix B presents a table of contents and a digest of selected sections of GAO's 1984 edition of federal accounting principles and standards.)

2. GAO reviews and approves or disapproves each agency's accounting system, internal audit procedures, and methods of internal control. In this regard, GAO continually updates the financial accounting and auditing principles and standards in accordance with which it will judge each agency's compliance.

In view of the broad and fundamental powers vested in GAO, it is too narrow to think of GAO as the auditing arm of Congress, although that is a popular impression that still lingers in the public mind. The authority and responsibility of GAO is abundantly documented in a long succession of laws passed by Congress.

The landmark legislation is known as the Budget and Accounting Act of 1950. This law is of comparatively recent origin, considering the long history of the government, and is explained by the great influx of professional accounting and auditing expertise into the government after World War II.

The years since have seen further expansion, clarification, and articulation of legislation along the lines outlined in the 1950 Act, notably in 1957, 1978, and 1982. The last mentioned law is known as the Federal Managers' Financial Integrity Act, as cited earlier.[4]

Adequacy of Statutes and GAO Directives

Existing statutes are adequate to bring about the improvement of the government's financial management system, and GAO is fulfilling its oversight responsibility. But it remains for agency managements to intensify their efforts to implement the clear, explicit, and compelling language stated in standing laws. The passage of each new legislation and reinforcement of past laws cannot help but raise the clout of GAO to see to it that the concrete provisions of the laws are observed fully.

It is correctly inferred from the foregoing that legislative requirements are necessarily broad as are also the mandates of the laws giving GAO authority and responsibility to establish financial management standards, particularly accounting standards. The result is that, at the practical level of implementation and enforcement, GAO's formulations, although professionally adequate, are still regarded by some agency managers as recommendations that they may adopt in the degree and manner that they judge to be suited to the conditions and circumstances of their operations, "with appropriate regard to costs and benefits," to use an oft-quoted phrase.

It is also to be acknowledged that, for the reasons noted, the federal government does not now have a uniform, consistent system of accounts and reports for all federal agencies to use. In the present state of this problem, GAO has wisely determined that for the time being no single system of accounting and auditing will meet completely the conditions and circumstances of all federal agencies. The magnitude of the problem is seen in more than 350 ongoing individual agency accounting systems currently in place. While over two-thirds of the agency systems have received formal approval of GAO, the oversight responsibility of GAO is a continuing task because changes in the standards are taking place as new operating problems surface for attention and treatment.

Agency conformance to GAO principles and standards recently received forceful language in the 1982 law previously referred to as the Federal Managers Financial Integrity Act, in these words:

Each agency head shall annually report to the President and the Congress, (i) his evaluation of the agency's financial system in relation to the principles and standards published by GAO, and (ii) what steps have been taken to correct instances of nonconformance to GAO's principles and standards.

Summary of GAO Mission

A summary statement of GAO's mission and responsibility, together with a thumbnail sketch of the Comptroller General who heads GAO's work, appears below.

The GAO is under the control and direction of the Comptroller General of the United States, appointed by the President with the advice and consent of the Senate, for a term of 15 years. The present Comptroller General is Charles A. Bowsher, CPA, a member of the public accounting profession before his appointment in 1981.

The duties and responsibilities of GAO are summarized in the following:

A) *Direct Assistance to the Congress at Its Request*
- Examines any specific matter;
- Conducts special audits, surveys, and reviews;
- Testifies before congressional committees;
- Assists in drafting legislation;
- Gives advice on congressional, administrative, and financial operations;
- Provides information services to the congressional budget office;
- Evaluates federal programs for their effectiveness and efficiency.

B) *Audit Authority Extends to All Federal Agencies*
- Has right of access to, and examination of, records and reports;
- Has power to request of any agency such information as it may need;
- Its scope of audit extends to all contractors who buy, sell, or receive goods and services from the federal government, including state and local governments, educational and other institutions, and contractors in the private sector.

C) *Authority to Recommend and Evaluate Agency Accounting Systems*
- Formulates accounting, auditing, and internal control principles and standards;
- In cooperation with Treasury and OMB, conducts a continuous program for the improvement of accounting and financial reporting;
- Develops, for the use of federal agencies, standard terminology and codes for federal fiscal, budgetary, and program-related data.

D) *Authority to Make Legal Decisions*
- Makes final determination as to the legality of actions of federal agencies regarding accountability for the use of money and property, including the

legality of all payments to federal personnel and parties external to the government;
- Makes final determinations of questions arising from government contracts and grants and other awards.

E) *Authority to Settle Claims and Make Debt Collections*
- Settles claims by and against the United States;
- Acts as collection agent of debts due the government upon request of agencies having past due accounts and notes receivable.

F) *Other Authority*
- The GAO "Policy and Procedures Manual for Guidance of Federal Agencies" is the official medium through which the Comptroller General formulates principles and standards for the subjects covered for the use of federal agencies and others who may be affected thereby.

COORDINATING REQUIREMENTS OF DIRECTING AUTHORITIES

It is generally recognized that financial managers of federal agencies face some special problems in keeping their accounts and reports in conformity with the requirements of three different directing authorities, namely, Treasury, OMB, and GAO. Overlapping accounting and reporting requirements have complicated the workloads of individual agencies and have contributed to agencies' problems of coping with the requirements laid down by each directing authority. Agency managements also have had to reconcile the external information requirements of the three directing authorities with their own internal management needs of communication and information. The problems associated with such conditions at times reach peak levels when extensive or sudden changes are imposed by the directing authorities.

The foregoing situation of overlapping controls and inefficient arrangements of information processing and reporting have been of concern to the directing authorities themselves. To find ways and means of reducing the problems by promoting greater compatability of information flowing to the directing authorities is the purpose of a continuing joint effort by the central authorities to this end. The work is organized under a coordinating agency staff operating under the name of the Joint Financial Management Improvement Program. But coordinating the separate requirements of the three directing authorities so as to reduce the differences in the reports prepared by individual agencies for each directing authority has been a slow process, although progress is being made. An obstacle to greater progress in this joint effort is that each directing authority is subject to different laws under which they must gather and report the data required of them. (The different laws illustrate the workings of "checks and balances" in government, clearly to the detriment of management efficiency.)

FEDERAL RESERVE SYSTEM: ADJUNCT TO TOTAL GOVERNMENT

All nations regulate money and credit through a government-owned or government-sponsored central banking system. In the United States, the functions of a central banking system are carried out by the Federal Reserve System, which was established by Congress in 1913. The system is officially sponsored by the government as an adjunct of total government but is otherwise independently owned and controlled, as explained further below.

Board of Governors

The Federal Reserve System is headed by its Board of Governors, located in Washington, D.C. All members of the Board are appointed by the President, with the advice and consent of the Senate. The Board is expected to act in concert with the President, but not in obedience to his will, which would undermine its independence. Board members serve 14-year-terms.

Federal Reserve Banks

Nationally, the system consists of 12 regional Federal Reserve Banks, located in Boston, New York, Philadelphia, Cleveland, Richmond, Atlanta, Chicago, St. Louis, Minneapolis, Kansas City, Dallas, and San Francisco. Each Federal Reserve Bank is a government-sponsored corporation that is owned and operated by member banks in the given region. A member bank is a commercial bank that has joined the Federal Reserve System and is thus subject to the regulatory provisions under which the system operates. Although the member banks in a given Federal Reserve region or district put up the capital required of their Federal Reserve Bank, the member banks elect only three of the nine members of the Bank's board of directors. Of the other directors, three are appointed by the Board of Governors, and three must represent "business, agriculture, or industry."[5]

Functions of Federal Reserve Banks

The day-to-day relationships of Federal Reserve Banks with the Federal government put the banks in the role of fiscal agents of the Treasury. The banks are the exclusive issuers of the national currency, even though the currency is either printed by Treasury's Bureau of Engraving and Printing or produced by Treasury's Bureau of the Mint, in the case of coins. If you look at a piece of paper money, you will in all likelihood see that it is called a Federal Reserve Note, payable by a specific Federal Reserve Bank, such as Atlanta, on demand. The note also says that it is legal tender (that is, money) for all debts, public and private. Federal Reserve Banks also act as banks of deposit, where the government deposits collections of taxes and against which it writes checks to pay its bills. The banks are exclusive agents for sales and redemptions of federal debt obligations.

Functions of the Federal Reserve Board

On broader matters, the Federal Reserve Board sets policies to assure liquidity of the country's commercial banks and to raise or contract the supply of money and credit. These policies are intended to influence employment, the general price level, and interest rates, either to help the country move out of a recession or to keep an economy from expanding too rapidly, thereby encouraging inflationary pressures. The Board's ways to achieve such objectives vary with conditions, but its principal tactic is to change the country's supply of money and credit, which consists of the total of private checking accounts plus cash held by individuals and firms. The specific actions of the Board include the following, with the fourth regarded by many as the most important:

1. Change member banks' reserves-to-deposits ratios, the amount of reserves in the form of cash on deposit with a Federal Reserve Bank that a member bank must hold against its various types of deposits. The higher this ratio is, the smaller the ratio that is left to measure the amount that a bank may loan out. Thus, if the ratio of reserves to deposits is raised from 10% to 12%, the amount loanable falls from 90% to 88%.

2. Change the discount rate for borrowing by member banks from the Federal Reserve Banks. The higher this rate is, the more expensive it is for a member bank to borrow from a Federal Reserve Bank.

3. Change the interest rate at which member banks may borrow from each other, making it more expensive or less expensive to borrow.

4. Conduct open-market operations in U.S. government debt obligations. Federal Reserve Banks sell some of their holdings (investments) in such securities to private investors, thus draining the deposits of commercial banks as the purchasers of the securities pay for them. In the opposite operation, Federal Reserve Banks buy the securities from private investors, thus pumping more money into the economy as they pay the private investors for the purchases.

Managed Money

Through the four actions outlined above, the Board of Governors has the power to raise or lower member bank reserve requirements, regulate the interest rate that each of the Federal Reserve Banks may charge for borrowings by member banks, regulate the interest rate at which member banks make loans to each other, and require the Federal Reserve Banks to buy or sell the government's debt obligations. The effect of any of those actions is to increase or decrease commercial bank credit and thereby raise or lower the country's total money supply. The dominant element in total money supply is checking accounts, because checks can be used as money. The workings of

EXHIBIT 3
Press Reports

Federal Reserve officials repeatedly have emphasized their concern that the economy's rapid growth, coupled with the federal government's huge budget deficits, will reignite inflationary pressures. Yesterday, Lyle E. Gramley, a member of the Federal Reserve Board, vowed that the Fed won't "cave in" to pressures to relax its anti-inflation drive.

"An easier monetary policy is not the way to lower interest rates," Mr. Gramley told a meeting of business economists in Chicago. He and several other Fed officials have warned in the past that pumping up the money supply would only heighten investor fears about inflation, thus adding to their reluctance to buy long-term fixed-income securities and leading to even higher interest rates.

Concerned About Deficits

Mr. Gramley also reiterated his deep concern about the government's massive budget deficits. He endorsed congressional efforts to begin paring the deficits but said that the steps proposed so far would do only enough "to keep the problem from getting worse, and that's about all."

Preston Martin, the Reserve Board's vice chairman, contends, however, that the economy isn't in danger of overheating. In an interview earlier this week that he initiated, Mr. Martin contended that investors have overreacted to recent government estimates that the economy grew at a rapid clip in the second quarter. The economy is slowing to "a more sustainable rate of growth," Mr. Martin said.

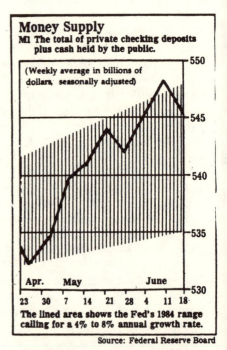

Money Supply
M1 The total of private checking deposits plus cash held by the public.

(Weekly average in billions of dollars, seasonally adjusted)

Apr. May June

23 30 7 14 21 28 4 11 18

The lined area shows the Fed's 1984 range calling for a 4% to 8% annual growth rate.

Source: Federal Reserve Board

The Federal Reserve yesterday estimated that the basic money supply, M1, averaged a seasonally adjusted $545.2 billion in the week ended June 18, down from a revised $548.3 billion the previous week. The prior week's figure was originally estimated at $548.2 billion.

The drop left M1 $3.1 billion below the upper end of the Fed's target range, which calls for 4% to 8% growth this year. M1 is the total of cash and checking deposits held by the public. Because the measure represents funds readily available for spending, many analysts consider it an important determinant of the economy and inflation.

the four actions of the Federal Reserve System give this country a managed money economy.

Gleanings from the Press

Exhibit 3 contains press reports from the *Wall Street Journal* that illustrate the sensitive problem areas of monetary and credit conditions in which the Federal Reserve Board and the Federal Reserve Bank take actions affecting the economy.

NOTES

1. Politics has been defined as the intervention of interest groups in the operation of the government. Interest groups are aligned and realigned as issues are discussed pro and con. In the ebb and flow of politics, some interest groups fade away and others appear for the first time with some issue, idea, or viewpoint to advance, support, and argue for government action.

2. The Congress is composed of (1) The House of Representatives, in which representation is based on population, and (2) the Senate, in which representation is based on the principle of state equality, with two senators for each state. Currently, there are a total of 435 members of the House of Representatives and 100 members of the Senate.

3. The latest effort along these lines is a recently enacted law titled The Federal Managers' Financial Integrity Act of 1982, passed by Congress on September 8, 1982. An OMB discussion of the problems tackled by this new law is found in OMB Circular A-123, bearing the title "Internal Control Systems," dated August 16, 1983.

4. To keep up with the evolution of these laws, including new laws as enacted, it is necessary to consult the *United States Code,* published by the Government Printing Office and available in public and college and university libraries. Look under Title 31, labeled "Money and Finance," and the chapters covering the budget, accounting, and auditing. Title 31 is updated every six years. The latest update is in the edition of 1983. Amendments to covering laws are reported in annual supplements to the Code. They are useful references between the comprehensive update every six years.

5. Most member banks are federally chartered as federal corporations, but some are chartered by individual states. Each Federal Reserve Bank pays dividends on its capital stock owned by the member commercial banks, but the annual dividend is fixed by law, and residual earnings of a Federal Reserve Bank are required to be paid to the federal government.

2.

CURRENT PROBLEMS OF FEDERAL FINANCIAL MANAGEMENT _____

SOME DIMENSIONS OF THE FEDERAL GOVERNMENT

The size and complexity of federal operations in the economy are enormous and difficult to comprehend. For example, the government's total payments for fiscal year 1983–1984 for needed goods and services were $852 billion or 24% of the gross national product (GNP).[1] This compares with $246 billion and 20%, respectively, eleven years earlier. The government's debt to holders of its notes and bonds was $1,577 billion on September 30, 1984. In 1973, the debt stood at $468 billion. In terms of people, the government payroll includes 2.7 million civilian employees and 2.1 million military personnel on active duty, for a total of nearly 5 million employees. The federal government's presence is found in virtually every nook and cranny of the country and in posts of duty extending around the world.

THE FEDERAL BUDGET AND FUND ACCOUNTING

How to finance such a large and diversified government is the annual task of the preparers of the President's budget. When preparing each year's budget, three fundamental questions must be answered: How much should the total budget be? How should the total be allocated or divided among the agencies and programs? And how should the total be financed, that is, what are the sources of the revenues and amount from each?

The preparation process for the annual budget involves a great deal of energy, time, and expense. Chapter 6 outlines the step-by-step process by which the budget is prepared. When the budget document reaches the final stage of review by Congress, it is thicker than a big city telephone directory, excluding the supplementary data that accompanies it.

All federal agencies (except as mentioned below) and their activities must be included in the President's budget because Congress is asked to provide money only for agencies and programs included in the budget. Congress reviews the budget, increases or decreases amounts requested, and then provides the money by making appropriations for the agencies and programs approved.

Appropriations and Funds

An appropriation always specifies the fund from which it is made. The fund structure of the government is discussed in detail later in this chapter, but it is mentioned briefly here in relation to budgets and appropriations that directly involve the work of Congress.

Most of the federal agencies and programs are budgeted and financed under the General Fund. Accordingly, the great bulk of appropriations are made from that fund, which receives all the general revenues of the government. In addition, there are business-type or self-supporting funds, namely, special funds, revolving funds, trust funds, and deposit funds, that make up the rest of the federal fund structure. The budgets of agencies and programs that operate under those funds must also be approved by Congress, which then appropriates the necessary money to finance the authorized programs. Following is a brief description of the process.

Special Funds

Special funds receive revenues that are specifically earmarked for their use. For example, fees received from oil companies drilling for offshore oil are earmarked for the Coast Guard's Oil Pollution Fund to finance the cost of cleaning up oil spillage caused by off-shore drilling activity. Based on an approved budget, Congress makes the appropriation for this program from the revenues earmarked for this fund. If revenues fall short of the budgeted amount, the related appropriation is automatically adjusted lower, and the given special fund is exhausted. Further financing would have to come from some other legally available appropriation for the purpose. As a fund type, special funds are relatively few and small.

Revolving Funds

Appropriations from revolving funds are made out of revenues earmarked for such funds. Revolving funds finance agencies and programs that buy and sell goods and services either to other agencies and programs of the government or to the general public. If a revolving fund of either type ends a year with an excess of revenues over appropriations, the excess is added to a revolving fund's ownership equity. If there is an excess of appropriation over revenues, that is, more was spent than was earned, the excess is deducted from the fund's equity at the beginning of the year.

Trust Funds

Like the revolving funds, appropriations from trust funds are made out of revenues earmarked for such funds. If a year ends with an excess or deficit of actual revenues over appropriations made, the excess or deficit is added to or deducted from a trust fund's ownership equity. Trust funds are legal accountable entities that are owned by the group designated as having the residual beneficial interest in the fund, that is, the fund's assets less its liabilities. However, trust funds are controlled by the government. That is why trust funds are said to be government controlled but not government owned.

Deposit Funds

Deposit funds lie outside the President's budget, but they are also subject to the constitutional principle that no money shall be paid out of the Treasury without being first appropriated by Congress. Congress authorizes, through specific legislation, a permanent appropriation of money to be disbursed by deposit funds. Naturally, no dollar limit is placed on such permanent appropriation because it would be impractical to do so. Financially, the assets of deposit funds are equal to their liabilities, which are reduced when the money held is disbursed to claimants in accordance with the terms and conditions under which the money was received.

Off-Budget Activities

Beginning in 1973, Congress enacted laws that permit a number of federal activities and programs to be budgeted and financed outside the President's budget. Congress reviews, analyzes, and approves off-budget programs and makes appropriations separately from the programs included in the President's budget. All monies appropriated for off-budget programs come from revenues earmarked for the revolving funds under which off-budget programs are carried out.

Congress has changed its mind from time to time as to which activities are to be budgeted and financed off-budget and which are not. The effect of excluding some federal agencies and programs from the President's budget splits the total federal budget into two parts, including two possible surpluses or deficits from operations. The rationalization for creating off-budget activities lies in the political sphere centered in Congress. Off-budget activities consist of making loans under specific loan programs deemed necessary by Congress. The loans are made either directly to qualified members of the public or to certain on-budget federal agencies. In the latter case, the effect is for an on-budget loan agency to liquidate some or all of its loans receivable by selling them to an off-budget agency, which then holds the loans until they mature or writes the loans off when they become uncollectible. Appropriations for off-budget activities currently run about 2% of appropriations for on-budget activities financed under the General Fund.

FINANCING THE FEDERAL BUDGET

In 1984, income taxes provided 53% and payroll taxes 36%, for a total of 89% of the government's revenues. Excise taxes provided 6%, and sundry taxes provided the remaining 5%. There are no federal property taxes.[2]

The public generally resists increases in tax rates unless the country is at war. So, unless tax rates are increased, actual revenues tend to fluctuate with the level of national income. National income swings up and down from one year to another depending upon whether the economy is expanding or contracting.[3]

Balancing the Budget

Logically, there should be annual surpluses (excess of revenues over expenditures) in years when national income benefits from a strong economy, but this has not occurred. In recent years, there has been only a close approximation to balancing the federal budget because Congress is always under pressure to increase expenditures for public services and national defense beyond the actual increase in national income. Traditionally, in years when the economy is in recession, the deficit is large. The historical demonstration of these relationships is indicated in Exhibit 4.

View of Some Economists

Although Presidents generally want a balanced budget, some economists urge acceptance of permanently unbalanced federal budgets together with a larger federal debt (resulting from borrowing to finance budget deficits) and continuing inflation of general prices. They believe this is necessary if the economy is to have a continuous high rate of economic growth and a low level of unemployment. The problem is accentuated by even greater pressure for unbalanced federal budgets

EXHIBIT 4
Federal Budget Surplus or Deficit in Recent Years

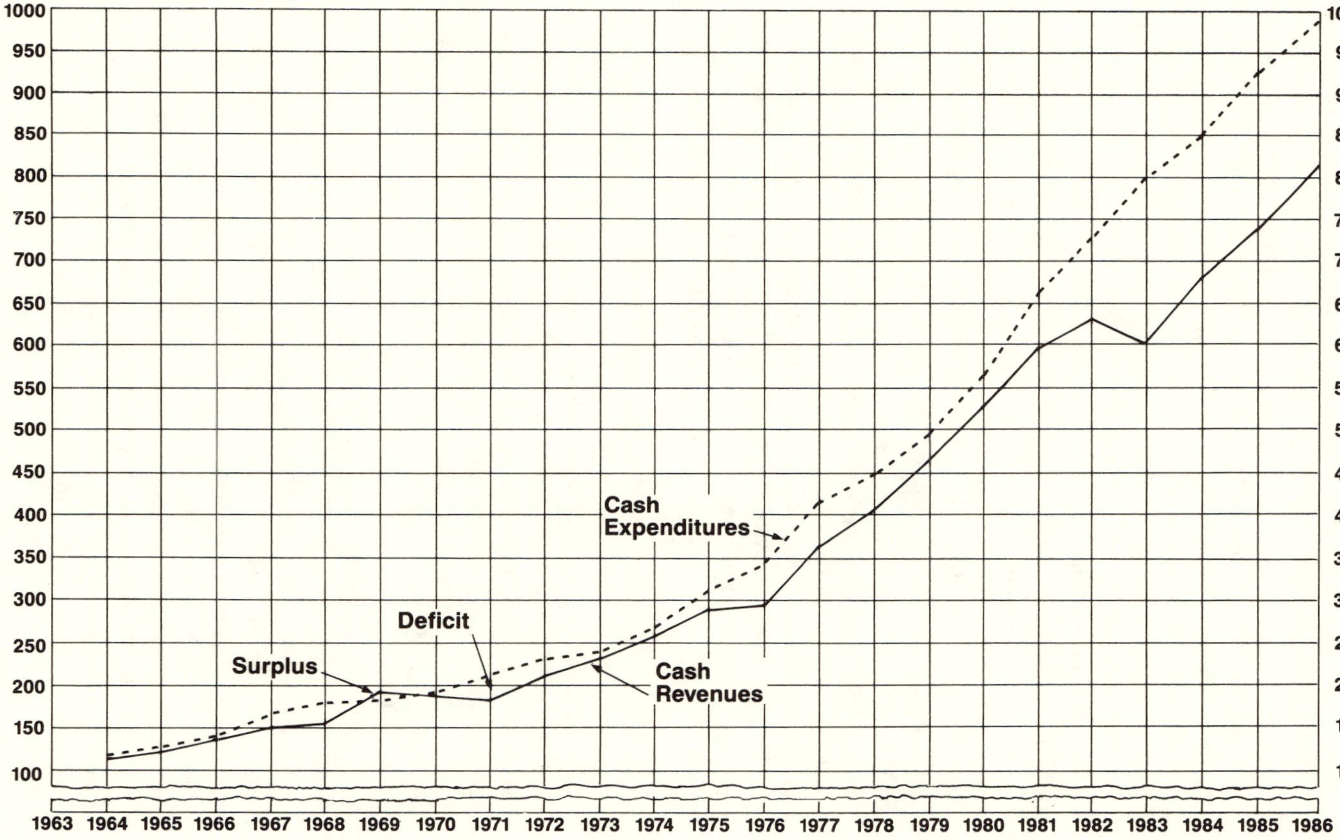

during years when the economy is going through a recession and growth of national income levels off temporarily or declines.

The roots of those factors are deep and complex, and a discussion of them is beyond the scope of this book, but the Appendix to this chapter does discuss the problems further. It appears that unbalanced federal budgets are here to stay.

Federal Deficits of the Last 20 Years

Exhibit 4 draws attention to the state of the economy and its effect on federal receipts and expenditures for the years 1964 to 1986. After the economy had moved out of the recession of the middle 1970s, it was faced with the forces of inflation. To an increasing degree, federal expenditures are directly linked to inflationary prices of goods and services. Most retirement and other social benefit payments are tied by law to the Consumer Price Index. Payments of Medicare programs are directly affected by the price of medical services. Interest on the federal debt is linked to market interest rates. The federal establishment pays more for goods and services because vendors operating in an inflationary economy must raise their prices. Therefore, social and economic changes in the private sector interact with those in the federal sector, each releasing forces changing the behavior of the other.

Perspectives

The above focus on federal deficits and the budgets that permit them is considered further in Exhibit 5, which discusses why federal budgets are so significant in setting national goals in securing and allocating resources. The discussion also sketches the historical trends, conditions, and decisions that have brought the state of contemporary federal budgets to where they are today.

Deficit or Surplus on a Cash Basis

The federal annual budget deficit or surplus is traditionally measured on the cash basis, that is, by the difference between cash revenues and cash expenditures, after excluding certain items. The items excluded are related to the government's debt (the public debt): sales of government debt issues (notes and bonds); redemption of the debt issues as they mature; and investments in government debt issues by government funds, notably, the trust funds. Federal debt issues are general obligations of the government that are issued (sold) as required (but not until required) to finance any deficiency in cash revenues. They are not issued to finance specific projects of a capital

EXHIBIT 5
What Is the Budget? How Did We Get Where We Are?

Our federal budget has many roles to play, and it performs a variety of very important functions that are seldom distinguished precisely. These distinctions are important if we are to clearly understand the role of the budget in our society.

Generally, the budget is how the President conveys to the people and the Congress his set of national priorities. These are contained in a specific set of expenditure and revenue proposals. They form the basis for debate on and decisions relevant to a number of important public policy questions. In particular, through the budget we decide what portion of our national output of goods and services or gross national products (GNP) will be used for our collection well-being. Within the total, we decide how these goods and services will be allocated among competing priorities, like national defense, income security, the administration of justice, the provision of a transportation and communications network, and the exploration of space.

The budget also serves as a device for redistributing our national income. Some individuals in our society are taxed, and the resulting revenue is used to enhance the living standards of others. These transfers can be from young to old, or they can occur among members of the same generation and income class.

The redistribution role played by the government has become increasingly important during the past 50 years. In 1929, for example, the federal government consumed slightly less than 1 percent of the resources that went to make up our GNP. In 1982, this resource use had grown to about 7 percent of GNP. On the other hand, all other federal expenditures rose from about 1 percent of GNP in 1929 to 17 percent in 1982. Thus, while the federal government's resource use has increased about sevenfold, its other expenditures, designed in part to redistribute income, have shown a seventeenfold increase. This change

has been most noticeable since the end of the World War II. For better or worse, we as a nation decided to assume at the national level various responsibilities that were once regarded primarily as the duty of the individual, the family, the church, or lower levels of government.

Besides its functions as an allocator of resources and redistributor of income, the federal budget has been used as a countercyclical and growth stimulus tool. This role for the budget is relatively new and is generally designed to maintain reasonably full employment over the course of the business cycle at reasonably stable prices, through both automatic stabilizers and discretionary changes in tax rates and expenditure levels.

Fiscal devices, such as progressive income taxes, unemployment compensation, farm price supports, and social security, were seen as a way to dampen automatically the effects of forces that would either weaken or strengthen private sector demand over the course of the business cycle. But it was always recognized that these built-in stabilizers could not do the whole job by themselves. Thus, they have been supplemented either by new programs or the expansion of existing programs and tax cuts whenever recession threatened or by the opposite mix of policy changes when inflationary pressures were present. It was through budget expansion or contraction that economists had hoped to make the business cycle a thing of the past.

In the 1960's, this cyclical stabilization role for the budget was superseded by one in which the budget deficit or surplus was oriented toward maintaining a fully employed growing economy. Discussions focused not on balancing the budget over the business cycle, but on budget balance relative to full employment. The actual deficit or surplus came to acquire little relevance to fiscal policy decisions. Major importance was attached to the position of the budget when the economy was operating at full employment.

nature in the manner common in local and state governments. In the federal government, maturing debt issues are normally redeemed with money obtained by issuing new issues to replace those that have matured. It is a way of perpetuating debt once it is first issued.

In theory, an annual budget deficit on the cash basis is financed by a matching increase in federal debt, and a budget surplus would be used to reduce the federal debt in an amount equal to the surplus for the given year. Such a relationship between annual federal deficits and surpluses and changes in the federal debt is an important concept in the fundamentals of federal government financing. The concept is discussed further in Chapter 3.

Cash Expenditures versus Appropriations

The appropriation for a particular year sets the limit to the amount that may be obligated by federal agencies; that is, the amount that may be spent on goods and services in current or future years. Experience shows that most, but not all, of an ordinary appropriation results in cash expenditures during the year for which the appropriation is made. Statistically, the experience shows that cash expenditures range between 80% and 85% of the amount appropriated for a given year, the remainder resulting in cash expenditures in later years. The phenomenon has important ramifications that will be discussed in a later chapter.

THE FEDERAL DEBT

Annual federal budget deficits keep pushing up the total federal debt, especially in periods of recession when unemployment rises together with the related rise in public welfare costs and federal revenues fall because of the decline in GNP. The latest data shows that the federal debt is nearing the $2 trillion mark. Economists tell us that every kind of debt, both public and private, is increasing in total amount. They also observe that the trends in the ratios of such debt to national income, as measured by the GNP, are not rising, except temporarily in times of recession.

Federal Debt in Relation to Other Debt

The government borrows money to pay for goods and services to the extent cash revenues are insufficient, that is, by the amount of the budget deficit for a given year. The year-by-year borrowings add up to the amount of the federal debt on any date.

Such government borrowings affect the country's financial markets

EXHIBIT 6
Distribution of Total Debt in the United States

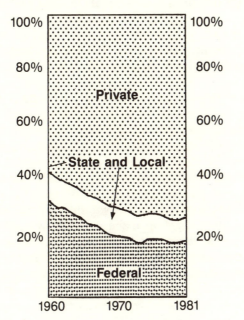

EXHIBIT 7
Federally Assisted Loans Outstanding at Year-End

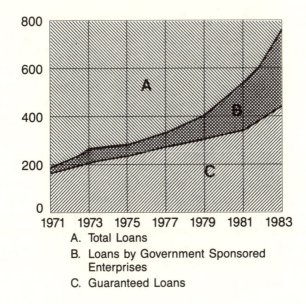

A. Total Loans
B. Loans by Government Sponsored
   Enterprises
C. Guaranteed Loans

in various ways. As an example, the government's borrowings drive up interest rates and leave less loanable money for private-sector borrowers. It is a tribute to the strength of the financial markets, therefore, that, notwithstanding the great increases in annual federal borrowings, the proportion of federal debt to total debt (public and private) has been decreasing over the years. Those relationships are presented in Exhibit 6, covering the years 1960 to 1981. During that period of years, the average annual rate of growth was 6.1% in the case of the federal debt, compared with 7.7% for debts of state and local governments and 10.3% for private debt.

Offsetting this trend, however, is the rise of federally assisted borrowings by others. The assistance takes the form of the federal government's guaranteeing or sponsoring loans by private individuals and firms to certain other private parties (either individuals or firms) under federal laws enacted for such purpose. Both types of assistance call for government supervision of the private lenders, and the guaranteed loans are contingent liabilities of the government. Government-sponsored lenders enjoy certain income tax exemptions among other special status conferred by the government. Borrowers find that the interest charged on government-guaranteed or -sponsored loans are at lower rates than comparable loans from other private sources. As indicated in Exhibit 7, government-sponsored loans are rising faster than government-guaranteed loans, but both types of loans in the aggregate are formidable, representing a combined amount of nearly $800 billion.

Federal Debt in Relation to GNP

To further illustrate the growth in the size of the federal debt, the amount is shown below as a percentage of the annual gross national product or GNP. The percentage declined in the 1960s, remained level during the 1970s, and appears to be rising in the 1980s.

Federal debt as a percentage of GNP:

Year	%
1960	48
1970	29
1980	28
1981	28
1982	30
1983	35

Economists regard this relationship as an indicator of the capacity of the country to absorb the cost of servicing (that is, paying) the interest on the debt and possibly the burden of redeeming the debt principal gradually in the future. The latter is a possibility that current consensus judges to be an improbability.

Resume of Federal Financial Operations

A study of the financing of government operations reveals several roles the government plays. It levies taxes and makes expenditures in accordance with approved budgets. It borrows money from the private sector when federal revenues fall below expenditures, and it lends money to private sector borrowers, as required by laws passed for such purposes. The lending is extended again under laws directing such actions by guaranteeing certain loans made by private lenders to private borrowers and by sponsoring the establishment of private lenders to private borrowers, both in an effort to make it advantageous for private lenders to lend money to disadvantaged private borrowers. The government, thus, not only serves as the operator of general government services but is a large borrower and lender of money in the private sector, thereby putting it in the banking business in the private sector.

FEDERAL FUND STRUCTURE IN THEORY AND PRACTICE

The federal fund structure is similar to that of state and local governments because they are patterned after the federal model. The dominant fund in the model, the General Fund, is surrounded by several other funds that are designed to be self-supporting and operated as closely as possible as business-type activities. The specialized nature of the other funds is indicated by their names: special funds, revolving funds, trust funds, and deposit funds. Each such specialized fund is accurately described as a fund type because the government uses as many separate funds of each type as may be managerially desirable for purposes of planning and controlling operations at different times and in different places. The number, size, and life span of individual funds fluctuates from time to time and from place to place in government operations depending upon the need for them as perceived by the government managers in accordance with governing legislation.

Fund Classifications

Frequently, the name of a fund is not indicative of its actual use. The practice is to be explained in terms of legislative history, agency prerogatives, and "legal necessities," all of which have resulted in pragmatic solutions. The reference to legal necessities is sometimes simply a euphemism for "legal expediency." To understand the purpose of a fund, look for substantive evidence of its intended nature and purpose; that is, how it is used rather than what it is called, or how it is classified in official government reports.

Expendable Funds

An expendable fund's resources consist of current assets, such as cash, receivables due within a current year, and so on. By definition, an expendable fund never includes noncurrent assets such as long-term investments, land, buildings and structures, equipment, or inventories of materials and supplies. An expendable fund has no liabilities that cannot be paid from existing current assets. An expendable fund has no permanent capital or equity, inasmuch as all of the fund assets can be used up or consumed in performing the services assigned to it. Although the rate of expenditures is a matter of budgetary control, nearly all expendable funds are subject to annual budgeting. That is the reason the typical life of an expendable fund in the federal government (indeed, in any state or local government) is one year. The foregoing characteristics of an expendable fund are those of a theoretical expendable fund. In practice, plans and controls are seldom so accurate, but the model of an expendable fund always exists as a matter of principle, supported by law, finance, and accounting. The General Fund is the example par excellence of an expendable fund. Special funds (which in state and local government are called "special revenue funds") are the other examples, except as follows.

Trust funds meet the criteria of expendable funds, if the trust in each case refers to the government's custodianship role as manager, but does not interfere with the expendability of trust funds, in accordance with the charter or mission of each trust fund. In the federal government, trust funds are typically expendable funds, as illustrated by the federal social security trust funds. Those funds are owned by the people with ownership rights, as previously noted.

Deposit funds are expendable funds because the funds' resources are held by the funds for full return or refund to the depositors in the manner agreed to when the deposits were received by the funds. For its duration, a deposit fund's assets are equal to its liabilities, leaving no fund equity.

By definition, then, only the revolving funds of the federal government are nonexpendable funds. Revolving funds are established with permanent capital to finance continuous operations during which resources are expended, recouped, and again expended, in a recurrent cycle. Goods or services are purchased, requiring payment to the vendors and working force. When, in turn, the fund sells goods or services to customers, money is recouped and the cycle is repeated by expending the money for a new round of purchasing and selling. A central strategy of the fund's management is to so price the goods or services sold that the fund will be reimbursed for the costs incurred: in theory no more and no less but in practice preferably a little more to provide for expansion and unforeseen contingencies.

ASPECTS OF THE GENERAL FUND

Unlike other funds that are identified at the outset with specific agencies and programs, the General Fund is not so identified initially. Identification comes at a later stage when Congress makes appropriations from the General Fund to individual agencies and programs. Each appropriation from the General Fund is called an appropriated fund. Each such appropriation from the General Fund creates a separate fund that is a complete financial and accounting entity, identified by agency, program, and the year of the appropriation.

Should the one-for-one relationship of appropriation and fund be observed also in transactions between an agency and Treasury? To put it in other words, should Treasury show in its books a separate account for each appropriation made by Congress to each agency, each year? (In the case of some federal agencies, such as a defense agency, the agency may receive more than one appropriation per year, thereby increasing the number of appropriations and corresponding funds to be accounted for each year.)

A combined (unified) appropriation account in the books of the Treasury for a given agency would not suffice because the U.S. Constitution states that "No money shall be drawn from the treasury, but in consequence of appropriations made by law." Treasury has been assigned traditionally the responsibility for detecting any violation of this law and reporting the violation to Congress. Treasury has met this responsibility by establishing a separate appropriation account on its books for each appropriation to each agency, each year, against which to charge disbursements from each appropriation. This is in keeping with the one-for-one principle of appropriation and fund, to which is added the further control of a matching account in the books of the Treasury for each appropriation.

To understand the above relationship, it is helpful if each appropriation is likened to a checking account in the books of a commercial bank. In Treasury's case, the "checking account" is a liability account in the name of a specific appropriation of a specific agency. The books of each agency carry a corresponding asset account, cash on deposit with Treasury, for each appropriation received. As a result, there is a

EXHIBIT 8
Agency X: Appropriated Fund 0201, Fiscal 1986—Statement of
Financial Position, October 1, 1985

Resources		Liabilities	
Cash on deposit with Treasury	$1,000	None	
		Fund Balance	
		Obligational Authority	$1,000
	$1,000		$1,000

three-way relationship between appropriation, appropriated fund, and the cash-on-deposit account with Treasury, resulting in three elements of control.

A given appropriation is accounted for in the books of an agency as a completely separate fund entity, known as an appropriated fund, with its separately identified equation, assets equal liabilities plus fund balance. Exhibit 8 is a simple illustration.

Controlling Overobligation

The one-for-one relationship outlined above enables Treasury to detect and report overdrawn appropriations of any fund, not just appropriated funds. However, only the management of an agency can prevent overobligation from happening. Only an agency can control its expenditures, more accurately, obligations, and thereby avoid overdrawing the Treasury balance of any appropriation. This is the reason for an express federal law, called the Anti-deficiency Act, which provides that the head of any agency is personally responsible for:

1. Establishing a system of financial control designed to prevent overobligation of any appropriation made to the agency;
2. Disciplining all offenders; and
3. Reporting to Congress all violations of the law, including identification of offenders and facts as to what disciplinary measures were taken.

The Act provides criminal penalties for violation. As would be expected, the Anti-deficiency Act is violated from time to time, for foolproof accounting systems are no more possible in government than in the private sector.[4]

ASPECTS OF REVOLVING FUNDS

In the federal government, revolving funds are used to finance and account for large segments of operations. Revolving funds are either public enterprise funds, dealing with the public, or intragovernment funds, dealing with other federal programs.

Public Enterprise Funds

Some large public enterprise funds are operated as government corporations.[5] The corporations are operated either as independent agencies or as subordinate agencies of executive departments or certain large independent agencies. However, some public enterprise funds are not conducted in corporate form (or name), they are usually subordinate agencies of executive departments or large independent agencies. Examples of these categories include:

(1) *Government corporations:*
   Operated as independent agencies
   • Tennessee Valley Authority
   • U.S. Postal Service
   Operated as subordinated agencies of other agencies
      Under Department of Agriculture:
   • Commodity Credit Corporation
      Under Federal Home Loan Bank Board, an independent agency:
   • Federal Savings and Loan Insurance Corporation
(2) *Unincorporated enterprises:*
   Operated as subordinated agencies of other agencies
      Under Department of Housing and Urban Development:
   • Federal Housing Administration Fund
   • Government National Mortgage Association
      Under Small Business Administration, an independent agency:
   • Business Loan and Guarantee Fund

Intragovernment Funds

Intragovernment funds are all managed and financed as subordinate activities of various executive departments or major independent agencies. The activities are distinguished between those engaged in production and services and those engaged in buying, storing, and selling materials and supplies. Examples include:

(1) *Production and Services.* Illustrative of these activities is the Department of Defense's shipyards, arsenals, clothing factories, and vehicle repair shops and General Services Administration's repair shops for the government's furniture and other equipment.

(2) *Materials and Supplies.* As examples, the Department of Defense operates supply centers that procure, store, and sell materials and supplies and General Services Administration buys, stocks, and sells general-use materials and supplies.

ASPECTS OF TRUST FUNDS

Trust funds play a more important role in the federal government than in state and local governments. The largest trust funds are really in the nature of special funds; that is, they receive revenues expressly earmarked for the purposes of a given trust fund and make expenditures from this fund only for the programs and people provided for under specific provisions of covering laws. The funds are associated with the country's social security programs. Revenues of the funds come from taxes levied on employees and employers who are members of these programs. Employees receive benefit payments under the programs in accordance with specific provisions of law.

Because the government manages the funds in a fiduciary capacity and does not own the funds, they are called trust funds to differentiate them from government-owned funds. The expendable nature of social security trust funds is usually lost to view by the public, which knows them only the way they are classified in government reports, namely, as trust funds.

There are some trust funds that are not expendable, but these are relatively few. There are also a few mixed permanent-expendable trust funds, mainly for employees' and survivors' retirement and disability annuities.

Another group of trust funds are established as public enterprises. Two examples are the Federal Deposit Insurance Corporation (FDIC) and the Veterans Life Insurance Funds. Government reports classify such activities as trust funds, although they logically belong to the category of public enterprise–type revolving funds. (Such funds are also known as revolving trust funds.)

To illustrate expendability of social security trust funds, the following data, covering the largest of such funds—the Federal Old-Age and Disability Insurance Trust Funds—exhibits the receipts and disbursements for the year ended September 30, 1982: (in millions)

Receipts	$152,129
Disbursements	156,644
Excess of disbursements over receipts	$ 4,515

APPENDIX: THE ECONOMIC BUDGET

Unlike the conventional fiscal or accounting budget of the government, which measures income and expenditures only in terms of the government's operation on the basis of cash flow, the economic budget encompasses the economy as a whole, public and private sectors taken together. The economic budget does not leave the vicissitudes of cash inflows and outflows of the government to the workings of a free economy operating under the market laws of supply and demand. In the economic budget, the interaction and interdependence of the private and public sectors is such that the two should not be viewed as separate, though related phenomena. Following is a brief discussion of the economic budget as advocated by the economists who want to see it adopted.

How to Avoid Recession

As long as the economy as a whole purchases all that is produced, it will continue to produce and purchase, and all economic signals are "go." But if some income is not put back into production to finance growth or if some goods and services produced are not purchased, a surplus of goods and services produced leads to a cutback in future production of goods and services. With less production, fewer workers will be employed and less capital equipment will be used, to mention two obvious consequences. With less income, people buy less of the goods and services produced, resulting in a further cutback in production. The process is repeated, and the downward spiral of economic activity continues, as does the accompanying recession.

The only way this downward spiral can be reversed is for the government to intervene. This it can do by accepting deficit operation of the government, which requires borrowing the money needed to meet the shortfall of receipts of taxes, thereby increasing the federal debt. Thus, deficit financing is an element of the economic budget.

How to Avoid Inflation

When producers of goods and services spend more than their income from production of the goods and services, they will resort to buying on credit, and paying higher prices for the goods and services they want. The result will be inflation, too much purchasing power chasing too little production, and an upward spiral of prices. Again, there is need for the government to intervene, this time to halt the upward spiral and bring it down to tolerable level. Governmental actions here are twofold: reduce purchasing power through higher taxes and lower the level of government spending, thereby bidding less for goods and services in the marketplace.

Pros and Cons of the Economic Budget

Economists advancing the above strategy claim the government should intervene in a period of recession by operating at a deficit and, in a period of inflation, by operating with a balanced budget or even with a budget surplus. Such compensating actions introduce the concept of the economic budget, intertwining the level of government operation with the level of activity in the private sector and in effect combining the impact of the public and private sectors in grappling with the major upturns and downturns of the economy as a whole.

As with most theories of economists, this one is logical, but its critics find the concept flawed for leaving out practical considerations. For one thing, some economists point out that there is no demonstrated ability of the government, short of a completely managed economy, to influence or direct the activities of the rest of the economy at the same time that it is implementing the economic budget.

NOTES

1. GNP stands for total national output per year of the goods and services of the United States at the market value of such output. Included are outputs of farms, other natural resources, manufacturing, wholesale and retail enterprises, and personal services enterprises. GNP is published by the Department of Commerce.

2. The charts and other data presented in this book are drawn from publications of the federal government for the periods and dates indicated, mainly from the President's Annual Budget, Annual Reports of the Department of the Treasury, Treasury Bulletin, and special reports by federal agencies.

3. This subject is discussed further in Chapter 3 in presenting differing viewpoints on what course taxation policies of the government should follow in the future.

4. For an interesting report of a number of celebrated instances of violations of the Anti-deficiency Act, see the *Journal of Accountancy* issue of February 1978. The article is written by Elmer B. Staats, who was then Comptroller General of the United States and head of the General Accounting Office.

5. Government corporations fall into three categories: government owned, financed, and operated; government operated but not government owned or financed; government sponsored and supervised but not government owned, operated, or financed, except when emergencies arise, as defined in the applicable laws.

Only corporations of the first type are financed under government revolving funds. Currently, one corporation exists in the second category, the Federal Deposit Insurance Corporation, which is financed under a trust fund. Examples of the third include Federal Reserve Banks, Federal Home Loan Banks, and Federal Land Banks.

3.

COMBINED FINANCIAL STATEMENTS: FUND CATEGORIES

INTRODUCTION

Chapters 3, 4, and 5 discuss federal financial statements that present combined selected data by major fund categories for the government as a whole. These statements are presented on a cash basis because the data are derived from the central records of the Treasury Department. They are significant because they focus on

1. The annual federal budget deficit or surplus and the federal budget as the determinant of the annual appropriations and
2. The fund accounting structure and process by which revenues and expenditures flow through the government.[1]

The financial statements present a consolidation of government-wide data. The accounting standards of consolidation, however, are not as complete or as uniformly applied as those used in commercial accounting. Therefore, the resulting statements are more accurately described as combined financial statements.[2]

In order to show the data as clearly and as simply as possible, the financial statements presented in this study were prepared by analyzing and condensing published data. The federal government does not publish an annual financial report in the manner common in state and local governments, which displays the data reported in terms of each major fund category. However, the Treasury Department has in recent years published an annual consolidated financial report for the government as a whole. The report represents an experimental effort to apply generally accepted accounting principles to government-wide data, including a fuller implementation of accrual accounting concepts than is actually used in federal accounting practice. In keeping with the objec-

STATEMENT 1
United States Government—Combined Cash Assets and Undisbursed Cash Balances by Funds, September 30, 19X1 (in millions)

COMBINED CASH ASSETS OF ALL FUNDS

Held by U.S. Treasury:

Currency, coin and other similar items		$ 457
Gold stock (Note a)		
Bank deposits:		
In Federal Reserve Banks, as fiscal agents	$ 3,520	
In other banks	15,150	18,670
Items in process of collection, etc.		934
Time deposits and other depository accounts		88
Monetary assets with International Monetary Fund (IMF)		
Deposits	4,617	
Special drawing rights (Note b)	578	5,195
Total held by Treasury		25,344

Held by Other Government Agencies		
		8,979
Total combined cash assets of all funds		34,323
Deduct: outstanding checks and similar items		7,656
Combined net cash assets		$26,667

Equities in Combined Net Cash Assets by Funds:

Undisbursed Cash Balances of Respective Funds:

General Fund (deficit)	(14,308)	
Special funds	7,090	
Revolving funds	20,886	
Total government-owned funds		13,668
Trust funds		9,627
Total budget-area funds		23,295
Deposit funds (subject to return to depositors)		3,372
Total fund equities in net cash assets		$26,667

Notes: a) The monetary gold stock of the U.S. Treasury is stated in its books at $11,152 million as of September 30, 19X1, as further discussed in the Appendix to this chapter.

b) Under the management of the IMF, five countries--the United States, the United Kingdom, West Germany, France, and Japan--have created a fund for settling international trade debts. The fund consists of a pool or "basket" of five currencies, as contributed by the five countries, in accordance with a mutually agreed-on formula. To operate the pool of currencies, use is made of a money unit called special drawing right (SDR), which serves as the medium of exchange or common monetary unit for the pooled currencies. Each member country currency in the pool is valued at the exchange rate for one U.S. dollar. The U.S. dollar equivalents of the currencies are then summed up to arrive at the value of one SDR in relation to one U.S. dollar. To illustrate the practical working of the SDR concept, assume that the West German Central Bank, the Bundesbank, wishes to use SDRs, which it is holding, to pay for a trade debt of $10,000 to the Federal Reserve Bank of New York. Using the day's quoted exchange rate of, say, $1.09273, the trade debt is settled for 9,151 SDRs (determined by dividing $10,000 by 1.09273 = 9,151), ignoring incidental fees for the transaction.

tives of an overall presentation, the report does not disclose data by fund categories but instead merges data for all funds; that is, consolidated data for all funds.

The financial statements presented in this chapter and in Chapters 4 and 5 were developed from a variety of official government sources and condensed from immensely detailed data. The principal sources were as follows:

1. Treasury's Annual Combined Statements of Receipts, Expenditures, and Balances of the United States Government;
2. Treasury Bulletin, published quarterly after 1981 and monthly in prior years;
3. Annual Reports of the Secretary of the Treasury;
4. President's Annual Budget documents.

The financial statements discussed in this chapter are:

Statement 1. Combined Statement of Cash Assets and Undisbursed Cash Balances by Funds, September 30, 19X1;

Statement 2. Cash Receipts and Disbursements by Funds, Year Ended September 30, 19X1;

Statement 3. Budget Receipts by Funds, Year Ended September 30, 19X1.[3]

COMBINED STATEMENT OF CASH ASSETS AND UNDISBURSED CASH BALANCES BY FUNDS

Statement 1 presents the combined cash assets of the government as a whole and the equities in the assets by the respective funds, as of September 30, 19X1. Excluded are foreign currencies acquired without dollar payments, which are discussed later, and also certain monetary assets invested in a number of international financial institutions operated by member governments, which are reported in Statement 8 (Chapter 5).

Cash Assets of the Government

The government's combined cash assets for all funds totaled $26,667 million as of September 30, 19X1, after deducting checks issued and outstanding. Statement 1 gives the composition of this cash in various categories.

Fund Equities in Net Cash Assets

In all, five fund categories are identified in Statement 1. Receipts and disbursements flow through these funds. Responsibility and accountability are also in terms of funds. Statement 1 shows that the General Fund is overdrawn by $14,308 million. The General Fund owes this sum of money to the other funds for borrowings made without explicit legislative authority and without interest.

The U.S. Treasury could easily and promptly repay the sum owed by the General Fund by borrowing from the public (the private sector) through issuing Treasury debt obligations and paying the current market rates of interest on the debt obligations issued. It is government policy, however, not to do this. Instead, Treasury uses an informal, interest-free method of borrowing, on behalf of the General Fund, money available from the other funds. The phenomenon is thus a manifestation of Treasury policy. The policy is not intended to merge or dissolve the distinctions between different fund categories. The same approach has been used in the past by Treasury to come to the aid of other funds. The government has provided other funds, notably revolving funds, interest-free capital from time to time, as deemed necessary, from money available in the General Fund.

Interfund borrowing, as a method of indirect and automatic borrowing at the discretion of Treasury, raises the question of the integrity and identity of separate fund categories and can be interpreted as undermining such integrity and identity.[4] The policy tends to blur distinctions between the several fund categories, although the bookkeeping of interfund borrowing is carried out correctly, fund by fund. However, this may be done to conform with the law requiring separate accounting for each fund type. Such an approach deemphasizes the independence of each fund type in response to solving higher national fiscal problems.

This combining of funds deserves further consideration. Although the unified budget concept, as adopted in 1969, combined government-owned funds in publications such as the President's Annual Budget, it is quite a different matter for the federal government to use the unified funds concept in Treasury reports, thereby merging totals for the several fund categories involved, namely, the General Fund, special funds, and revolving funds, and calling them federal funds. The inference seems to be that separate accountability of each fund type is neither necessary nor desirable as government policy. If the reason is to enable comparison between budgetary and actual data, a better way may be a different reporting format. Otherwise, the interested public must depend upon researchers to construct fund-by-fund data by analyzing the details of published government reports, usually in labyrinthian depths extractable only by patient and laborious effort by accountants versed in federal accounting. Without such research, important relationships between major fund categories would lie buried and unavailable for study and analysis by anyone interested in

STATEMENT 2
United States Government—Combined Cash Receipts and Disbursements by Funds, for the Year Ended September 30, 19X1 (in millions)

BUDGET AREA FUNDS

	Government-Owned Funds					Total Budget Area Funds	Deposit Funds	All Funds
	General	Special	Revolving	Total	Trust Funds			
Budget receipts	$403,669	$1,100	(a)	$404,769	$197,843	$602,612		$602,612
Budget disbursements	436,786	93	32,990	469,869	190,675	660,544		660,544
Budget surplus (or deficit)	(33,117)	1,007	(32,990)	(65,100)	7,168	(57,932)		(57,932)
Other receipts or disbursements	(660)(b)	--	(21,005)(c)	(21,665)	--	(21,665)	1,823(d)	(19,842)
Adjusted budget surplus (deficit)	(33,777)	1,007	(53,995)	(86,765)	7,168	(79,597)	1,823	(77,774)
Appropriations and loans								
From other funds	1,443	--	56,576	58,019	20	--	--	--
To other funds	(56,596)	(1,443)	--	(58,039)	--	--	--	--
Excess of receipts (or disbursements) before debt Transactions	(88,930)	(436)	2,581	(86,785)	7,188	(79,597)	1,823	(77,774)
Debt transactions:								
Net proceeds from sales of obligations, less redemptions	90,092	--	(530)	89,562	--	89,562	--	89,562
Net investments in U.S. government obligations (e)	--	--	(931)	(931)	(9,363)	(10,294)	(1,997)	(12,291)
Net debt receipts (or disbursements)	90,092	--	(1,461)	(88,631)	(9,363)	79,268	(1,997)	77,271
Total excess of receipts (or disbursements)	1,162	(436)	1,120	1,846	2,175	(329)	(174)	(503)
Undisbursed balances:								
September 30, 19X0	(15,470)	7,526	19,766	11,822	11,802	23,624	3,546	27,170
September 30, 19X1	$(14,308)	$7,090	$20,886	$13,668	$9,627	$23,295	$3,372	$26,667

Notes:
a) Stated net of receipts.
b) Consists of loss on seignorage (loss on coin production), $450 million, and loss on sale of gold (from international transactions), $210 million.
c) Represents off-budget revolving funds.
d) Stated net of disbursements.
e) Stated net of sales (+) and purchases (-).

understanding the structure and process of the federal financial management system.

COMBINED STATEMENT OF RECEIPTS AND DISBURSEMENTS BY FUNDS

Statement 2 shows the combined cash receipts and disbursements of all funds of the government for the year ended September 30, 19X1.

Concepts of Receipts and Disbursements

Receipts include only tax receipts. Disbursements represent only payments to individuals—civilian and military—on the federal payroll and to vendors outside the government for purchases of goods and services. Statement 2 uses government terminology of budget receipts and budget disbursements, and, depending on the difference between the two, budget surplus or budget deficit. As previously noted, the prefix budget refers to the fact that the data are classified in the same way as budgeted items are in the President's budget proposals (budget estimates) for an upcoming year. The data in Statement 2 are actuals and result from actual transactions in the covered year, and the prefix budget is used for the reason explained.

Official Treasury reports stop with the first three lines in Statement 2. Excluded are all debt and investment transactions and appropriation and loan transfers between funds. In Statement 2, the excluded items appear below budget surplus or deficit. They are added in order to complete the report, making it a summary of all cash receipts and all cash disbursements under the fund categories shown. The data below line 3 show how the budget deficit was financed; namely, by appropriations and loans between funds and by borrowing from the public and thereby increasing the national debt. Certain receipts and disbursements included in Statement 2 have been netted by Treasury as discussed below.

Netting of Certain Debt Transactions

To keep the data condensed, disbursements for redeeming (or paying off) matured debt have been netted against receipts from issuance of new debt obligations. There is no breach of accounting principle here because receipts from issuance of new debt obligations may be treated properly as the source of money to pay off matured debt obligations.

Netting of Certain Investment Transactions

In the case of revolving, trust, and deposit funds, receipts from sales of investments in federal debt securities have been netted against disbursements for purchases of the investment securities. As of September 31, 19X1, approximately 21% of the federal debt securities were held as investments of revolving, trust, and deposit funds. Thus, a significant percentage of this debt is held within the government as investments in other funds.

Netting of Receipts and Disbursements of Revolving Funds

The practice of netting cash receipts and disbursements is further evidenced by the omission of receipts of revolving funds, the receipts being offset against the disbursements of those funds. Many billions of dollars of receipts are thus omitted from the report. The reasoning behind such nettings are explained below.

In the case of intragovernment revolving funds, no useful purpose is served by swelling receipts and disbursements by interfund transactions within the government. Receipts of revolving funds are disbursements of other funds (for whom work was done or to whom materials and supplies were sold). Similarly, disbursements of revolving funds, to the extent they reimburse other funds for work done by them for revolving funds, are receipts of other funds.

In the case of public enterprise revolving funds, since receipts of these funds are compensation for services to the public and return of loans made to other funds, such receipts should not be added to tax receipts. To offset the receipts omitted, a matching amount of disbursements is also omitted, leaving net disbursements to be reported in Statement 2.

Netting of receipts and disbursements as described reduces the informational value of government reports. This is especially true in the case of public enterprise revolving funds. Known as proprietary receipts, they are made up of interest, rent, royalties, and sales of products and services. Proprietary receipts are of interest in studies of the interaction of the public and private sectors of the economy. If the information cannot be presented in the report itself, such disclosures could be made in supplementary exhibits.

SURPLUS OR DEFICIT OF WHICH FUND?

Statement 2 separates results of operations by funds and groups of funds. Data under budget area funds must be distinguished between government-owned funds and trust funds, which are government controlled but not government owned. Assets of trust funds are held by the government as trustee for the beneficiaries of trust funds. Control over trust funds is as much a matter of law as it is a case of discretionary direction by the government managers. Differentiation between funds and fund groups requires an analysis of which fund or fund group has a surplus and which has a deficit.

Deficit of General Fund

Line 3 of Statement 2 shows that the deficit of the General Fund was $33,117 million, which was increased to a total operating cash deficit of $88,930 million as summarized in Exhibit 9.

To finance the $88,930 million deficit, the government borrowed $90,092 million from the public and used the excess of $1,167 million to decrease overdrawn cash balances at the beginning of the year.

Deficit of Government-Owned Funds

The budget deficit of the combined funds owned by the government, as shown by line 5, column 4, the $86,765 million was financed as shown in Exhibit 10.

Note that the operating deficit for government funds taken together is $86,765 million, whereas the operating cash deficit for the General Fund alone is $88,930 million.

Deficit of All Budget Area Funds Combined

A third measure of deficit operations is the combined amount for all budget area funds, that is, all of the funds that are included in the President's budget. The deficit for all such funds combined is shown on line 5 of column 6 as $79,597 million. This deficit was financed as shown in Exhibit 11.

The government borrowed $89,562 million from the public, thereby increasing the federal debt by this amount. How was this money used? It replenished the cash caused by the deficit in the amount of $79,597, and revolving and trust funds increased their investments in federal debt securities by $10,294 million, the reason for which is not obvious. To meet the combined use of $89,891 million ($79,597 plus $10,294) in the face of having borrowed only $89,562 million, it was necessary to draw down the cash balance at the beginning of the year by $329 million.

Concept of Unified Funds

The concept of a unified budget that includes all funds (other than deposit funds) in the President's Annual Budget document began in 1969, when trust funds were no longer excluded as they had been in the past.[5] Treasury then began to use the unified-funds concept in

EXHIBIT 9
General Fund Deficit

		(in millions)
Budget deficit (per line 3)		$33,117
Loss on seignorage (coin production)	$450	
Loss on sale of gold (international monetary transactions)	210	660
Budget deficit (per line 5)		33,777
Transfers to other funds (net)		55,153
Operating cash deficit (per line 8)		$88,930

EXHIBIT 10
Combined Funds Deficit

		(in millions)
Borrowing from the public (increase in federal debt)		$89,562
Deduct:		
Increase in federal agencies' investments in federal debt obligations (purchases of federal debt securities)	$ 931	
Payment of loans to trust funds	20	
Addition to cash balance of government-owned funds at the beginning of the year	1,846	2,797
		$86,765

EXHIBIT 11
Budget Area Funds Deficit

		(in millions)
By borrowing from the public (increase in federal debt)		$89,562
Deduct:		
Increase in federal agencies' investments in federal debt obligations (purchases of federal debt securities)	$ (10,294)	
Add:		
Amount by which the cash balance at the beginning of the year is reduced	329	(9,965)
		$79,597

after-the-fact reporting in Treasury publications to correspond to the unified budget data in the President's Annual Budgets. In a statement of receipts and disbursements like Statement 2, only totals of budget area funds are published, as shown in column 6 of Statement 2. Some published Treasury reports do separate government-owned funds, called federal funds, from trust funds, but government-owned funds are never separated in respective totals for the General Fund, special funds, and revolving funds. This is the present policy of the government with respect to publications for external users. Of course, internally, budget estimates and actual results are compared in the most minute segments useful for management planning and control, fund by fund, agency by agency, and at each management level within these funds and organizations.

The unified funds concept was urged by economists and others interested in making studies of national income. It was believed that federal data combining all of the government's funds (other than deposit funds) would reveal important cash flows between the federal and private sectors of the economy. Except for such purposes, however, the combined data on lines 1, 2, and 5 in column 6 have little or no significance.

OFF-BUDGET FUNDS

Statement 2 includes so-called off-budget funds in the column for revolving funds (column 3). This was done to avoid a separate column for the off-budget funds, but official Treasury reports exclude off-budget funds data from budget-area funds. In the year reported in Statement 2, disbursements of off-budget funds totaled $21,005 million. The phenomenon of off-budget funds is of recent origin, dating from 1971. This policy of excluding certain activities from the President's budgetary control was understandably not the President's, but by direction of Congress, which wanted certain activities to be budgeted and financed separately by Congress.

Nature of Off-Budget Funds

Off-budget funds are in the nature of public enterprise revolving funds that are government owned and controlled directly by Congress. The exclusion of off-budget funds from the President's budget is required by law and must be interpreted as legislative policy to which the President has agreed. Agencies managing off-budget funds are engaged mainly in administering loan programs under laws explicitly requiring such programs. The most important of such agencies is the Federal Financing Bank, which operates as an arm of Treasury. Debts

STATEMENT 3
United States Government—Budget Receipts by Funds, Year Ended September 30, 19X1 (in millions)

Description	General Fund	Special Funds	Trust Funds	Total
Income taxes				
From individuals (including FICA taxes) less refunds of $47,299	$285,551	--	--	$285,551
From corporations, less refunds of $12,596	61,137	--	--	61,137
Total income taxes	346,688			346,688
Social security taxes				
Employment taxes and contributions, including FICA taxes collected from employers	--	--	$117,757	117,757
Federal disability insurance	--	--	12,418	12,418
Federal hospital insurance	--	--	30,361	30,361
Railroad retirement taxes	--	--	2,457	2,457
Unemployment insurance	--	--	16,129	16,129
Supplementary medical insurance	--	--	3,319	3,319
Federal employee retirement contributions	--	--	3,909	3,909
Other retirement contributions	--	--	76	76
Total social security taxes			186,426	186,426
Excise taxes (a)	33,162	935	6,742	40,839
Estate and gift taxes	6,787	--	--	6,787
Customs duties	8,023	--	60	8,083
Miscellaneous receipts				
Dividends from earnings of the Federal Reserve System	12,834	--	--	12,834
Other receipts	745	165	45	955
Total receipts	$408,239	1,100	193,273	602,612
Transfer of revenue sharing	(4,570)	--	4,570	--
Total receipts per Statement 2	$403,669	$1,100	$197,843	$602,612

Note: a) Excise taxes represent mainly gasoline sales taxes, but also include tobacco and alcohol sales taxes. Revenues from gasoline taxes are earmarked for various government trust funds, such as for highway, airport and urban mass transit projects.

of off-budget agencies are included in the total federal debt. In the past, Congress has changed the list of off-budget agencies from time to time, adding to the list or returning certain agencies to the category of budget-area revolving funds, usually because of pressures from lobbying groups.

Off-budget funds are at present composed of the following:

Postal Service Fund

Rural Electrification and Telephone Fund

Federal Financing Bank

Rural Telephone Bank

Strategic Petroleum Reserve Fund

Synthetic Fuels Corporation

U.S. Railway Association

SOURCES OF GOVERNMENT REVENUES

Statement 3 sets forth the government's major sources of revenues. It presents the details of the respective fund categories that also appear in Statement 2. A summary of the sources of revenue is shown in Exhibit 12. Exhibit 13 shows receipts by source for the years 1973–1985.

Revenues are categorized when received by the respective funds that are legally entitled to them. The major portion goes into the General Fund because it is the source of money on which the great bulk of the government's programs depend for financing.

TAXATION PROBLEMS IN THE MIDDLE 1980s

Statement 3 not only discloses the sources of revenues, but also reflects taxation policies of the government. Both the Congress and executive branch constantly walk a tightrope in wrestling with taxation policies. On the one hand, tax policies must avoid stifling the economy by excessively annually draining off resources (money) from the public, leaving it less to spend or save. It is primarily through savings that capital is provided for investment in and expansion of the economy. On the other hand, the government must meet its financial responsibilities. It must also keep the economy financially healthy and growing. Otherwise, economic stagnation will cause a downward spiraling effect on all the indicators of social and economic well-being.

Federal policy makers are faced with a twofold, usually conflicting, responsibility: stimulating the economy by cutting taxes and raising taxes to help the needy members of society who cannot support themselves. The latter include students seeking education and training, the unemployed seeking assistance, and the retired depending upon the government in whole or in part for their living. Somewhere in this thicket of taxation problems is the rising cost for national defense, in both absolute terms and as a percentage of the total cost of running the federal government.

EXHIBIT 12
Sources of Revenue

(in millions)

Source of Revenue	Amount	Percent
Individual income taxes	$285,551	47%
Corporate income taxes	61,137	10
Social security taxes	186,426	31
Excise taxes	40,839	7
Estate and gift taxes	6,787	1
Other receipts	21,872	4
	$602,612	100%

EXHIBIT 13
Budget Receipts, 1973–1988

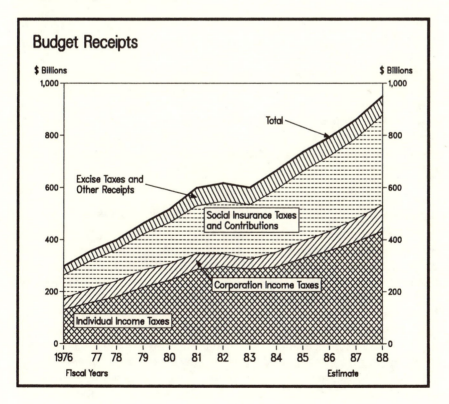

The actual effect of taxation policies is reflected in the amount and source of annual federal revenues. Recent trends in these amounts and sources are noteworthy and are presented in Exhibit 13. All taxes are trending upward, with sharpest increases taking place in the social security taxes and individual income taxes.

Taxation policies are debated extensively in Congress and in the media during every session of Congress. The debate consists of proposals and counterproposals; for in this area there are two sides to each issue, always with some group getting or losing money depending upon which way an issue is settled.

Increase Taxes by Revision of Tax Law (Tax Reform)

Many ideas have been put forth for increasing taxes by revising the present tax laws. For example, some suggest

1. Replacing the present completed-contract method of computing earnings with the percentage-of-completion method under which a contractor reports earnings according to the percentage of the contract completed during each year.
2. Eliminating tax-exempt revenue bonds issued by state and local governments for the purpose of industrial development, housing, and similar privately owned and controlled activities.
3. Eliminating investment tax credits for the purchase of energy-saving equipment and structures as an unnecessary subsidy to businesses.

Those who propose these and other revisions claim that such deductions from taxable income of taxpayers have crept into tax law undeservedly or are no longer legitimate incentives to business even if they once were.

Improve System of Tax Collection and Enforcement

Each new administration takes a fresh look at how tax collection and enforcement could be improved. The purpose is to reduce the size of the underground economy, which is the name given to the amount of taxes not collected because of unreported taxable income or other false tax return items. One method proposed is to widen the sources of taxable income that are subject to withholding by payors, for example, withholding on interest and dividends payments. Another proposal is to raise the percentage that corporations currently pay during the year from 80% to 90% of estimated income taxes for the given year. A third proposal is to augment the staff of the Internal Revenue Service in order to increase the efficiency of enforcement and collection activities. In 1983, the incumbent administration proposed an increase of 5,000 personnel for these purposes. Invariably, those who object to these proposals counter with rationalizations suited to their points of view.

Increase Personal and Business Income Tax Rates

Finally, some advocate increasing income taxes that individuals and firms pay by raising the tax rates. Some want to raise tax rates as a matter of first priority and resort. Others want to make this objective a matter of last priority and resort. The specifics of why each side takes the position it does can easily fill a book on this subject, and so must be left to specialized study. Briefly, those who oppose increases in tax rates to reduce the deficit believe that the level of government expenditures should first be pared down to stop built-in, self-feeding forces that push up such expenditures out of sheer momentum. They believe that the government will just spend all additional revenues generated by tax increases. Fundamental as this thinking is, the conditions of the middle 1980s, with unprecedented huge federal deficits from operating the government, inject a new factor for consideration, namely, how to eliminate such deficits and keep them from occurring in the future.

President Ronald Reagan has stated that an expanding economy, aided and abetted by a pared down level of government spending, will reduce and remove the federal deficits without increasing taxes. Others disagree. Nobody objects to reducing fraud, waste, and abuse in running the government, as well as finding ways and means to increase its efficiency and effectiveness of operation. The challenges, however, are more difficult. They include coping with how to reduce unemployment, how to support the higher cost of health care and the higher cost of public education that state and local governments find difficult to finance by themselves, and how to increase aid to individuals and families in order to bring them up to minimum standards of living, as defined in official government studies as the poverty line. Given the conditions and realities of the middle 1980s, including the problem of coping with large federal operating deficits, many believe (although they don't want it) that an increase in taxes is required for the government to meet its responsibilities and reduce the deficit, thereby bringing down the national debt.

WHERE THE MONEY WENT

Statement 2 shows that total government disbursements from all budget area funds came to $660,544 million (per line 2, column 6).

EXHIBIT 14
Statement of Disbursements—United States Government (in billions)

By National Functions		By National Agencies	
National defense	159.8	Legislative branch	1.2
International affairs	11.1	The Judiciary	.6
		Executive Office of the President	.1
General science, space, and technology	6.4	Funds appropriated to the President	7.0
Energy	10.3	Department of Agriculture	26.0
Natural resources and environment	13.5	Department of Commerce	11.5
		Department of Defense—Military	156.1
Agriculture	5.6	Department of Defense—Civil	3.1
Commerce and housing credit	3.9	Department of Health and	
Transportation	23.4	Human Services	228.1
Community and regional development	9.4	Department of Housing and Urban	
Education, training, employment, and		Development	14.0
social services	31.4	Department of the Interior	6.8
		Department of Justice	2.8
Health	66.0	Department of Labor	30.1
Income security	225.0	Department of State	1.9
Veterans benefits and services	23.0	Department of Transportation	22.5
		Department of the Treasury	93.4
Administration of justice	4.7	Environmental Protection Agency	5.2
General government	4.6	National Aeronautics and Space	
General purpose fiscal assistance	6.9	Administration	5.4
		Veterans Administration	22.9
Interest	82.5	Foundation for Education Assistance	13.1
		Office of Personnel Management	18.1
		Other independent agencies	17.6
Undistributed offsetting receipts	−27.0	**Undistributed offsetting receipts**	−27.0
Total per Statement 2, Col. 6	660.5	**Total per Statement 2, Col. 6**	660.5

Before this money was disbursed, it was subjected to reviews by both the administration's executive branch and congressional oversight committees. Each budget program and program subdivision benefitted from the sequential scrutiny known as planning, programming, budgeting, and vouching of disbursement requests. What were the purposes for which the money was spent and what agencies spent it? Exhibit 14 presents answers to the questions in terms of specific agencies and specific program or functional descriptions.

Sources and Dispositions of Money

Where the budget dollar came from and where it went for the year ended September 30, 19X1 are shown in Exhibit 15 as respective percentages of total sources and total dispositions. (Actuals are about the same as the budget estimates used in the charts.)

EXHIBIT 15
The Budget Dollar

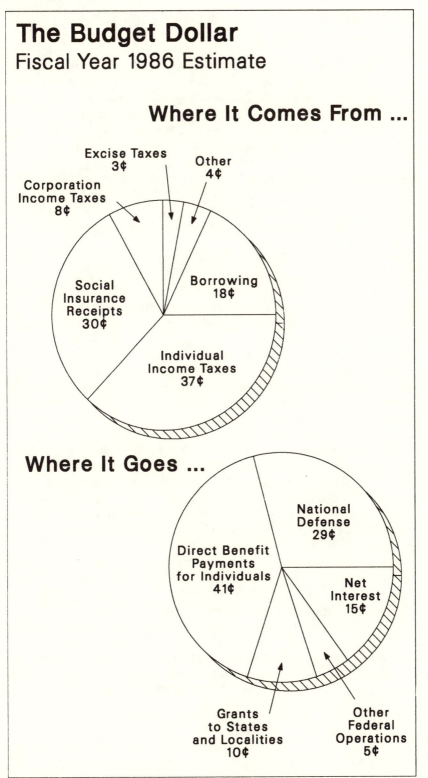

The Budget Dollar
Fiscal Year 1986 Estimate

Where It Comes From ...

Excise Taxes 3¢

Other 4¢

Corporation Income Taxes 8¢

Social Insurance Receipts 30¢

Borrowing 18¢

Individual Income Taxes 37¢

Where It Goes ...

National Defense 29¢

Direct Benefit Payments for Individuals 41¢

Net Interest 15¢

Grants to States and Localities 10¢

Other Federal Operations 5¢

FOREIGN CURRENCIES ACQUIRED WITHOUT DOLLAR PAYMENTS

This chapter is concluded with a discussion of the unique practice of acquiring foreign currencies without paying for them in dollars. The currencies are acquired by Treasury from governments as consideration for sales to them of surplus agricultural products and for economic and military aid under standing agreements. (Foreign currencies are also acquired by U.S. agencies with dollar payments from commercial sources to finance overseas operations.)

When acquired, the foreign currencies are in the form of bank deposits to the credit of the U.S. Treasury in the banks of foreign countries. The Treasury draws against these bank deposits in accordance with applicable federal laws and international agreements.

Disbursements of the Currencies

The foreign currencies are required to be disbursed within the contracting countries. As a general rule, disbursing is done in a roundabout way.

First, the currencies are "purchased" by federal agencies that have payments due in the countries where the foreign deposits are located. Secondly, the federal agencies then draw against the bank deposits transferred, in effect sold to them, to pay for obligations incurred by them resulting from their activities in the foreign countries. Of course, these activities, like any other, are included in the agencies' budgets and related appropriations. In more procedural language, what happens is that the dollar equivalents of the foreign currencies "purchased" by the agencies are charged against their appropriation accounts in the books of the Treasury. In the same Treasury books, the credits offsetting the sales of currencies are recorded as miscellaneous receipts of the General Fund, except when by law the proceeds of the sales must be remitted to designated agencies.

As an agency views it, foreign currencies purchased in the above manner have the effect of converting some of its appropriation dollars into foreign currency, which becomes part of the agency's total cash assets until disbursed. The drawback is that the foreign currency can only be spent in the country in which it is deposited. Apart from this restriction, subsequent disbursements of the foreign currency are handled like any other disbursement on the books of both the agency and U.S. Treasury. (Foreign deposits, however, never leave the control of Treasury until they are disbursed by the agencies.)

Free-Use Transfers

Some of Treasury's foreign currencies are actually transferred free of charge, that is, without charging the appropriation accounts of the recipient agencies. Such free-use transfers are controlled by specific legislation that specifies the conditions to be met for such transfers. Free-use transfers are subject to separate control procedures issued by the Office of Management and Budget. The effect of such tight controls is to place free-use transfer accounts in the same category as appropriation accounts.

Sales for Dollars

Approximately $1,083 million of the foreign currencies were sold during the year ended September 30, 19X1 at prevailing exchange rates. The sales were made to federal agencies for official use, namely, for use in making disbursements in the foreign countries involved, as approved by covering budgets and corresponding appropriations. The alternative would have been to buy the foreign currencies from regular commercial sources.

In summary, an agency conducting activities in a foreign country can acquire some of its foreign currency needs through purchases from Treasury or by receiving free-use transfers from Treasury (if it met the qualifications) or by buying foreign currency from commercial sources, depending upon the options it had under applicable U.S. laws and regulations. In the last-mentioned option the actual purchases must be made through Treasury's regular disbursing officers.

APPENDIX: U.S. TREASURY'S STOCK OF GOLD

Since early history, the U.S. Treasury has purchased from private owners and held a stock of gold. In an unprecedented action, Congress passed the Gold Reserve Act of 1933, which increased this gold stock sharply by requiring private owners of gold to exchange such gold for paper currency. Accompanying this requirement was another historic development in that paper money was no longer redeemable in gold at the Treasury. The effects of this and related measures was to take the United States off the gold standard and replace it with managed money, that is, paper currency, as the lawful money of the country. Today, the monetary role of Treasury's gold stock is of little or no significance. In 1975, a new law was passed making it legal once more for private owners to have gold in their possession, like any other commodity.[6]

Book Value of Treasury's Gold Stock

Under enabling legislation, Treasury has increased, from time to time, the book value (or price) at which it carries gold stock in its accounts. The latest increase in this book value occurred in 1973, when it was raised from $38 per ounce to $42.22, an increase of 11.11%. In popular terms, the increase in valuation is called a 10% devaluation of the dollar, computed as follows: $38 = .90x; x = $42.22. Devaluation of the dollar consists of raising the dollar value of gold, requiring more dollars to buy or sell an ounce of gold.

Every time Treasury raises the book value of its stock of gold, a windfall gain results. Thus, the last time this was done, in 1973, a gain of $1.157 billion resulted from the action. In the accountant's language, the carrying or book value of the gold asset was debited by this amount, and a matching credit was made to the General Fund balance, as a "special event" transaction. The 1973 devaluation increased the book value of Treasury's gold stock from $10.410 billion to $11.567 billion, representing an increase of $1.157 billion, or 11.11%.

Gold Stock Fund

This fund was created when the Gold Reserve Act of 1933 required Treasury to purchase gold from private owners. To finance purchases, Treasury paid for the gold in cash, that is, paper currency, thereby reducing its cash balance. Treasury then replenished the cash paid out by issuing (selling) gold certificates to the Federal Reserve Banks by an amount matching cash paid out. The gold certificates, a type of debt, are secured by pledge of the gold asset in the Gold Stock Fund. There was a further provision in this arrangement that, if any portion of the gold stock is sold in the open market, the cash received must be used to redeem some of the gold certificates.

Treasury pays no interest on the gold certificates outstanding. However, the gold certificates are not in the nature of equity securities but debt obligations bearing no interest and originating in the manner described. The financial status of the Gold Stock Fund, as of September 30, 19X1 (the same report date as used in Statement 1) shows the asset, gold stock, at its then book value of $11.52 billion on the basis of $42.22 per ounce, and an offsetting liability for gold stock certificates outstanding of $11.52 billion. (The market value of gold at September 30, 19X1 was $450 per ounce.)

There were no purchases or sales transactions during the year ended September 30, 19X1. Treasury's gold stock is kept mainly at Fort Knox, Kentucky; other places include several United States Mints, and the U.S. Assay Office in New York City.

EXHIBIT 16
Gold Stock Fund Transactions

	Debit	Credit
1) Buy gold; finance purchase through General Fund.		
Gold	42.22	
Payable to General Fund		42.22
2) Issue gold certificates to Federal Reserve Bank(s) to receive cash to pay off debt to the General Fund.		
Payable to General Fund	42.22	
Gold certificates		42.22
3) Sell gold in the open market.		
Cash	450.00	
Gold		42.22
Payable to General Fund		407.78
4) Redeem gold certificates; transfer gain on sale to the General Fund.		
Gold certificates	42.22	
Payable to General Fund	407.78	
Cash		450.00

Transactions in the Gold Stock Fund are illustrated in Exhibit 16 through a number of simplified entries.

NOTES

1. As used here, budget receipts, budget disbursements, and the resulting budget surplus or deficit are all "actuals," representing year-end, after-the-fact data. The prefix budget refers to the fact that the data classifications are the same as those used in preparing the President's budget proposals for an upcoming year. As an illustration, budget receipts represent actual receipts, as distinguished from estimated receipts in the budget for an upcoming year.

2. Statutory requirements and traditional treatments of data in government reports create certain limitations for the researcher in the analysis and

interpretation of published federal data. No two independent researches of the data would therefore arrive at government-wide financial statements showing the same content as found in the exhibits in this book. In presenting, explaining, and interpreting the content of the exhibits, the authors believe that the information is as fairly put together as their judgments enabled them to do. More specifically, the authors believe that the financial statements portray fairly the financial positions of the respective fund categories and the financial results of the respective fund categories for the dates and periods represented.

3. The data covers a recent year, referred to as 19X1, since some adjustments have been made to delete minor aberrations in the interests of improving the presentation as models for study.

4. Special funds, revolving funds, and trust funds are restricted-purpose funds. Their respective resources are required by law to be expended only for legally designated purposes. If loans are made between funds, they must be made and repaid in the manner provided by covering legislation and in conformance with fund accounting principles. In recent times, the basic legislation of this subject is found in the Budget and Accounting Procedures Act of 1950, as amended from time to time in subsequent years. In reading the above, Treasury would no doubt respond that it has implied authority, under governing legislation, to utilize funds deposited on behalf of the government, in accordance with its best judgment.

5. Recent press reports indicate that a growing number of members of Congress are interested in excluding trust funds from the unified budget concept, favoring separate handling and reporting of trust funds in order to highlight the financial plight of pending insolvency of such funds (mainly social security funds).

6. In the United States today, money consists of coins and paper currency (25%) and demand deposits in banks known as checking accounts (75%), all regulated by the Federal Reserve System. This concept of money has evolved gradually over the past 150 years to the degree that it has completely replaced gold or paper currency backed by (redeemable in) gold as the country's money supply. Of course, gold as a commodity is accepted by everybody as a store of wealth. The total supply of gold is relatively small, and annual production of newly mined gold is small, 70% of which comes from South Africa.

4.

COMBINED FINANCIAL STATEMENTS: THE GENERAL FUND

The General Fund is the federal government's mainstream fund, as it is for state and local governments. Flowing through this fund are all receipts and disbursements and all resources and liabilities not earmarked for any other specific fund. This chapter discusses and illustrates four financial statements of the General Fund:

Statement 4. Changes in Undisbursed Balances, Year Ended September 30, 19X1

Statement 5. Budget Receipts, by Major Sources, Year Ended September 30, 19X1

Statement 6. Changes in Undisbursed Balances, by Major Agencies, Year Ended September 30, 19X1

Statement 7. Summary of Financial Position, September 30, 19X1

STATEMENT OF CHANGES IN UNDISBURSED BALANCES

Statement 4 shows receipts and disbursements of the General Fund for fiscal year ended September 30, 19X1. Proper recording of transactions under the classifications indicated in the Statement, namely, appropriated (designated Appropriated Funds), unappropriated, and unappropriated balance, is essential. Each appropriation to an agency is accounted for as a separate expendable fund. Each agency thus administers each appropriation received as an appropriated fund. These concepts were discussed in Chapter 2.

STATEMENT 4

United States Government—Changes in Undisbursed Treasury Balances of the General Fund, Year Ended September 30, 19X1 (in millions)

Description	Appropriated Funds	Unappropriated Balance	Total (a)
Budget receipts	--	$403,669	$403,669
Other receipts or disbursements (net)	--	(660)	(660)
Total receipts of revenue	--	403,009	403,009
Net proceeds from sale of debt obligations	--	90,092	90,092
Total receipts for year	--	493,101	493,101
General Fund appropriations:			
Initial	$490,782	(490,782)	--
Transfers	(26,609)	26,609	--
Withdrawals	(4,248)	4,248	--
Net appropriations	459,925	(459,925)	--
Appropriations and interfund loans and land repayments (net)			
From special funds	--	1,443	1,443
To revolving funds	--	(56,576)	(56,576)
To trust funds	--	(20)	(20)
	--	(55,153)	(55,153)
Total deductions	--	(515,078)	--
	459,925	(21,977)	(437,948)
Disbursements (b)	(436,786)	--	(436,786)
Net increase (or decrease)	23,139	(21,977)	1,162
Undisbursed Treasury balance:			
September 30, 19X0	220,209	(235,679)	(15,490)
September 30, 19X1	$243,348	$(257,656)	$(14,308)

Notes: a) The data in total column agrees with corresponding items in
Statement 2, column 1.
   b) Net of appropriation reimbursements.

Appropriated Funds versus Unappropriated Balance

The relationship between these two accounts can be demonstrated with a simplified set of summary data (Exhibit 17) that traces the general activity in a typical operating year.

At the beginning of the year, a total of $10 billion of cash was in the appropriated funds (known as general appropriated funds) and there was an unappropriated balance of $6 billion. Therefore, the General Fund began the year with total cash resources of $16 billion.

On the books of the Treasury, appropriations are credited to separate appropriated fund accounts, each such account also identified by agency and representing an appropriated amount subject to use in accordance with the agency's approved budget. Appropriated funds began

EXHIBIT 17
Summary Data

(in billions)

Activity/Balance	Appropriated Funds	Unappropriated Funds	Combined Balance
Undisbursed Treasury balance, at beginning of year	$ 10	$ 6	$ 16
Budget revenues and other receipts	--	180	196
Appropriations by Congress	175	(175)	196
Budget disbursements by agencies	(150)	--	46
Undisbursed Treasury balance, at end of year	$ 35	$ 11	$ 46

the year with $10 billion, received appropriations of $175 billion, made disbursements of $150 billion, and ended the year with $35 billion.

The year's receipts totaled $180 billion. Under the law, the receipts must first be credited to the unappropriated balance. Congress makes appropriations out of the unappropriated balance. (Article 1, Section 9 of the Constitution states that "no money shall be drawn from the Treasury but in consequence of appropriations made by law.") Appropriations for the illustrative year totaled $175 billion, leaving a year-end unappropriated balance of $11 billion, represented by cash on deposit with the Treasury.

Receipts exceeded appropriations by $5 billion ($180 billion minus $175 billion). This resulted in a surplus (termed "budget surplus") of receipts over appropriations, and explains why the unappropriated balance at the end of the year was $5 billion greater than at the beginning. Congress considers such surplus (or deficit) when considering the level of appropriations for an approaching year. The year's surplus of $5 billion and the starting unappropriated balance of $6 billion, together amounting to $11 billion, are of great interest to Congress when thinking about the financing of a new year.

Statement 4 presents the receipts and disbursements figures for the General Fund, summarized in Statement 2, and breaks the data down between appropriated funds and unappropriated balance. Statement 4 shows that receipts are first credited to unappropriated balance, which is the source of appropriations to the agencies in the form of appropriated funds. Statement 2 merges these two procedural steps.

Significance of Statement 4

Statement 4 presents the appropriated funds in Treasury's central accounts, recorded on the cash basis. In Chapter 8, the record keeping by individual agencies for appropriations received is presented on the same basis used by Treasury (cash basis) and also on two additional bases, the accrual basis and the obligation basis. The differences between the cash, accrual, and obligation bases are timing differences; that is, when transactions are recorded. Agencies would have no difficulty in keeping accounts on all three bases by expanding the accounting system to accommodate the additional accounts, and financial statements could be prepared on either or all bases, depending upon the purpose of the statement.

The accrual basis is found at some agencies, but accrual concepts are utilized in varying degrees from agency to agency. Generally, agencies operating revolving funds have the widest applications of accrual concepts.

Statement 4 also shows that appropriated funds are subdivisions of the General Fund, from which appropriations are made. Government receipts from taxes and other general revenues, plus receipts from sales of debt obligations, are first deposited in the Treasury and credited to the General Fund. Receipts remain under the control of the General Fund, in its unappropriated balance, until appropriations are made.

Statement 4 illustrates the use of internal accounting controls. All expenditures must come out of appropriations made. Control over appropriations is thus tantamount to control over expenditures, even though the control is indirect. Congress is in control of the unappropriated balance and the resources represented, from which it makes appropriations. Agencies are in control of appropriated funds, which are the source of expenditures. This pattern of controls is found in every level of government—local, state, and federal.

Some of the facts and relationships disclosed in Statement 4 will be discussed in the following paragraphs.

Receipts

Net revenue receipts of the General Fund for fiscal year 19X1 totaled $403,009 million. In addition, net receipts from sales of government debt obligations were $90,092 million. Therefore, the total amount credited to the unappropriated balance of the General Fund was $493,101 million.

Appropriation Transfers

Appropriations out of the General Fund aggregated $459,925 million to appropriated funds, $56,576 million to revolving funds, and $20 million to trust funds. In the other direction, the General Fund received appropriations from special funds in the amount of $1,443 million. Transfers of money between funds are common today because of the government's unified fund concept, discussed in Chapter 3.

Reimbursements

Reimbursements represent collections for goods provided or for work done for others, either other federal agencies or other organizations within the same agency. Collections of this nature reimburse the agency performing the activity for costs it has incurred. The practice is a proven method for transferring appropriated funds between activities, from those buying to those selling. In Statement 4, reimbursement receipts and payments have been offset against each other in the combining process.

Disbursements

Statement 4 shows that $456,786 million of appropriated funds were disbursed as payment for goods and services received, exclusive of intragovernment transactions as noted previously.

The item of $90,092 million under receipts, described as net proceeds from sales of debt obligations, is the difference between receipts from sales of new debt obligations and disbursements for redeeming matured debt obligations. The netting also was shown in Statement 2. Since disbursements can only be made out of appropriated funds and receipts can only be credited to unappropriated balance, such netting departs from established principles.

To conform with established principles, disbursements to redeem matured debt obligations should have appeared as a charge in the appropriated funds column on a separate line, so as to distinguish them from disbursements for goods and services. Consistent with such treatment, receipts from sales of new debt obligations would be shown on a gross or actual basis in the unappropriated balance column.

Transactions with Other Funds

The General Fund appropriated and loaned $56,576 million to revolving funds and $20 million to trust funds. The General Fund also received appropriation transfers of $1,443 million from special funds. Treasury determined these transactions to be necessary to meet certain fluctuating capital needs of several funds. The practice suggests a togetherness of the funds that cuts across fund distinctions that normally should be observed. Providing capital to revolving funds is considered equivalent to appropriations unless they are loans. In the case of loans, they are receivables to the lender fund and payables to the borrowing fund. Loans received or repaid would thus seem not to have anything to do with increasing or decreasing the unappropriated balance of the General Fund. No distinctions are drawn between appropriations and loans between funds, at least in the published reports.

Transactions of the types described above between the General Fund and the other funds that directly affect the unappropriated balance of the General Fund may surprise the reader. Some say that such practices circumvent congressional procedures and thus are a way of staying outside the jurisdiction of Congress. In Treasury's view, however, they are flexible means to cope with the financing problems of the individual funds. Right or wrong, the practices have come to be known as back-door financing.

Undisbursed Balances

Statement 4 shows that the General Fund is overdrawn by $15,470 million at the beginning of fiscal year 19X1 and by $14,308 million at the end of the year. The overdrawing was made possible by borrowing from the cash assets of other funds, and the overdrawn amount of $14,308 million at the end of the year correctly states the cash deficit position of the General Fund as a whole.

The overdrawn amount of $257,656 million in the unappropriated balance results from overappropriation. Though huge in amount, it is correctly measured, and is made possible by a phenomenon within the General Fund. The reason why the General Fund can still operate when faced with a cash deficit of this magnitude is the existence of undisbursed Treasury balances of $243,348 million in appropriated funds. Demands for disbursements are made upon appropriated funds, not against the unappropriated balance (except for direct loans and appropriations to other funds, notably, revolving funds). So for purposes of disbursements, there is $243,348 million of available cash.

Treasury's ability to cope with a tremendous deficit in unappropriated balance is not hard to understand. It simply relies on the time disbursements lag behind appropriations. The $257,656 million cumulative deficit, to repeat, is a case of overappropriation by this amount. It resulted from annual deficits over a long period of years.[1]

STATEMENT 5
United States Government—Revenue Receipts of the General Fund,
Year Ended September 30, 19X1 (in millions)

Income Taxes	Individuals	Corporations		
Withholdings from pay	$255,917	--		
Direct collections	76,981	$73,733		
Total	332,898	73,733		
Refunds	(49,347)	(12,596)		
Total income taxes	$285,551	$61,137	$346,688	86%
Excise taxes			33,162	8%
Estate and gift taxes			6,787	2%
Custom duties			8,023	2%
Total taxes and duties			394,660	
Miscellaneous revenues:				
Dividends from earnings of the				
Federal Reserve System (a)			12,834	3%
Other revenues			745	
			408,239	
Transfer to trust funds for general				
revenue sharing			(4,570)	(1%)
Total per Statement 2, line 1			403,669	
Other additions or (deductions):				
Loss on seignorage			(450)	
Loss on sale of gold			(210)	
Total			$403,009	100%

Note: a) Mainly interest earned on holdings (investments) of U.S.
government debt securities (generally referred to as the
government's public debt).

The Treasury saves a lot of interest by not selling additional debt obligations so as to remove the cumulative deficit from the books.

STATEMENT OF REVENUE RECEIPTS

Statement 5 presents the major sources of revenue of the General Fund. Income taxes provide 86% of the total revenues. This highlights the reliance of the government's tax system on income taxes. In fact, income taxes and payroll taxes (earmarked for social security trust funds) make up practically 88% of all federal taxes, as shown in Statement 3.

Revenues not Shown

Statement 5 does not show several kinds of receipts from the public that were used to help finance the activities of certain agencies, as

EXHIBIT 18
Actual versus Budgeted Income Taxes (in millions)

	Actual	Budget	Actual over (under) Budget	
			Amount	Percent
Individual income taxes	$285.5	284.0	1.5	.5%
Corporation income taxes	61.1	66.0	(4.9)	(7.0%)
	$346.6	350.0	(3.4)	(1.0%)

required by law. Examples in the case of the General Fund are interest, rent, royalties, and sales of government surplus property.

Statement 5 also does not show receipts from other important sources. Conspicuous among these is the receipts from sales of government debt obligations. These receipts are accounted for as nonrevenue receipts and appear in Statements 2 and 4 under a separate category, but they are as much a part of general receipts of the government as receipts from taxes. Another class of receipts omitted are appropriation reimbursements, which are netted against disbursements in Statement 4.

Actual versus Budgeted Revenue Receipts

Statement 5 does not compare actual revenue receipts with budgeted receipts for fiscal year 19X1. General Fund exhibits of state and local governments customarily do make such comparisons. In Exhibit 18, the comparison between actual and budgeted items is shown for only income taxes.

The variance of $3.4 billion under budget represents the net results of various economic factors. One may be the net effect of changes in tax law, not anticipated in budget preparation. Another may be changes in taxes caused by growth or decline in the tax base, again as not accurately estimated in the budget. An expanding economy creates more taxable income. A declining economy causes lower taxable income. In the case of personal income taxes, there is the element of automatic changes due to rise or fall of personal income tax rates, depending upon whether the economy is expanding or contracting. This factor can push taxpayers into higher or lower tax brackets, compared with an earlier period.[2]

STATEMENT 6
United States Government—Changes in Undisbursed Balance of Appropriated Funds (General Fund), by Agencies, Year Ended September 30, 19X1 (in millions)

	Balance September 30 19X0	Appro-priations	With-drawals	Transfers	Disburse-ments	Balance September 30 19X1
Legislative branch	$ 377	$ 1,252	$ 30	$ (27)	$ 1,222	$ 350
The judiciary	67	656	18	--	641	64
Executive Office of President	19	103	4	--	99	19
Funds appropriated to President	31,439	11,970	1,118	--	7,496	34,795
Department of Agriculture	3,352	26,076	279	(3,288)	22,431	3,430
Department of Commerce	1,886	2,035	49	49	2,222	1,699
Department of Defense, Military	83,544	177,003	1,702	(106)	156,656	102,083
Department of Defense, Civil	939	3,051	3	(21)	3,086	880
Department of Education	12,777	14,897	102	(5)	15,081	12,486
Department of Energy	9,529	12,318	68	(14)	12,811	8,954
Department of Health/Human Services	13,584	73,317	116	(12,563)	60,554	13,668
Department of Housing/Urban Development	13,591	13,240	210	--	11,566	15,055
Department of the Interior	1,846	4,566	55	(39)	4,516	1,802
Department of Justice	950	2,325	12	--	2,699	564
Department of Labor	3,563	12,974	123	--	13,119	3,295
Department of State	523	2,211	55	--	2,002	677
Department of Transportation	7,417	14,601	59	(80)	11,983	9,896
Department of the Treasury						
Interest on public debt	--	95,589	--	--	95,589	--
Operating functions	13,859	10,776	46	(162)	11,473	12,954
Environmental Protection Agency	13,122	4,667	18	--	5,250	12,521
National Aeronauts/Space Administration	1,917	5,542	28	--	5,425	2,006
Veterans Administration	3,333	22,454	67	--	22,317	3,403
Independent agencies (total)	2,575	51,250	86	(10,353)	40,639	2,747
	220,209	562,873	4,248	(26,609)	508,877	243,348
Less: intragovernmental transactions and proprietary receipts from the public	--	(72,091)	--	--	(72,091)	--
	$220,209	$490,782	$4,248	$(26,609)	$436,786	$243,348

STATEMENT OF CHANGES IN UNDISBURSED
BALANCES, BY AGENCIES

Statement 6 gives a breakdown of the summary data in the appropriated funds column of Statement 4 in terms of major agencies of the government. Although it appears to be relatively detailed, it is still very condensed, with but one line of data for each listed agency. Necessarily, the line on each agency gives only the total of its appropriated funds. The data are for the General Fund only.

Statement 6 first breaks down the summary data for the government as a whole to the specific agency organizations that perform the tasks of the federal government, which thus provides an organizational view. Second, Statement 6 identifies the major functions into which the work of government is divided. This provides a functional operating view.[3] Third, Statement 6 presents an overall view of the government's appropriated funds structure. Changes in the status of appropriated funds are triggered by appropriations (+), withdrawals (−), transfers (+ or −), and disbursements (−), all of which are accounted for by responsible agencies which, as their names suggest, are mission oriented, stated in general terms. The specific programs and subprograms, of course, are not visible in the summary single line figures for each agency.

The three-way overview contributes to an understanding of the fiscal affairs of the federal government (or any other government). The three ways—organizational, functional, and funding—merge because each is a different aspect of the same thing. The list of agency organizations also is the list of its broad functions, and its list of appropriated funds through which funds are funnelled to the places and for the purposes authorized.

To illustrate, the Department of Labor is the federal organization that administers the functions of dealing with protection and welfare of workers. The Department is financed by appropriated funds assigned to it. This three-way arrangement holds for the department as a whole and, equally, in the progressive subdivision of organizational unit, set of functions, and appropriated funds, irrespective of operating level, location of activity, or specific mission.

Ideally, in government as in business, no well-defined function or mission should be fractured or split into more than one organization being responsible for it, nor should it be subjected to split financing, meaning financing through overlapping appropriated funds. In other words, the more specific the line of responsibility, the line of operating jurisdiction, and the line of funding, the closer a situation is to achieving the ideal. Congress and the executive branches recognize this principle and its implementation is getting better year by year. However, changes in programs—adding new ones and dropping or modifying old ones—that occur every year because of political, social, or economic reasons have a tendency to slow down progress.

Additional Disclosures in Statement 6

Statement 6 presents other important data and concepts as discussed in the following paragraphs.

Appropriation Details

The line item summary for each agency shown in Statement 6 is supported by appropriation details. The details are accounted for under two categories, namely, by operating program and by object. This is illustrated below for the Coast Guard, a component activity of the Department of Transportation (except in war times, when the activity is transferred to the Department of the Navy).

Amounts for each category are omitted because they are not readily available only for the General Fund in published reports of the government.[4]

Appropriation details by program. Search and Rescue, Aids to Navigation, Marine Safety, Marine Environmental Protection, Enforcement of Laws and Treaties, Marine Science and Polar Operations, and Military Readiness.

Appropriation details by object. Personnel Compensation, categorized into full time, part time, other civilian personnel, military personnel, and special services; Personnel Benefits, categorized into civilian, military; Travel and Transportation, categorized into persons, things; Communications; Utilities; Rent; Printing, Reproduction; Supplies and Materials; Equipment; Land and Structures; Insurance Claims and Indemnities; Interest; Other Services.

Disbursements

The disbursements shown in Statement 6 are presented in accordance with the same principles described in Statement 4, which are repeated here for emphasis. Disbursements are shown net of appropriation reimbursements. Disbursements do not include amounts disbursed for redeeming Treasury debt obligations or for appropriations and loans to other funds. Those items are charged directly to unappropriated balance.

The disbursement figures embrace a wide variety of payments including operating expenses; capital outlays for land, buildings, and equipment; materials and supplies purchased; and loans and investments made. Diverse as these purposes are, they represent money disbursed and all of them result from appropriations made to appropriated funds. The breakdown of the purposes for which appropriations

EXHIBIT 19
Changes in Undisbursed Balances (in millions)

Balance, start of year			$220,209
Appropriations		$490,782	
Transfers	$ 26,609		
Withdrawals	4,248	30,857	459,925
			680,134
Disbursements			436,786
Balance, end of year			$243,348

and related disbursements are made is published by operating programs and object classification but not for the General Fund separately. The data in Statement 6 are stated on the cash basis.

Undisbursed Balances

For fiscal year 19X1, the changes in the undisbursed balances were as shown in Exhibit 19 (in millions).

The additions during the year of $459,925 million exceeded disbursements of $436,786 million, resulting in an increase in year-end totals of undisbursed balances of $23,139 million. Why is there such a relatively large undisbursed balance, especially since each year's increment (excess of inflows over outflows) is relatively small?

Perhaps the main reason for the large undisbursed balances is that appropriations for capital outlays are made on a continuing, no-year basis; therefore, they are made available until used. Capital outlay appropriations thus continue over a number of years until actually disbursed. Typically, disbursements for capital expenditures are not completed until three, five, or more years after the year of appropriation and capital projects almost always involve large sums of money.

A second reason for the large balance is the behavior of one-year appropriations for ordinary operating requirements. Disbursements for appropriations that cover purchases of materials and supplies (including repair parts of all kinds) and major service contracts (for example, repairs of buildings), often lag a year or more behind appropriations.

Finally, regardless of purpose, appropriations are made in terms of obligational authority, which means authority to incur obligations by issuance of contracts and orders. Actual disbursements to pay for obligations incurred naturally come later. How much later will depend upon the span of time between date of appropriation and date of disbursement. In the federal government, this span of time often takes several years, depending upon how soon after appropriation the contracts and orders are issued; how soon after issuance of contracts and orders they are completely carried out; and how soon after completion of contracts and orders they are fully paid.

APPROPRIATIONS VERSUS DISBURSEMENTS

A question raised from time to time is whether Congress should exercise closer control over disbursements than it presently does. Advocates of such an approach admit that disbursements can be made only under standing appropriations; nevertheless, they feel that Congress can have a more direct control over disbursements. This concept is found in one of the recommendations of the second Hoover Commission.

Those who make such proposals really want to give Congress control over the timing of disbursements. Since authority to make disbursements is governed by appropriations, timing of disbursements is the only thing left that Congress could control. But is such a control possible? The question has been discussed seriously within congressional appropriation committees and the consensus seems to be that congressional control over timing of disbursements raises more problems than it solves.

Since disbursements are effects of incurring obligations, then acts of obligating are matters of internal agency management. If Congress is to step in and exercise control over disbursements of an agency, it must first take over the agency's active management, which is inconceivable. Even agency managers have problems over timing of their disbursements. It is inherently a difficult thing to do. To use a figure of speech, a spigot cannot be turned on and off to regulate the flow of disbursements during a particular year, like the flow of water. The "spigots" of appropriations are turned on, of necessity, when programs are funded one, two, or more years ahead of the disbursements flow and automatically set the rate of flow of disbursements. Although the two flows are related to each other, one following and being governed by the previous one through time, the two flows are otherwise radically different. The considerations and decisions that set appropriation flows are more or less independent of those that subsequently control disbursement flows.

EXHIBIT 20
Appropriations Compared with Disbursements

Year Ended June 30	Appropriations	Disbursements						
		19X1	19X2	19X3	19X4	19X5	19X6	19X7
Prior years	$200*	$130	$ 70					
19X1	225	80	80	$ 65				
19X2	250		92	88	$ 70			
19X3	300			105	95	$ 86	$ 14	
19X4					?	?	?	?
		$210	$242	$258	?	?	?	?

*Balance forward.

Forecasting Disbursements

The above discussion is not intended to create the impression that estimates for next year's disbursements are not possible. Such forecasts are made regularly and with a reasonable degree of accuracy, but the forecasts are conditioned on appropriations already made or under active consideration by Congress (as in studies of an upcoming budget). The technique of relating appropriations and disbursements is illustrated in Exhibit 20. Assume that the forecast is prepared in 19X3 for fiscal year 19X4 and that the method of forecasting has been in use for the past several years. Amounts are in billions.

From the data in Exhibit 20, it is apparent that in its 19X3 deliberations as to how much it should appropriate for fiscal year 19X4, Congress is faced with the fact that some $165 billion have been committed already for disbursing in 19X4 by reason of past appropriations. The only way this sum can be reduced is by legislative recission of appropriations previously made but not yet obligated accompanied by cutting back on authorized programs or by citing agencies to cancel existing contracts and orders. Under any of such actions, public outcry against program reductions, disruption of agency plans and arrangements, and likely legal suits by contractors seeking damages for contract cancellations would all combine to give Congress problems more formidable than those it was seeking to alleviate.

Using analyses similar to the foregoing, OMB regularly forecasts disbursements in relation to appropriations. In a recent year's budget

STATEMENT 7

United States Government—Financial Position of the General Fund, September 30, 19X1 (in millions)

	Appropriated Funds	Unappropriated Funds	Total
Fund resources			
Undisbursed Treasury balance	$243,348 (a)	--	(b)
Accounts receivable (c)	26,121	--	$ 26,121
Anticipated reimbursements (unfilled customers orders)	10,357	--	10,357
Anticipated appropriations to cover contract authorizations	242,434	--	(b)
Anticipated future receipts to cover appropriations and authorizations (d)	--	$500,090	500,090
Total	522,260	500,090	536,568
Fund obligations			
Accounts payable and accrued liabilities	53,223	--	53,223
Contracts and orders outstanding (unfilled orders with vendors)	413,823	--	413,823
Payable to appropriated funds	--	243,348	(b)
Payable to other funds (to cover borrowings resulting from overdrawn cash account with Treasury)	--	14,308 (e)	14,308
Anticipated appropriations to cover contract authorizations	--	242,434	(b)
Total	467,046	500,090	481,354
Unobligated fund balances	$ 55,214	--	$ 55,214

Notes: a) Per Statement 4.
     b) Eliminated in consolidation.
     c) Taxes receivable are not accrued unless due; taxes past due are stated at face value until collected or written off as uncollectible.
     d) A logical, though improbable, fund resource, depending upon the interpretation used (as discussed further in the text).
     e) Per Statements 1 and 4.

analysis, for example, the appropriations recommended by the President to Congress totaled $568 billion, of which $361 billion or 63% was forecast to be disbursed in the upcoming budget year and $207 billion or 37% in later years. It was also forecast that, in the upcoming budget year, disbursements would total $500 billion, representing $361 billion or 72% under appropriations for that year and $139 billion or 28% under appropriations made for prior years.

STATEMENT OF FINANCIAL POSITION

The last statement in the series is a summary of the General Fund's financial position as of September 30, 19X1 in Statement 7.

Appropriated Funds

Anticipated Reimbursements

This amount represents the value of orders received for goods and services that are in the process of being filled. The amounts involved will become accounts receivable for goods delivered or work done. By anticipating reimbursements and recording them as a fund resource, the serving agency is able to create an offsetting obligational authority to incur expenditures necessary to fill the orders. When the accounts receivable are collected, the cash expended previously will be recouped. (The procedure is similar to recording the budgetary item "estimated revenue" in local government.)

Anticipated Appropriations

In certain cases, agencies receive authorization from Congress to enter into contracts for capital expenditures. This contract authorization enables an agency to incur obligations, but does not permit it to disburse money to pay for the obligation. Disbursements cannot take place until Congress makes the related appropriation, which may take a year or so after contract authorization. As noted above, anticipated appropriations are offset on the books of an agency by a matching credit to obligational authority, which permits it to incur obligations. It is considered impractical to distinguish obligational authority created in this manner from that created through actual appropriation. As a result, the two sources of obligational authority are credited in the agency's books to the same account (unobligated balance). When Congress makes appropriations to cover contract authorizations previously granted, the affected agency transfers the amount appropriated from anticipated appropriations (an asset) to undisbursed Treasury balance (cash).

Obligations

The federal government's accounting for obligations is similar to the methods used by state and local governments, but there are exceptions. Contracts and orders outstanding include legal commitments for purchases of goods and services from vendors both within and outside the government.

In preparing the statement, receivables and payables between appropriated funds have not been eliminated, even though consolidation procedure requires such eliminations. The reason for not eliminating such items is that to have done so would have netted out important interfund relationships.

Unobligated Balances

Fund resources less obligations incurred give the unobligated balances of the General Fund, as for any other constituted fund. Statement 7 shows that unobligated balances total $55.214 billion. This amount relates only to continuing or "no year" appropriations. All other appropriations are made for one year and expire at the end of each year. All of the unobligated amount, $55.214 billion, is available for obligating until used up, barring unforeseen conditions such as contract cancellations.

Unappropriated Balance

The unappropriated balance shows no present resources and $500.09 billion of obligations, resulting in a deficit of that amount. The obligations are payable to the appropriated funds and the other funds. However, the obligations shown are only correct technically in terms of fund accounting principles as would be the indicated deficit described below.

Rationale for Presenting a Deficit Condition

It was both legal and proper for the General Fund to follow the will of Congress and make appropriations and reduce the unappropriated balance. Equally legal and proper were the actions of the appropriated funds in recording appropriations received as additions to their cash balances on deposit with the Treasury. However, receipts fell behind appropriations. In the circumstances, the General Fund was compelled to incur obligations to the appropriated funds and other funds with the result that the financial position of the General Fund as of September 30, 19X1 shows excess obligations of $500.09 billion in its unappropriated fund; in other words, a deficit in this amount.

The deficit can be removed, at least in the amount of obligations to the appropriated and other funds—$257.656 billion—by Treasury borrowing the needed money and increasing the public debt. Upon receipt of the cash, the General Fund could pay its obligations. However, this is not done because there is no need for Treasury to obtain this money by borrowing in the marketplace and thus incur the cost of interest. There is no indication that the time lag of disbursements behind appropriations will not continue in the future. As of September 30, 19X1, the lag has created some $243.348 billion of undisbursed Treasury balances of the appropriated funds. That appears to be more than ample to meet foreseeable disbursements of the appropriated funds, which alone are authorized to make disbursements on behalf of the General Fund. The overdrawn or deficit condition of the unappropriated fund, therefore, becomes a matter of secondary concern.

The deficit condition noted cannot, however, be passed over lightly. The trend over the years is to keep raising the level of this deficit. The ability of the government to live with a deficit is generally accepted by all. No one questions the ability of the government to pay its obligations as they mature, as long as the government's credit remains good. And why should it not, considering that it is backed with the full authority of Congress? The ability of Congress to accelerate cash receipts by raising taxes or increasing debt so as to reduce or eliminate the deficit is the reason for treating the $500.09 billion item as a fund resource instead of as a fund deficit in Statement 7.

Will the General Fund as a whole ever have resources equal to its appropriations? The reply that this situation is not necessary, or that the Congress can, if it so wished, bring this condition about is reassuring. However, in the debate as to whether the condition will ever be realized, the skeptics outnumber the optimists.

Data not Shown in Statement 7

Three significant items are omitted from Statement 7 as an exhibit of the financial position of the General Fund, in keeping with its nature as an expendable fund. These are the General Fund's nonfund resources, nonfund liabilities (generally referred to as the public debt), and contingent liabilities (see chapter 5).

NOTES

1. The overappropriated position of the General Fund is aggravated further by the existence of contingent liabilities. These represent guarantees of loans made by private lending institutions and insurance commitments on other types of loans also made in the private loan market. All such contingent liabilities have been explicitly authorized by Congress under covering legislation. Chapter 5 gives a brief discussion of contingent liabilities.

2. To illustrate this phenomenon, in years of inflation there is a "creep" in the tax bracket due to an increase in a person's pretax income that is traceable to the factor of inflation, as shown by a cost-of-living pay increase. This has been the subject of congressional concern. The problem has been identified as "inflation-induced tax bracket creep," the effect of which is to offset, in whole or in part, any cost-of-living pay increase, as an example, that was received to allow for inflation.

The Economic Recovery Tax Act of 1981 includes a provision which, for the first time, makes a correction for the inflation factor through a formula method known as indexation. The provision goes into effect in the 1985 tax year;

however, Congress may change its mind and repeal this provision. Congress may decide that too much tax revenue would be sacrificed by indexation because its effect is to lower marginal tax rates and thereby decrease average tax rates. Indexation logically works both ways as a correction method, depending upon whether the economy is expanding, accompanied by higher general prices, or contracting accompanied by lowering of general prices (deflation).

3. As noted in Chapter 2, there is an effort for a more formal functional classification of government activities, but the effort is still under development. For the present, this effort is not greatly different from the functions provided in terms of major organizations.

4. Appropriation details are recorded in the accounts of each agency in terms of the object classification in the ageny's chart of accounts. Charges to the accounts are coded by program for purposes of monthly and annual reporting in the agency's financial statements. Some charges are allocated to programs by formula method.

5.

OTHER COMBINED FINANCIAL STATEMENTS ___

This chapter presents and discusses the following government-wide combined financial statements of the federal government as of September 30, 19X1 (except as noted):

Statement 8.   *Nonfund Assets Owned.* Assets acquired through the General Fund, through which their purchase or construction was financed.

Statement 9.   *Summary of the Public Debt.* Liabilities incurred mainly by borrowings of the General Fund; the liabilities are treated as nonfund debt because they are not payable from a designated fund but are considered to be general debt of the government.

Statement 10.   *Financial Position of Revolving Funds.* Includes intragovernment and public enterprise–type revolving funds.

Statement 11.   *Financial Position of Trust Funds.* Government managed but not government owned.

Statement 12.   *Financial Position of Federal Old-Age and Survivors Insurance Trust Fund.* As of September 30, 1983.

Statement 13.   *Changes in Fund Balance of Preceding Fund.* For the year ended September 30, 1983.

Statement 14.   *Financial Position of the Government as a Whole, by Funds and Nonfund Entities.*

Statements 8 and 9 highlight that the federal government, like state and local governments, owns certain assets and owes certain debts that are outside the duly constituted funds; namely, the General Fund, special funds, revolving funds, and trust funds. The government's nonfund assets are primarily noncurrent assets, and the government's nonfund debt represents noncurrent debt, as will be further discussed in this chapter.

Generally, nonfund assets are used by federal agencies other than those managing revolving funds. Each agency using nonfund assets probably purchased or constructed such assets with money financed under the General Fund. As will be discussed further in Chapter 7, an agency that purchased, constructed, or received a transfer of nonfund assets from another agency maintains a two-tiered set of asset accounts. The first tier represents assets that are shown in the balance sheet of an expendable fund and can be used to pay for the fund's current or future debts. The second tier consists of assets that are held for use or consumption in the normal operation of the given agency and will not be convertible into cash for the purpose of expenditure, that is, for paying the fund's current or future debts. Second-tier assets are shown in a supplement to the balance sheet of an expendable fund.

ORIGIN AND DISPOSITION OF NONFUND ASSETS AND LIABILITIES

Nonfund assets, consisting mainly of physical property and certain loans and investments required under certain government aid programs, are initially financed by the General Fund. A combination of tradition, custom, and accounting practice has, however, disassociated the assets from the General Fund. Similarly, the money received from issuing debt obligations, popularly called the public debt, is added to the cash balance of the General Fund. The resulting debt is not associated with the General Fund, again as a result of tradition, custom, and accounting practice.

Materials, supplies, land, buildings, and equipment are used and, as applicable, used up under the category of nonfund assets as their respective life cycles are completed. Any proceeds received from the sale or disposition of the assets are credited to miscellaneous receipts of the General Fund, thereby increasing the General Fund's unappropriated balance. Other nonfund assets such as loans and investments are handled in a similar way: money received from their liquidation is also credited to the miscellaneous receipts of the General Fund, which also increases the unappropriated balance of the General Fund.

Nonfund liabilities represented by the public debt are equally disassociated from the General Fund, even though, to repeat, the proceeds from the sales of such debt were added to the cash balance of the General Fund. Statement 2 highlighted this treatment. Like general taxes collected, proceeds from the sale of debt increased the unappropriated balance of the General Fund, which then became available for appropriations in accordance with the President's budget, as approved by Congress. When issued debt matures, it is repaid by refunding it; that is, new debt is issued for the express purpose of paying off old debt that has matured. This refunding process is the responsibility of the Treasury, under specific authority of Congress, and is completely disassociated from the General Fund.

Measurement of Nonfund Assets and Liabilities

The total respective amounts of the government's nonfund assets and liabilities, as presented in Statements 8 and 9, are large by any standard. Of the asset categories shown, physical property is more difficult to value than loans and investments.

Generally, controls over materials, supplies, and the other items of property are not of the level of standards of accountability usually found in the private sector. Frequently, physical custody and control does not consist of maintaining the assets in good condition or at a satisfactory level of utilization or protection. Nor is physical custody and control always equated with satisfactory measurement of acquisition value (purchase price). Repair history, age and expected life, and final disposition by sale, transfer, or removal from service is other information that is often either missing or incomplete.

Granted that lawful agencies do have possession and use of nonfund assets and government-owned assets are placed under the responsibility of a specific agency for its custody and use, still the standards of property management and accountability to which the assets are subject are another problem.

STATEMENT OF NONFUND ASSETS

Assets acquired by expenditures from the General Fund are presented in Statement 8, although the assets are not treated as nonfund assets of the General Fund. They are considered general assets of the government during their entire life cycle from beginning to end, similar to the treatment of general assets owned by state and local governments. Following is a discussion of certain assets, other than materials and supplies and foreign currencies acquired without dollar payments (see Chapter 3).

Fixed Assets

The federal government owned $279.7 billion of fixed assets as of September 30, 19X1. Every imaginable type of asset is included under land, buildings, and equipment, for example, military items such as ships, shipyards, aircraft; assorted manufacturing plants, shops, labo-

STATEMENT 8

United States Government—Nonfund Assets Owned, September 30, 19X1 (in billions)

Foreign currencies acquired without dollar payments stated in U.S. dollars by using appropriate foreign exchange rates			$ 1.01
Loans receivable, less allowances for losses, from borrowers under financial aid programs (including some foreign aid programs)			34.20
Investments in certain international public financial institutions, under existing foreign aid programs, at cost			19.90
Investments in revolving funds, representing the government's equity in the funds, per Statement 10			71.20
Subtotal			126.31
Inventories of materials and supplies, at cost			17.50
Physical facilities:			
Land, at cost		$ 10.80	
Structures and facilities	$ 96.40		
Equipment	187.40		
Leaseholds	1.50		
Total cost	285.30		
Less accrued depreciation	16.40		
Total book value		268.90	
Total physical facilities			279.70
Other assets (unclassified), at cost less allowances for losses			108.80
Total nonfund assets owned			$532.31

Notes: a) The nonfund assets presented in this Statement were financed almost entirely by the General Fund.

   b) In the case of loans receivable, additional loans of this nature are made by revolving funds, as shown in Statement 10.

   c) Depreciable property is stated at approximate cost, and the accumulated depreciation shown is probably an estimated measure, considering the magnitude of the task of keeping adequate property accounts. The percentage of accrued depreciation, 5.5%, is a relatively low measure. However, the data presented in this Statement are a good reminder of the problem of accuracy of accrued depreciation.

   d) The relatively large amount of unclassified assets suggests that the reports from the agencies of such items were less than satisfactory.

   e) Materials and supplies include stockpiled items having military end use.

   f) In general, Statement 8 is prepared from several sources of published data and should be interpreted as subject to a significant margin of conjecture. Nevertheless, the data presented in Statement 8 are a useful picture of the types of nonfund assets and the approximate dollar values of these assets as reported in various government-published sources.

ratories; practice fields; roadways and waterways vehicles and railroads; and many other items needed to conduct and facilitate the business of government.

One-sixth of the United States (mostly in the West) is federally owned; excluding Alaska. This total rises to one-third if Alaska is included, and rises further if the outer continental shelf and off-shore islands owned by the government are added.

Depreciation

Fixed assets are excluded from the balance sheets of expendable funds because such assets are not available for obligating or for paying bills. If depreciable assets are excluded as fund assets of expendable funds, provisions for depreciation on such assets are also omitted. Therefore, no charges for depreciation are included in an operating statement of an expendable fund. The expenditure was made when the depreciable property was acquired. Depreciable property will have to be replaced eventually if it is used in an ongoing program; property wears out or becomes too expensive to maintain or is caught up with obsolescence.[1] When property is replaced, the new costs are treated as expenditures of the period in which replacements take place, the same as if they were new items not related to the items replaced.

A provision for accumulated depreciation and amortization of $16.4 billion is presented in Statement 8. However, it does not represent accumulated charges to the operations of the expendable funds making use of them. It is a statistical measurement resulting from engineering estimates by property managers who wish to recognize the life cycle of depreciable property they manage to help them plan for future replacements.

Engineering and accounting experts develop schedules or life expectancy tables, normally by property class or group. These tables furnish periodic depreciation and amortization amounts that can be recorded formally: debit government's equity accounts and credit asset contra accounts identified as "accumulated provision for depreciation." Property ledgers can then be kept current with respect to accumulated depreciation.

Loans Receivable

Approximately $34.2 billion of loans receivable are outstanding as of September 30, 19X1. All of the loans are made from the General Fund out of appropriations to individual agencies. Loans are made under several aid programs authorized by Congress intended to assist various groups or individuals, including homeowners, businesses, state governments, educational institutions, and war veterans.

The loans usually earn interest (though the interest is generally well below market rates) and are paid back at maturity. The loans are shown net of allowances for uncollectibles, but the adequacy of this provision is not generally known. Repaid loans, together with related interest, are treated as miscellaneous receipts of the General Fund and are therefore added to the unappropriated balance of this fund. Thus, repaid loans and interest received are not considered as liquidation of fund resources because there are no such fund resources to be liquidated.

The cycle begins when Congress makes appropriations from the General Fund for the aid programs. Next, the loans are made and treated as expenditures, which are charged against appropriations as irrevocably as for the purchase of fixed assets. The cycle ends when loans and related interest are collected and credited to the General Fund's miscellaneous receipts. New appropriations by Congress are necessary to make such miscellaneous receipts available for other purposes. Covering legislation may direct that repaid loans shall be made to some designated loaning fund that operates as a revolving fund.

Investments in International Aid Programs

Statement 8 shows that $19.9 billion are invested in certain international financial institutions with money appropriated from the General Fund. The investments fall under the government's foreign aid programs, particularly to third world nations.[2] The total of $19.9 billion includes cash of $10.8 billion that is committed but not yet disbursed. The life of the investments is uncertain and they represent capital investments. The cycle begins, as for loans, with money appropriated by Congress from the General Fund. Only institutions specified in the appropriation can qualify for the investments authorized. Expenditures follow as investments are made by the responsible agencies. It is uncertain when, if ever, such investments will be liquidated. If and when such investments are liquidated, the money received will be treated as miscellaneous receipts of the General Fund. Reentry of such receipts into the appropriation process cannot take place without new appropriations by Congress.

Investments in Revolving Funds

The financial relationship between the General Fund and the government's revolving funds is shown in Statement 8. It shows that the government's owner equity in its revolving funds totals $71.2 billion. This is measured by the difference between the total assets of $304.1 billion and total liabilities of $232.9 billion, as set forth more fully in Statement 10. Revolving funds are more important generally in the federal government than in state and local governments. The $71.2 billion is made up of two elements: the contributed capital that resulted from appropriations from the General Fund and accumulated net earnings from operations.

The General Fund's relationship to revolving funds follows a pattern similar to its relationship with loans and investments but with a significant difference. As to the similarity, Congress makes appropriations from the General Fund to revolving funds, and money is disbursed to the revolving funds. (Statement 2 shows this flow of money.)[3] The difference appears at this point. The money received by the revolving funds becomes fund assets of the funds to be held and used by them indefinitely, in accordance with the charters under which revolving funds operate. Moreover, the money so received is credited to invested capital on the books of the revolving funds, using accounting standards similar to those observed in commercial accounting. When and if for any reason a given revolving fund is discontinued, the proceeds from liquidation, less payments due creditors, will flow back to the General Fund, where it will be credited to miscellaneous receipts and thus added to the unappropriated balance.

Accounts for Nonfund Assets

The respective agencies that have management control over nonfund assets also have responsibility for the proper accounting records. Thus, Treasury's central accounts include foreign currencies acquired without dollar payments. The several agencies managing loans and investments are required to keep suitable records of the status of such loans and investments. Periodic reports are prepared, in accordance with the standing directives, for Congress, Treasury, OMB, and other higher authorities. The government's equity in revolving funds is reported in the financial statement of each revolving fund. Finally, each agency having and using materials and supplies and property items such as land, buildings, and equipment is required to maintain detailed records of its accountability of the respective items. Self-balancing accounts using double-entry bookkeeping is a good system of record management. To record the receipt of an asset, debit an account for the cost of acquisition and credit the amount for the government's equity in the item in the appropriate property ledger.

STATEMENT OF THE PUBLIC DEBT

Statement 9 gives a summary of the government's nonfund indebtedness, popularly known as the public debt or federal debt. This debt stood at $998.4 billion dollars, described as total direct Treasury obligations. When the several additional items appearing further down in

STATEMENT 9
United States Government—Summary of the Federal Debt, September 30, 19X1 (in billions)

	Debt Amount Payable	Debt Subject to Statutory Limitation
(A) Direct Treasury obligations		
Public issues:		
Marketable obligations		
Treasury bills (due within one year)	$223.4	
Treasury notes (due from one to five years)	363.6	
Treasury bonds (due after five years)	96.2	$683.2	$683.2
Nonmarketable obligations		
Savings bonds series	68.5	
State and local governments series	23.2	
Foreign governments series		
Payable in dollars	15.4	
Payable in foreign currencies	5.0	
Other debt	.1	112.2	112.2
Treasury debt not subject to statutory limitation		.6
Total public issues		796.0
Special issues (nonmarketable) to U.S. Government agencies		
Civil Service Retirement Fund	80.8	
Old Age Survivors Insurance Trust Fund	20.7	
Hospital Insurance Trust Fund	18.1	
Unemployment Trust Fund	12.8	
Federal Deposit Insurance Corporation	11.2	
Highway Trust Fund	9.1	
National Service Life Insurance Fund	8.0	
All Other	40.3	201.0	201.0
Matured debt on which interest has ceased		.5	.5
Debt bearing no interest		.9	.9
Total direct Treasury obligations		998.4	997.8
(B) Government agencies' debt securities issued under special financing authorities		
Guaranteed debt securities issued by government agencies		
Export-Import Bank	.4	--
Department of Defense	.5	--
Department of Housing and Urban Development	.4	1.3	.4
Debt securities not guaranteed by the United States issued by:		
Department of Housing and Urban Development	2.9	1.2
Postal Service	.2	--
Tennessee Valley Authority	1.7	4.8	--
Total federal debt		$1,004.5	$999.4
Statutory limitation of federal debt at report date		$999.8

the statement are added, the total public debt as of September 30, 19X1 is increased to $1,004.5 billion.[4]

The federal government, as in the case of state and local governments, does not consider such general indebtedness as a part of the General Fund but as a stand-alone item or simply as the government's nonfund indebtedness.

EXHIBIT 21
U.S. Government Public Debt

	1955	1960	1965	1970	1975	1980	Est. 1985
Public Debt	$273	$284	$314	$370	$533	$893	$1,828
Index	100	104	115	135	195	327	670

Although the purpose of every increase in the government's public debt (technically described as direct Treasury obligations) is to furnish the General Fund with money needed to make up the shortfall of current tax receipts, the debt itself is excluded as an obligation of the General Fund. This is consistent with the character of the General Fund as an expendable fund.[5] However, the public debt is not accounted for by any other duly constituted fund, such as a sinking fund that would be used to accumulate tax receipts to pay off the public debt outstanding in some systematic manner. Apart from what fund may properly account for the public debt is the broader issue of whether the government can repay (that is, redeem) the public debt. If and when conditions in the future do enable the government to begin to repay its public debt, the payments will be treated as expenditures from current tax receipts of the payor fund designated for the purpose.[6] Presently, current tax receipts to finance the annual payments of interest on the public debt (through the General Fund) amount to approximately $100 billion.

Historical Record of a Rising Public Debt

The public debt of the government has steadily increased during the past several decades, and dramatically so in recent years, as noted in Exhibit 21 (in billions). The attribute of the public debt as probably a perpetual debt appears to be a realistic interpretation of history. For the foreseeable future, the efforts of any political administration seem to lie in curbing the increase, not in reducing the level of debt.

Accounts for Nonfund Indebtedness

Treasury's central records include detailed accounts of the public debt, which are summarized in Statement 9. Treasury's records are single-entry accounts, but they readily can be converted into self-balancing, double-entry accounts. A balance sheet can be prepared from the information so recorded. Essentially, each item of debt is recorded by a debit to "future receipts to be provided" and a credit to "debt item payable." Exhibit 22 shows one way for preparing a summary report:

EXHIBIT 22
**Statement of Status of the Public Debt of the United States Government
as of September 30, 19X1**

```
Resources                              Liabilities

To be provided by future receipts      Total public debt
   from:                                   representing direct U.S.
                                           Treasury obligations,
   (a) Planned surplus of tax              issued and outstanding
       revenues over disbursements
       for operations and                    Held outside the
                                             government          $793.0
   (b) Planned refunding by which
       proceeds from sales of new            Held by federal
       debt issues are used to               agencies            205.4
       redeem maturing outstanding                              ======
       issues                 $998.4                            $998.4
                              ======                            ======
```

```
Since resource (a) is improbable, resource (b) is the only
   practical method of redeeming debt as it becomes due.
```

MAJOR CLASSES OF THE PUBLIC DEBT

Several major classes of the public debt are shown in Statement 9:
public issues, special issues, and agency issues.

Public Issues

Public issues are subdivided into marketable and nonmarketable
obligations and debt not subject to limitation. Marketable issues include debt items that are sold to the public.[7] They can be held by
investors to maturity or sold in the financial market to other investors.
Nonmarketable issues are sold to the special investor categories listed.
They include debt items such as Series E Savings Bonds that are sold
to individuals. Interest on Series E bonds is paid when the bonds mature and is measured by the difference between the amount paid for
the bonds by the individual and the maturity value of the bonds. If an
investor in Series E bonds wants to convert them into cash prior to
maturity, he or she receives the redemption value of the bonds based
upon a standard redemption timetable applicable to the bonds.

Special Issues to Federal Agencies

Certain debt items are sold directly by Treasury to federal agencies
that manage the large trust funds. The Civil Service Retirement Fund

alone holds $81 billion of such obligations for investment. Federal trust funds are required by law to restrict their investments to federal debt obligations. Special issues of this nature are nonmarketable in the sense that they cannot be bought and sold in the financial market.

Agency Debt Issues

Some federal agencies are authorized by Congress to borrow directly from the investing public. Such borrowings are relatively small, as indicated in Statement 9. But Statement 9 does not include all debt of this nature; such agency debt issues are described in Statement 10 covering revolving funds.

MANAGING THE PUBLIC DEBT

The public debt is in reality a federal institution that deserves further discussion and analysis.

Refunding

A large portion of the public debt classified as direct Treasury obligations is short term, maturing within one year. However, the short-term nature is only legalistic and technical. It has little or no economic significance. The short-term obligations bear the lowest interest rates, but they must be continually refunded, that is, replaced with other short-term debt. In the single year ending September 30, 1983, the government issued new debt securities totaling $2.378 trillion, of which $2.143 trillion or 90% represented the refunding of maturing debt securities (many with terms of less than a year).

Seasonal Pattern

There is a certain seasonal pattern in the level of the public debt. The level rises toward the end of the calendar year, then falls during the early months of the next calendar year, when more taxes are collected. However, under the government's policy of pay-as-you-go tax collections, the seasonal fluctuation tends to be minimal.

Debt Ceiling

It is a prerogative of Congress to set a limit or ceiling on the public debt, including guaranteed debt of certain agencies. The limitation keeps getting higher periodically; that is, Congress keeps setting a higher and higher debt limit. These actions are related to the appropriations made by Congress, but they are separate and distinct actions of

Congress. Appropriations by Congress predetermine the level of future disbursements. The related need for money over and above anticipated tax receipts then forces Congress to take the other action, namely, to increase the debt limit in order to permit borrowing the difference.

A formal limitation on the public debt set by Congress is a strong tradition. Occasionally, when there is a somewhat tardy increase of the currently existing debt ceiling, a situation of near crisis grips the government until the debt ceiling is raised sufficiently to permit the required increase in the debt.

Investors in the Public Debt

Holders of the public debt represent a cross section of the entire business community and government agencies. Exhibit 23 is a summary of the investors as a percentage of the total.[8]

U.S. government agencies owned as investments a total of $205.4 billion of the government's public debt, representing some 21% of the total, $998.4 billion. Restricted-purpose funds are the source of the money for making such investments. The reasons for this approach are that the government needs the money for general operations and that the several funds have surplus money to invest and earn income. The practice of government agencies in using spare cash (until it is needed) for such investments, however, is only partly a matter of earning income. Thus, Treasury securities are by law the only type of investments that restricted-purpose funds are permitted to make. As a further control, the government agencies that do invest are issued debt securities that are nonmarketable; that is, they are not traded in the financial market.

The excess cash of restricted-purpose funds is also used, as noted in the discussion of Statement 1, to meet day-to-day cash needs of the General Fund. The overdrawn cash position of the General Fund, made possible by automatic borrowing from restricted-purpose funds, has become a familiar phenomenon of federal financing policy. The practice enables Treasury to use the spare cash of other funds to aid the General Fund, free of interest charges for the amounts borrowed.

Substantial investments in the public debt are also made by the Federal Reserve Banks. The amount invested is around $124.3 billion, representing 12% of the total, $998.4 billion, at the date of the report. Federal Reserve Banks buy and sell Treasury obligations in the financial market, a practice that is well known in financial markets. The Banks buy or sell the obligations in a concerted effort to carry out monetary policy as directed by the *Federal Reserve Board*. In general, the Banks buy to increase the nation's money supply and sell to reduce

EXHIBIT 23
Summary of Investors

U.S. government agencies	21%
Federal Reserve Banks	12%
Commercial banks	11%
Individuals	11%
Foreign and international investors	13%
State and local government agencies	10%
All other	22%
	100%

the money supply.[9] Earnings of the Federal Reserve Banks over and above a stated return on the equity of their stockholders are annually handed over to the Treasury.

Treasury's Bureau of the Public Debt

It takes a staff of approximately 2,500 currently to manage the federal debt. Though redeeming matured debt and issuing new debt are the main functions, the work involves a lot of related activities as well. Management of the public debt takes Treasury into the financial markets almost daily. Exhibit 24 illustrates a few instances as reported in late summer 1984.

STATEMENT OF FINANCIAL POSITION OF REVOLVING FUNDS

Statement 10 sets forth the combined financial position of the government's revolving funds. A total of $304 billion of assets are at work in the activities represented. Included are both internal (that is, intragovernment service) and public enterprise revolving funds.

The largest asset shown is the $176 billion for loans outstanding, a measure of the credit activities of the government under the various aid programs, domestic and foreign. The other items in the statement are self-explanatory, but two items are noted as follows. One is materials and supplies that are held for sale to user agencies. The other is manufacturing facilities to make and sell products, either to user agencies or the public.

EXHIBIT 24
Press Reports

Treasury Note Sale Brings 12.78% Yield, Lowest Since Feb. 28

By a WALL STREET JOURNAL Staff Reporter

WASHINGTON—The Treasury sold $6.53 billion of five-year, two-month notes at an average annual yield of 12.78%.

The yield was down from the 13.93% average annual yield at the previous auction of similar notes May 30 and was the lowest since 11.84% on Feb. 28.

The Treasury received bids totaling $16.74 billion and accepted those in a range of 12.77% to 12.78%, including $522 million of non-competitive bids at the average return. The Treasury accepted 96% of the bids it received at the high yield. The average price was 99.742.

The coupon interest rate was set at 12¾%, down from 13⅜% in May and the lowest since 11¾% in February. The notes will be dated Sept. 4 and mature Nov. 15, 1989.

By EDWARD P. FOLDESSY
And TOM HERMAN
Staff Reporters of THE WALL STREET JOURNAL

NEW YORK—Bond prices edged lower as dealers were disappointed by investors' lackluster response to the Treasury's $5.5 billion auction of new 10-year notes.

The average yield on the notes was 12.65%. That was down from 13.16% at the previous sale of similar securities May 9, but it was higher than many dealers had been estimating.

Dealers were "a little disappointed with the way the auction went," said Peter Treadway, senior vice president and chief economist at Cralin & Co. The mood was in sharp contrast with the optimism that swept through the credit markets Tuesday when both U.S. and foreign investors bid aggressively for $6.5 billion of three-year Treasury notes.

The government will complete its three-part, approximately $16.75 billion quarterly financing operation today with the sale of about $4.75 billion of new 30-year bonds.

Treasury Sale of Notes Will Raise Fresh Cash Totaling $1.65 Billion

By a WALL STREET JOURNAL Staff Reporter

WASHINGTON—The Treasury plans to raise about $1.65 billion in fresh cash Wednesday with the sale of about $8.5 billion of two-year notes to redeem maturing notes valued at $6.85 billion.

The new notes will be dated Aug. 31 and mature Aug. 31, 1986.

Bids for the notes, available in minimum denominations of $5,000, must be received by 1 p.m. EDT Wednesday at the Treasury or at Federal Reserve banks or branches.

Cash Management Bills Sold by Treasury At a Yield of 11.28%

By a WALL STREET JOURNAL Staff Reporter

WASHINGTON—The Treasury sold $8 billion of 20-day cash management bills at an average annual yield of 11.28%.

The sale was needed to help bridge a low point in the Treasury's cash balances and wasn't comparable to previous auctions.

The department received bids totaling $30.99 billion and accepted those in a range of 11.25% to 11.3%. Noncompetitive bids weren't accepted. The Treasury accepted all the bids it received at the high yield. The average price was 99.373. The bills will be dated Aug. 31 and mature Sept. 20.

Separately, the Treasury said it plans to raise about $525 million in new cash Tuesday with the sale of about $13.2 billion in short-term bills to redeem maturing bills valued at $12.69 billion.

The auction will be held Tuesday, rather than the customary Monday, because of the Labor Day holiday.

The offering will be divided evenly between 13-week and 26-week bills, which will be dated Sept. 6 and mature Dec. 6, 1984, and March 7, 1985, respectively.

Bids for the bills, available in minimum denominations of $10,000, must be received by 1 p.m. EDT Tuesday at the Treasury or at Federal Reserve banks or branches.

STATEMENT 10

United States Government—Combined Statement of Financial Position of Revolving Funds, September 30, 19X1 (in millions)

Assets

Undisbursed Treasury Balance			$ 20,886
Accounts receivable, less allowances for losses			28,805
Investments in U.S. government debt issues			16,169
			65,860
Loans receivable under financial aid programs, less allowances for losses			176,200
Inventories of materials and supplies, at cost			29,214
Physical facilities			
Land, at cost		$ 1,114	
Structures and other facilities	$ 15,403		
Equipment	7,153		
Leaseholds	159		
Total cost	22,715		
Less accrued depreciation	3,677		
Total book value		19,038	
Total physical facilities			20,152
Other assets (unclassified), at cost less allowances for losses			12,659
Total Assets			$304,085

Liabilities and Government's Equity

Accounts payable and accrued liabilities			54,699
Agency debts:			
To the public for debt securities issued		$ 16,449	
To Treasury for loans		141,800	
To other funds for loans and advances		19,967	
Total agency debts to the foregoing			178,216
Total liabilities			232,915
Government's equity (excess of assets over liabilities)			71,170
Total Liabilities and Government's Equity			$304,085

Notes: a) This exhibit includes only assets and liabilities appropriate in a business-type balance sheet suitable for revolving funds. Excluded are (in billions):
   From assets, anticipated future receipts for unfilled customers orders $15.4
   From liabilities, reserves for commitments on contracts with vendors 38.4

b) Revolving funds are subject to contingent liabilities as guarantors or insurers of loans made by private lending institutions, including government-sponsored private lending institutions. As of the report date, contingent liabilities of this nature were as follows (in billions):
   - by federal budget agencies $343.4
   - by off-budget agencies   16.6
   - by government-sponsored, private firms   .8
   Total contingent liabilities $360.8

c) The government's equity, $71.17 billion, represents capital contributions by the General Fund plus accumulated earnings and less accumulated deficits of individual revolving funds, as of the report date.

Revolving funds generally account for their activities on the accrual basis. In principle, if its costs (including depreciation) are to be recovered from others (including the public) they should be measured as accurately as conditions permit. Although full recovery of costs by serving activities is desirable, it is not actually achieved because of the extra time and effort that is necessary to establish the costs to the

STATEMENT 11

United States Government—Combined Statement of Financial Position of Trust Funds, September 30, 19X1 (in millions)

Assets

Undisbursed Treasury balance	$ 9,627
Accounts receivable less allowance for losses	3,474
Anticipated reimbursements (unfilled customers' orders)	42
Investments in U.S. government debt issues, at cost	184,956
Anticipated future receipts to cover contract authorizations	34,975
Total assets (see note)	$233,074

Liabilities and Fund Equity

Accounts payable and accrued liabilities	18,897
Contracts and orders outstanding (unfilled orders with vendors)	33,744
	52,641
Fund equity	180,433
Total liabilities and fund equity	$233,074

Note:

Following are the ten largest agencies in terms of trust-fund assets managed:

Department of Health and Human Services	$ 50,134
Department of Transportation	33,386
Executive Office of the President	20,411
Department of Labor	14,940
Veterans Administration	9,631
Department of the Treasury	1,336
Department of the Interior	1,093
Department of State	887
Department of Agriculture	468
Department of Defense--Military and Civilian	252
Total (representing 57% of total trust funds assets)	$132,538

satisfaction of users that are billed for the costs. Typically, when accumulated losses handicap the operation of a revolving fund, Congress makes appropriations from the General Fund to replenish resources. Appropriations received by a revolving fund are credited to its invested capital.

Currently, there are some 163 separate revolving funds in operation. Some are huge, even for the federal government, but the total covers large and small alike. The distribution of 105 of those funds, identified by the organizations that manage them are: Department of Defense, 24; Department of Housing and Urban Development, 19; Department of Health and Human Services, 11; Department of Transportation, 11; Veterans Administration, 11; Department of Commerce, 10; General Services Administration, 10; and Department of Agriculture, 9.

STATEMENT OF FINANCIAL POSITION OF TRUST FUNDS

Statement 11 exhibits the combined financial position of the government's trust funds. As previously noted, trust funds are government managed, not government owned. Ownership of trust funds is vested in the people who have beneficial interest in them.

The asset item "anticipated future receipts to cover contract authorizations" covers anticipated receipts for purposes of covering budget authority to incur obligations beyond the amounts otherwise available. The item is also known as unfunded contract authority. When receipts are realized through appropriation by Congress, they are recorded as increases in undisbursed Treasury balance (debits) and decreases in anticipated future receipts to cover contract authorizations (credits).

As indicated in Statement 11, most of trust funds' assets (79%) consist of investments in the federal public debt. This reflects a certain time lag between collections of dues, taxes, and other required contributions and expenditures for benefit payments to members of the several programs. Experts in this field claim that the trends show a shorter time lag between receipts and payments as receipts fall behind scheduled payments. The effect of such trends is to reduce the necessity of investing spare cash in the funds until it is needed to meet benefit payments.

Trust funds are mainly in the nature of pension funds and assorted types of other funds covering disability, medical service, life insurance, hospitalization, and unemployment plans. Following is a recently published list of federally managed trust funds:

Airport and airway trust funds

Black lung disability trust fund

Civil service retirement and disability fund

Employees health benefits fund—Office of Personnel Management

Retired employees health benefits fund—Office of Personnel Management

Employees life insurance fund—Office of Personnel Management

Federal disability insurance trust fund

Federal hospital insurance trust fund

Federal supplementary medical insurance trust fund

Federal old age and survivors insurance trust fund

Foreign service retirement and disability fund

Highway trust fund

Judicial survivors annuity fund

Library of Congress trust funds

National service life insurance fund

Pershing Hall Memorial fund

Railroad retirement account

Railroad retirement supplemental account

Unemployment trust fund

U.S. government life insurance fund

FEDERAL OLD AGE AND SURVIVORS PENSION FUND

The centerpiece of the social security program is the Federal Old Age and Survivors Insurance Trust Fund. This pension fund covers tens of millions of retired workers other than federal military and civilian personnel. The question that is asked frequently about this fund is whether its resources are adequate to meet future pension payments. An analysis of the nature of the fund will help provide the answer.

The adequacy of the fund is best tested by its ability to collect annually contributions from employers and employees, identified as FICA taxes, sufficient to meet pension payments required under the covering laws. It must collect enough to pay retired workers. When those now working retire, they in turn will be supported from contributions of a new generation of workers, and so on.

The fund's assets are intended to meet requirements of the covered programs and balance the receipts and disbursements so that at no time would the fund be insolvent.

That approach is far from the use of actuarial methods familiar in the operation of pension plans in the private sector and in state and local governments. However, many believe that conventional plans found elsewhere would be difficult and perhaps impossible to use because of the hugeness of the problems that would be faced. The size and complexity of the task is believed to be such as to make the concept unworkable. Specialists on the subject, however, are divided.

The ideal of getting receipts and disbursements of this pension fund to flow in balance with each other is becoming more and more difficult lately because receipts are falling behind disbursements. This condition is a matter of great concern to the government and to the public. Remedies advanced for meeting the problems fall into three categories: increase FICA taxes, reduce benefit payments, or make some appropriations from the General Fund.

None of the remedies, however, singly or in combination, will change the fundamental concept of pay as you go, which is contrasted with the conventional concepts of funding future benefits used in the private sector and most public retirement plans.

STATEMENT 12

United States Government—Statement of Financial Position of Federal Old Age and Survivors Insurance Trust Fund, September 30, 1983 (in millions)

Assets

Undisbursed Treasury balance	$ 1,153
Investments in U.S. government debt issues, at cost	25,503
Accounts receivable, less allowances for losses	1,208
Other assets (unclassified)	79
Total assets	$27,943

Liabilities and Fund Equity

Accounts payable	12,485
Loans from other trust funds	17,519
Contracts and orders outstanding (unfilled orders)	1
Total liabilities	30,015
Fund deficit	(2,072)
Total liabilities less fund deficit	$27,943

Statement 12 shows the financial position of this fund as of September 30, 1983. Liabilities exceed assets, resulting in a deficit of $2,072 million. Statement 13 shows that for fiscal year 1983 receipts from all sources were $150,489 million, compared with total disbursements of $153,892 million, resulting in a deficit of receipts of $3,403 million.

STATEMENT 13

United States Government—Statement of Changes in Fund Balance of Federal Old Age and Survivors Insurance Trust Fund, Year Ended September 30, 1983 (in millions)

Receipts

Appropriations (see note)	$116,508	
Deposits by states	13,999	
Military service credits	18,544	
Net earnings on investments in federal debt issues	1,299	
Other receipts	139	
Total receipts		$150,489

Expenditures

Benefit payments	150,893	
Administrative expenses	1,552	
Other payments (unclassified)	1,447	
Total expenditures		153,892
Excess of expenditures over receipts during year		(3,403)
Fund balance, September 30, 1982	1,159	
Direct credits	172	
Fund balance as adjusted		1,331
Fund balance, September 30, 1983 (deficit)		$ (2,072)

Note:
In more descriptive language, this is receipts from payroll taxes.

Retirement Provisions for Federal Personnel

Like any employer, the federal government must provide for retirement payments to retired personnel. Civilian federal retirees are paid from the Civil Service Retirement and Disability Fund and other similar trust funds established for the purpose. The inadequacy of these funds from an actuarial view points up the same problems discussed above for other social security trust funds.

Military personnel who retire are now paid on a pay-as-you-go basis by annual appropriations from the General Fund. The military retired and disabled payrolls are understandably large, being approximately $18 billion in 1984. Under consideration are proposals to finance payments to military retirees through one or more trust funds, similar to the plans used for civilian federal retirees. If the proposals are adopted, both active military personnel and the government would contribute to the building up of the required trust funds. In that eventuality, the issue of whether the trust funds shall be operated on basically the pay-as-you-go concept or the actuarial concept would have to be faced.

FINANCIAL POSITION OF THE U.S. GOVERNMENT, BY FUND AND NONFUND ENTITIES

Statement 14, the final one in the series, gives a bird's eye view of the financial position of the government as a whole. Shown is the combined financial position of each major fund category, the combined financial position of all nonfund assets, and the combined financial position of the public debt. To emphasize their stand-alone nature, the nonfund assets are described as general assets. A similar description of general indebtedness should be ascribed to the nonfund debts, but the term "public debt" is widely used.

The data in Statement 14 have been previously discussed. It presents the financial position of the government as a whole. The statement also gives a comparative picture of the several parts which together constitute the financial system of the government. However, the data in each part (or column) are a universe of their own.

To the extent that the data in this Statement result from cash transactions, the data source is Treasury's central records, as published. To the extent that the data shown result from noncash transactions, the data source is reports to Treasury from the field, that is, from individual agencies operating in Washington and elsewhere. Finally, the data in the statement reflects the method of fund accounting whereby the business of government is conducted by separate fund and nonfund entities with the items and amounts shown.

In the main, the government uses the cash basis of accounting to meet Treasury controls, the obligation basis to meet congressional con-

STATEMENT 14
United States Government—Financial Position by Fund and Nonfund Entities, September 30, 19X1 (in billions)

Assets (a)	General Fund	Special Funds	Revolving Funds	Trust Funds	Deposit Funds	Nonfund Entities General Assets	Nonfund Entities Public Debt	Combined (Memo)
Undisbursed Treasury balance	$(14.3)	$7.1	$ 20.9	$ 9.6	$3.4	$ 1.0		$ 26.7
Foreign currencies in U.S. dollars								1.0
Accounts receivable (b)	26.1	.3	28.8	3.5				58.7
Loans receivable (c)			176.2			34.2		210.4
Investments in U.S. government debt issues (d)		.1	16.2	185.0	4.1			(e)
Anticipated reimbursements	10.4							10.4
Anticipated future receipts to cover contract authorizations				34.9				34.9
Sundry investments and assets						19.9		19.9
Government's equity in revolving funds						71.2		(f)
Materials and supplies inventories (d)			29.2			17.5		46.7
Land (d)			1.1			10.8		11.9
Structures, equipment, etc. (d)			22.7			285.3		308.0
Accumulated depreciation			(3.7)			(16.4)		(20.1)
Anticipated future receipts: To cover appropriations and contract authorization	500.1							500.1
From surplus of receipts over expenditures and from sales of new debt to redeem matured debt							1,004.5	1,004.5
Unclassified assets			12.7			108.8		121.5
Total	$522.3	$7.5	$304.1	$233.0	$7.5	$532.3	$1,004.5	$2,334.6

STATEMENT 14 continued

	General Fund	Special Funds	Revolving Funds	Trust Funds	Deposit Funds	General Assets	Public Debt	Combined (Memo)
Liabilities and government equity								
Accounts payable and accrued liabilities	53.2	.2	54.7	18.9				127.0
Contracts and orders outstanding	413.8	2.0		33.7				449.5
Agency debt issues			178.2					178.2
Treasury debt issues (public debt)							1,004.5	799.1(e)
Liability for deposits					7.5			7.5
Government's equity	55.3	5.3	71.2	180.4		532.3		773.3(f)
Total	$522.3	$7.5	$304.1	$233.0	$7.5	$532.3	$1,004.5	$2,334.6

Notes: (a) Minor items have been merged to condense data.
     (b) After provision for losses.
     (c) In addition to such direct loans, the government is guarantor or insurer of loans made by private lenders, creating contingent liabilities of this nature totalling $360.8 billion (per Statement 10).
     (d) At cost or estimated cost; if acquired by gift or eminent domain, the items are stated at estimated value at date of acquisition.
     (e) Asset line total, $205.4 billion is eliminated against Treasury debt issues of like amount.
     (f) Asset line total, $71.2 billion is eliminated against government equity of like amount.

trols, and the expenditure basis to meet individual agency management controls. At agency level, a multi-basis accounting is necessary in order to produce data required for all three bases. Agency accounting is further complicated by the fact that one agency may conduct operations under more than one type of fund and more than one fund within each type of fund where, as in the case of appropriated funds, it is necessary to maintain a separate fund for each appropriation.

Should the Data of Statement 14 Be Combined Further?

The method of preparing a grand summary of assets, liabilities, and residual equities as found in the last column is simply to cross foot each line of numbers, line by line, and in doing so to eliminate the more obvious interfund relationships described in notes e and f.

But what good may such a summary serve? Does not such a grand summary have the effect of suppressing the great heterogeneity of the data involved?

The summarization can satisfy a legitimate curiosity, and, besides, the notation in the heading of the column that the data is a "memorandum" clearly calls attention to the combining step that produced it. Nevertheless, it remains to be seen what value the combined information may have. Some would say that the summarization appears too much like an accounting exercise for the sake of accounting. Using a metaphor, they suggest that the eye of the accountant's camera might shoot a view that is breathtaking, but the picture's value for serious thought and action is another matter. In this view, an evident rational purpose of the grand summary would be necessary first before the resulting picture could be deemed to have significance to those for whom it is prepared, namely, the general public, Congress, or the incumbent President and his administration.

NOTES

1. In the federal government, an exception must be noted in the handling of proceeds of sales of certain specified surplus property. Such proceeds do not revert to the General Fund as miscellaneous revenues; instead, they are permitted to be added to the appropriations of the agencies concerned. However, the exception is limited to the amount necessary to reimburse the agencies for costs incurred to salvage and sell the property or to replace it (in the case of certain equipment). The purpose of the exception is to encourage and expedite disposal of property no longer needed.

2. Foreign aid is carried out under four broad categories: grants, loans, capital investments in international financial institutions, and other assistance such as sales of surplus agricultural products.

3. See Chapter 3.

4. The federal public debt has risen rapidly of late. As of October 31, 1985, the debt stood at $1,824 billion.

5. A general principle observed at all levels of government is that obligations of any expendable fund should exclude debt that is not repayable from present assets of that fund. In other words, unexpended resources of the fund are normally expected at least to equal the fund's unliquidated liabilities.

6. Such procedure is commonplace in state and local government redemptions of their general indebtedness. Using a payor fund for the purpose, the general indebtedness (nonfund debt) is systematically paid off as scheduled maturities take place, usually under some installment plan for repayments. Lest this be overlooked, state and local government general indebtedness are controlled by ceilings or limitations set either in state constitutions or state statutes. Such ceilings or limitations, in the case of the federal government, are solely in the hands of the Congress.

7. Marketable issues are also sold to certain government agencies, including Federal Old Age and Survivors Fund and Federal Deposit Insurance Corporation.

8. Financed by revolving funds, $16.2; trust funds, $185.0; deposit funds, $4.1; and special funds, $.1; totalling $205.4, per Statement 12.

9. When the banks buy, the cash paid out increases the money supply in circulation; when the banks sell, the cash proceeds of the sales decrease the money supply. For a review of the discussion on this subject, see Chapter 1. Recall the measure of money supply as being bank checking account balances plus cash held by the public.

6.

BUDGETING AND FUNDING CYCLE OF A FEDERAL AGENCY

Although a close-up view of the budgeting and funding cycle of a single federal agency may be interpreted as a rather microscopic treatment and hardly equal to the task of penetrating the huge federal establishment, every federal agency, large or small, uses a similar structure of budgeting and funding. The system of accounting and reporting owes its existence to federal laws that, by long tradition and precedence, are enacted and enforced in accordance with a uniform pattern of implementation. Therefore, since the whole is made up of its parts, a study of a single agency will truly be a minute activity of the total federal government and a prototype of the many parts that make up the whole.

It is both feasible and simpler to use one agency out of the vast number of agencies as a satisfactory model of all. All federal agencies have similar financial systems; that is, their systems or procedures of accounting, financial planning, funding, and financial control, notwithstanding their different missions, functions, sizes, and complexities of organizations.

Our illustrative agency is called the National Air Safety Board, NASB, which is the alias for the real federal agency represented. The educational value of the illustration has been enhanced and the presentation made more effective by simplifying the data presented.

ORGANIZATION OF NASB

NASB is in its eighth year of operation. It was formerly a part of the Department of Transportation but became an independent agency under a law enacted by Congress and now reports directly to Congress. NASB maintains close ties with both the Department of Transportation and the Federal Aviation Agency.

Powers and Duties

NASB is the designated agency of the government for air transportation safety. Its powers and duties as stated in the law creating the agency are as follows:

1. Investigate and determine the facts, conditions, circumstances, and probable causes of accidents involving aircraft;
2. Prepare written reports of such accidents and make them available to the public at reasonable cost;
3. Prepare and issue periodic reports to the Congress, and federal, state, and local agencies concerned with safe air transportation; recommend and advocate ways and means of reducing aircraft accidents; and propose corrective steps to make air transportation as safe and as free from risk of injury as is possible;
4. Conduct research into the adequacy of safeguards and procedures to prevent or reduce recurrent accidents involving aircraft; and
5. Establish liaison with counterpart agencies of other national governments to advance international cooperation in prevention or reduction of aircraft accidents.

Plan of Management

As established by law, the governing board of NASB consists of five members, including a chairman. They are all appointed by the President, subject to the terms, conditions, and responsibilities of management outlined below.

1. Members of the board shall be appointed by the President, by and with the advice and consent of the Senate. No more than three members of the board shall be of the same political party. At any given time, no less than two members of the board shall be individuals with field experience in accident reconstruction, safety engineering, or transportation safety.
2. The terms of office of the members of the board shall be five years and are renewable for second five-year terms.
3. Any member of the board may be removed by the President for inefficiency, neglect of duty, or malfeasance in office.
4. The chairman shall be designated by the President and shall serve for a term of two years as the board's chief executive officer; three members of the board shall constitute a quorum for the transaction of any function of the board.
5. The board shall establish and maintain distinct and appropriately staffed bureaus, divisions, or offices in its headquarters offices and in the field as necessary for the conduct of its affairs.
6. The board shall have a seal that shall be judicially recognized.

7. Subject to the civil service and classification laws, the board is authorized to select, appoint, employ, and fix the compensation of such officers and employees as shall be necessary to carry out its powers and duties under this Act.

Organizational Chart

NASB's chart of organization, showing board members as responsible for general management, a managing director, two staff functions dealing with law and public relations, and five operating units identified by individual programs appears as Exhibit 25.

FUND STRUCTURE OF NASB

NASB is financed almost entirely out of expendable funds appropriated by Congress from the General Fund. The agency rents the office space it uses. The agency's budget does not include capital items such as land, buildings, and equipment, except for some office equipment that is purchased as needed.

One trust fund is used to receive donations from airlines for advancing research in air transportation safety. The trust fund contributes to

EXHIBIT 25
NASB Chart of Organization

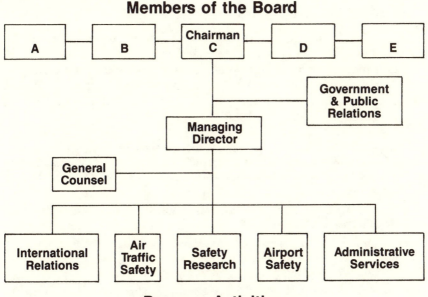

the support of certain research projects conducted by the agency's research laboratory. There is no revolving fund to finance any agency activities at present, but the board is considering the feasibility of establishing one or more of such funds for certain activities. As an example, consideration is currently being given to creating a revolving fund to finance an air safety school for the training of air safety inspectors and accident investigators who are employees of airports, as well as employees of the agency itself. The programs are now budgeted and financed under the agency's appropriations from the General Fund.

BUDGETING AND FUNDING CYCLE

The remainder of this chapter will discuss the steps in budgeting and funding to which every federal agency, including NASB, is subject. We will not repeat the name of our illustrative agency in the discussion of each step, because all agencies are required to observe the same basic procedures.

Major Steps in the Budget Process

The budget process of the government extends over a period of 18 months before the applicable fiscal year begins. The major steps in the budget process are discussed in the appendix.

THE BUDGET CALENDAR

The federal financial process begins with the formulation of the annual budget. The following calendar of budget preparation and submission indicates the timetable of the work, including the lead time needed in moving an annual budget from stage to stage. It will be assumed that the budget is for the year that begins on October 1, 1984 and ends on September 30, 1985.

1983 Spring and Summer.—Using guidelines received from agency headquarters, each organizational unit puts together the results of its planning/ programming effort into a financial budget conforming to official formats for the purpose.

1983—Fall. Agency budget in total, and in all its parts moves to OMB for review, changes, and approval.

1984—January. Congressional consideration of the budget of each agency, big or small, as received from OMB.[1]

1984—Spring and Summer Months. In Congress, a budget is first considered and acted upon by the House of Representatives. This step ends up with the "House Bill" (proposed law), which then moves to the Senate for its separate consideration, changes, and approval. (Senate changes in a House Bill moves a budget into a "conference" in which House and Senate conferees iron out their differences.)

1984—On or before October 1. OMB receives back the budget it sent to Congress, hopefully recognizable and bearing a resemblance to the budget that was sent to Congress. This is the draft of the budget that Congress has acted upon by appropriating a sum of money equal to the approved budget. It is also known as the funding step. It is this congressionally approved budget that federal agencies use to crank up their financial operation for an upcoming year.

Congressional Review, Changes, and Approval of the Budget

A common expression heard in the halls of Congress that the presidency proposes, Congress disposes, is especially apt in the case of the federal budget. Congress rarely accepts any part of the President's budget as originally formulated and submitted. The budget is subjected to strenuous congressional scrutiny, and some parts get more attention than others. In the role of reviewer of budgets, Congress is motivated as much politically as it is by a desire to find the most effective use of the dollars in the national interest. The following paragraphs outline the procedure.

Congressional work on a budget begins in the House of Representatives where hearings are held before the House Appropriation Committee. After changes and final approval, the budget is forwarded to the Senate, where it undergoes a similar process of review and change at the hands of the Senate Appropriation Committee. Inevitably, the two versions of the budget lead to the meetings of a Conference Committee that reconciles the two drafts and ends up with a final draft that is agreeable to the conferees representing the House and Senate Appropriation Committees. At this point, the approved appropriation bill is passed first by the House and then by the Senate, and is ready to be sent to the President for his signature.

Once an appropriation bill is enacted into law, attention turns to its execution through established channels and stages, ending with the funding of each agency included in the approved budget and related appropriation.

STEPS IN THE FUNDING PROCESS

Although the steps associated with the funding process tend to overlap as outlined below, there is a chronological order for the process as a whole that starts with formal approval of an agency's programs and ends with making the money available for them.

Authorization of a Program

In this initial step, Congress enacts legislation authorizing programs or functions for each agency. A pattern of hearings, discussions, and related research, as necessary, precede authorizing legislation. In many instances, authorizations are valid from one year to another, as amended. In other instances, authorizations are granted annually for one year at a time. An authorization of a program or function is often accompanied by a "price tag," that is, a monetary limit on the amount that can subsequently be appropriated for the stated purposes. As a final point, political inputs by interest groups of the public may significantly shape the content and boundaries of programs in the authorization stage.

Typical wording of a law authorizing a set of programs for an agency (and, in addition, authorizing an appropriation for the programs) would be as follows: Be it enacted by the Senate and House of Representatives of the United States of America in Congress assembled, that there is hereby authorized to be appropriated in fiscal year 19XX, not to exceed $XXX, for necessary operating expenses in accordance with the provisions of Section X of the Act of 19XX as amended, establishing the (name of agency).

Appropriation for a Program

In the next step, Congress passes the law providing an appropriation of money to an agency after it has examined, changed, and approved the agency's budget.

Every agency, without exception, must undergo this step. Oftentimes, an appropriation law incorporates the appropriations to a number of different agencies under one act, but there is a separate and distinct "title" or section under the act for the appropriation to each agency, the same as if it were a separate law providing an appropriation for the particular agency.

A rather extended description of the annual budgeting-and-funding cycle appears in the Appendix to this chapter. A brief sketch of it follows.

Whether for authorization of a set of programs for an agency, or for later providing an appropriation for it, the process starts with hearings of the proposals on behalf of an agency before the duly designated committees. The task continues with discussions pro and con within the committees (and related subcommittees) and later on the floors of the House and Senate when draft legislation is under debate. The end of this line is not reached until the President either vetoes the legislation or affixes his signature of approval on it, thereby making the legislation the "law of the land."

It would be unrealistic to conclude this sketch without a mention of the role of lobbying in the political and legislative process. The most understanding explanation of lobbying in this sense is that it provides direct input by the public, primarily through employed representatives, in the deliberations of Congress.

As in the case of authorization language, the wording of an appropriation is by tradition and custom quite standardized and stylized, as in the following example: Be it enacted by the Senate and House of Representatives of the United States of America in Congress assembled, that the following sum(s) is appropriated out of money in the Treasury for the (name of agency) for the fiscal year ending September 30, 19XX for necessary operating expenses, $XXX.

Apportionment to an Agency

This step is in the hands of the President's OMB, which formally declares that a given appropriation is made available for obligating. Such action of OMB is referred to as making an apportionment under a given appropriation. If for any reason an agency is provided with more than one appropriation, the funding steps are carried out separately for each appropriation all the way down to the lowest level of funding of that agency. Well established procedures assure a smooth handling of an appropriation once it is enacted into law:

(a) A certified copy of the appropriation law is sent by the President's Office to Treasury.

(b) Treasury draws a warrant certifying the appropriation and sends the warrant to the given agency. A copy of the warrant and related documents is transmitted at the same time to OMB for its information and attention.

(c) The agency receiving the Treasury warrant makes a formal request for apportionment by OMB, which then responds by making the apportionment.

The period for which OMB makes an apportionment is normally the fiscal year covered by the approved budget. Sometimes OMB will make an apportionment for a lesser period, such as for one-quarter of a year at a time, or it will temporarily hold back or reduce a given appropriation to an agency. There have been cases in which holdbacks or reductions of this nature turned out to be permanent. OMB's reason for taking actions that delay, reduce, or prevent an appropriation to an agency is explained usually in terms of unforeseen developments that have intervened since the related budgets were approved by Congress, thereby requiring the change in funding action as taken. OMB informs interested offices of its actions in this connection. The principal notification is of course to Congress through its applicable standing committees, which are furnished supporting explanations. Such communication maintains good working relations between the legislative and executive branches.

Allotments within an Agency

The funding process is concluded with an allotment of an apportionment to each individual organizational unit of an agency. In larger agencies, intermediate levels of management transmit allotments to subordinate units, but the funding action is still regarded as making allotments.

In the large agencies, an extra funding action is introduced in the interests of better internal control. The action is known as allocation. Thus, an apportionment to such an agency by OMB is used by the agency's headquarters staff to make allocations to a number of intermediate levels of management who then make allotments to subordinate organizational units.

In the case of our illustrative agency, NASB, an apportionment goes through one more funding step; that is, when the agency headquarters staff makes an allotment to each regional office (of which there are four), an allotment to the research laboratory, and an allotment to finance headquarters activity, for a total of six allotments.

Budget Revisions during the Year

To facilitate an agency's handling of unforeseen needed goods or services, the budget and related funding can be revised through built-in flexibilities. Revisions at a given level of management and control require corresponding revisions at all levels subordinate to it. Each management and control level is expected to change existing plans, as dictated by new and unanticipated conditions. Thus, each such level is a good point for controlling and modifying existing plans. The changes (when not caused by discovery and correction of errors) usually involve transferring amounts from one budget segment to another at the level concerned as exigencies arise. However, a subordinate level may be ordered by a higher level to reduce (or raise) its total budget, with guidelines on how the changes should have an impact on program details.

HALLMARKS OF AN AGENCY'S FINANCIAL SYSTEM

A tight financial system surrounds the federal funding process. At the core of this system is the Anti-deficiency Act (Sec. 3679, 31 U.S. Code, p. 665), the violation of which signals the risk of criminal proceedings. The Anti-deficiency Act personalizes responsibility for exceeding the approved budget and the consequent mishandling of the related appropriation (the identity of a given appropriation is never lost, no matter how many times the appropriation is subdivided down the chain of funding). As previously noted, the Anti-deficiency statute is explicit; the head of an agency shall establish a system to prevent overobligation and overexpenditure in relation to an approved budget, report violations to the President and the Congress, and punish violators, including criminal penalties in the more serious cases.[2]

The punitive measures of the Anti-deficiency law do not make a system. Of the positives working for an effective financial system are strategic actions that are built into everyday financial operations of an agency.

Regulations to Implement the Law

The head of each agency prepares detailed regulations (generally as drawn up by the agency's legal staff) to implement the provisions of the Anti-deficiency Act. Among other things, the regulations require that the given agency specifically subdivide each appropriation within the amount apportioned by OMB. The subdivision is required to be carried out through all levels of management (or command, in the case of the military departments), thereby providing a visible, verifiable chain of subdivision of the funding down to the lowest or allotment level. The effect of this requirement is to stamp on the financial system a clear and straightforward method of control.

Each appropriation (or subdivision of it) to an organizational unit of an agency is equal to the approved budget of that unit, and it is both an authorization and a limitation on the unit for incurring obligations and expenditures.

Dual Control by Fund and Budget

Each appropriation provides an appropriated fund. Therefore, if an appropriation is subdivided, the appropriated fund is also subdivided. This creates a fund as an object of control. The other control is the approved budget that must be equal to and match the amount of the related fund. Responsibility for staying within the two limitations rests directly with the head of the organizational unit, irrespective of where this unit is located or how high or low its level of operation in the management (or command) hierarchy.

Flow of Funding Actions to Create Funds

Exhibit 26 shows the manner in which funding actions create funds to finance related budgets (and the programs they represent).

EXHIBIT 26
Flow of Funding Actions

Action	Resulting Fund	To Finance Budget of
1. Congress authorizes programs and funding	No fund	No budget
2. Congress appropriates money	Appropriated fund X	Total budget of agency X
3. OMB declares money is available for obligating	Apportioned fund X	Total budget of fund X
4. Agency allots money to its operating units	Allotted fund for each operating unit	Budget of each operating unit

Budgeting and Funding Is for Obligational Authority

The amount budgeted and funded for any agency (and its subdivisions) is stated in terms of authority to obligate. If an agency is budgeted and funded, say for $50,000, it may incur obligations up to $50,000, and sooner or later pay it. The resources an agency buys with this money is governed by the related budget that is very explicit. For example, the money is to be used for "operating expenses, '$'X'"; "motor vehicles, '$'Z'"; or "Q physical facility, '$'Y'"; and so on.

PERIODIC FINANCIAL STATEMENTS

NASB, like other agencies, prepares and submits monthly financial statements for internal and external reporting. If an agency's organization is multi-level, financial statements of lower levels are combined with headquarters data to arrive at totals for the agency as a whole. In the larger agencies, information may go through several intermediate stages before agency-wide data is accumulated. In principle, each feeder point combines the financial statements received from lower levels with those of its own level; the resulting summaries are then transmitted to the next higher level for the next round of combination.

For external reporting, each agency prepares and submits the data required by the authority to whom it is addressed, using the standard accounting and reporting formats prescribed by that authority. Thus, monthly financial statements sent to Treasury include a monthly statement of transactions and a monthly statement of accountability, showing cash receipts and disbursements, with beginning and ending cash balances as shown by agency records. Treasury then combines the data for all agencies in order to generate data for the entire government.

A separate set of financial statements is prepared for each appropriated fund at each level of funding. Combination is always in terms of a given appropriated fund because accountability, all through budgeting, funding, obligating, and paying, is in terms of a particular appropriated fund existing at each point of funding within an agency organization.

For example, if an agency is appropriated $1 million for fiscal year 19X9, the resulting appropriated fund is identified as the agency's 19X9 appropriated fund all through the life of that fund. Each subdivision of the appropriated fund within the agency carries a similar identity and accountability, such as agency X, 19X9 allotted fund, branch 21; agency X, 19X9 allotted fund, branch 22; and so forth.

Furthermore, if Congress makes several separate appropriations to an agency, it does so under a separate law for each appropriation. Thus, if an agency receives three separate appropriations, accountability and reporting are also separated. The agency is required to account and report separately for each appropriation received for the stated year. The separate identities are preserved in all the funding subdivisions that may characterize the operation of an agency.

INTERNAL TRANSACTIONS

If an organizational unit receives goods or services from other organizational units—either within the same agency or a different agency in the federal government—the requesting unit must stand the cost and pay for it to the supplying unit. The practice is known as reimbursing the supplying unit for goods or services received from it, similar to a buyer and seller. A given organizational unit oftentimes plays the role of both buyer and seller of goods or services. When it acts as a seller, it receives payment from the unit to which it sells. When it acts as buyer, it pays other units. A pricing system is, of course, necessary and it must be acceptable to buyer and seller, but the arrangement is essentially a matter of the buyer reimbursing the seller for costs incurred.

In the accounts, the buying unit includes the costs in its approved budget like any other expenditures. The supplying unit includes the reimbursement in its obligational authority as if it is an appropriation.

The principle of reimbursements is applied realistically and is avoided if it is not practicable to do so, such as when the amounts involved are nominal and the paperwork does not justify it. For example, an agency would not bill and collect on giving a box of paper clips to the organizational unit across the hall, or for the temporary use of a photocopy machine in an emergency. As a general guide, it is usually considered unnecessary to invoke the reimbursement principle if the organizational units are financed by the same allotted fund. In such cases, goods or services received by one unit from another must be subjected to more informal methods of control.

Revolving Funds

The sale and purchase of goods and services between organizational units, as incidental to regular operations, fits neatly into the regular financial system. On the other hand, it may be advisable to create a revolving fund whose entire or primary role is to serve others on a cost reimbursement basis. Our illustrative agency believes that its research laboratory is approaching the point of development where it should be formally organized as a revolving fund instead of continuing as an incidental seller of services to others.

The principle of a revolving fund reinforces the need for cost reimbursement. Users of goods and services furnished by others are usually not cost conscious or cost conservators unless they bear some or all of the costs through the reimbursement process. If they are furnished free goods and services, they probably would use or consume the resources received in ignorance of the costs and overuse or waste them.

RELATION BETWEEN TREASURY AND A FEDERAL AGENCY

The funding process calls for close interaction between Treasury and a particular federal agency. The discussion following highlights this interaction.

Accounts of the Federal Government

Each federal agency maintains its own internal accounting system to record and control its financial transactions. Treasury also does through its central accounts and related records, which are designed to produce government-wide accounting data representing assets and liabilities that are directly generated by the stream of cash receipts and disbursements made or to be made shortly, not unlike current assets and current liabilities as generally known.

To fulfill its responsibility, Treasury keeps its central accounts and related records in close relationship with individual agency accounts in the field by means of an elaborate network of communication and information flow, which works in two directions. In one, they relay accounting actions by the agencies to the Treasury. In the other, they

EXHIBIT 27
Journal Record of Transactions

TREASURY'S CENTRAL ACCOUNTS FOR THE GENERAL FUND

a) Collect general taxes
    Undisbursed Treasury balance, GF   300
        Unappropriated balance, GF   300

b) Make appropriations
    Unappropriated balance, GF   325
        Unobligated appropriation, GF
            Agency X   320
        Unobligated appropriation, GF
            Interest on public debt   5

c) No entry

d) Pay on account; checks outstanding
    Unobligated appropriation, GF
        Agency X   302
        Checks outstanding, GF   302

e) Pay checks outstanding
    Checks outstanding, GF   299
        Undisbursed Treasury balance, GF   299

f1) Receive proceeds of sale of public debt issues
    Undisbursed Treasury balance, GF   25
        Unappropriated balance, GF   25

f2) Anticipated resources   25
        Public debt issues   25

g1) Receive proceeds of sale of public debt issues to
    refund maturities
    Undisbursed Treasury balance, GF   10
        Public debt issues   10

g2) Redeem matured issues
    Public debt issues   10
        Undisbursed Treasury balance, GF   10

h) Pay interest on public debt
    Unobligated appropriation, GF
        Interest on public debt   5
        Undisbursed Treasury balance, GF   5

AGENCY X'S ACCOUNTS FOR ITS APPROPRIATED FUND

b) Receive appropriation
    Undisbursed Treasury balance   320
        Unobligated balance, appropriation   320

c) Purchase, receive goods and services
    Unobligated balance, appropriation   313
        Accounts payable   313

d) Pay on account
    Accounts payable   302
        Undisbursed Treasury balance   302

Transactions not affecting agency accounts: a, e, f1, f2, g1, g2, and h.

relay accounting actions by Treasury to the agencies. Needless to say, the communication and information flow must be made in a timely manner in both directions and must be controlled and reconciled.

Control and execution of transactions are widely decentralized. They occur all over the United States and at locations overseas and

EXHIBIT 28
Treasury and Agency Accounts

CENTRAL ACCOUNTS OF TREASURY

Undisbursed Treasury Balance

	Debit	Credit	Balance
a)	300		300
e)		299	1
f)	25		26
g1)	10		36
g2)		10	26
h)		5	21

Anticipated Resources

	Debit	Credit	Balance
beginning	50		50
f)	25		75

Checks Outstanding

	Debit	Credit	Balance
d)		302	302
e)	299		3

Unappropriated Balance, GF

	Debit	Credit	Balance
a)		300	300
b)	325		(25)
f)		25	--

Unobligated Appropriation, GF, X

	Debit	Credit	Balance
b)		320	320
d)	302		18

Unobligated Appropriation, GF, Int.

	Debit	Credit	Balance
b)		5	5
h)	5		--

Public Debt Issues

	Debit	Credit	Balance
beginning			50
f)		25	75
g1)		10	85
g2)	10		75

Trial Balance, end of year

Undisbursed Treasury balance	21	
Anticipated resources	75	
Checks outstanding		3
Unappropriated balance, GF		--
Unobligated appropriation, GF, X		18*
Unobligated appropriation, GF, Int.		--
Public debt issues		75
	96	96

*The sum of $7 is transferred to expired
balance account, per report from agency X
at end of year, assuming appropriation
was for one year:

Unobligated appropriation, GF, X	7	
Expired balance, GF, X		7

ACCOUNTS OF AGENCY X

Undisbursed Treasury Balance

	Debit	Credit	Balance
b)	320		320
d)		302	18

Accounts Payable

	Debit	Credit	Balance
c)		313	313
d)	302		11

Unobligated Balance, Appropriation

	Debit	Credit	Balance
b)		320	320
c)	313		7

Trial Balance, end of year

Undisbursed Treasury balance	18	
Accounts payable		11
Unobligated balance, appropriation		7*
	18	18

*Transferred to Expired Balance, by
year-end closing entry:

Unobligated balance, appropriation	7	
Expired balance		7

take time to process and put into the communication and information stream. The flow of transaction papers moving from agency offices in the field to Washington, especially, is large and continuous, 24 hours a day, seven days a week. Finally, the communication and information stream is practically entirely in terms of cash receipts and disbursements.

Illustration

The ongoing relationship between Treasury and agency offices is illustrated in Exhibits 27–29 by using a few basic transactions. Detailed data-processing steps are omitted, although they are necessary to the maintenance of good internal controls. The illustration assumes but one agency, and some everyday transactions that affect only Treasury in Washington. Assume that the public debt stood at $50 at the start of a fiscal year; also, assume the transactions following:

(a) Treasury collects general taxes of $300.

(b) Congress makes appropriations for agency X, $320; for interest on the public debt, $5.[3]

(c) Agency X buys and receives goods and services costing $313.

(d) Agency X pays on account, causing checks outstanding of $302.

(e) Treasury pays checks aggregating $299.

(f) Treasury receives $25 from sale of public debt issues (this is a borrowing operation).

EXHIBIT 29
Treasury's Central Accounts

United States Government

Statement of Receipts and Disbursements, General Fund, Year Ended September 30, 19XX

Budget receipts	$300
Budget disbursements	307
Budget deficit	7
Net proceeds from public debt issues	25
Undisbursed Treasury balance, end of year	$ 18

United States Government

Statement of Changes in Undisbursed Treasury Balance, General Fund, Year Ended September 30, 19XX

	Appropriated Funds	Unappropriated Balance	Total
Receipts from taxes		$ 300	$ 300
Net proceeds from sale of public debt issues		25	25
Appropriations	$ 325	(325)	
Disbursements	(307)		(307)
Undisbursed Treasury balance, end of year	$ 18	--	$ 18

(g) Treasury receives $10 from additional sales of public debt issues for the express purpose of redeeming matured public debt (this is known as a refunding operation).[4]

(h) Treasury pays $5 interest on the public debt outstanding.

APPENDIX: THE BUDGET PROCESS

The budget process has four main phases: executive formulation and transmittal, congressional action, budget execution and control, and review and audit. Each of these phases is interrelated with the others.[5] (See Exhibit 30.)

Executive Formulation and Transmittal

The budget sets forth the President's financial plan and indicates his priorities for the federal government. The President's transmittal of his budget to the Congress early in each calendar year is the climax of many months of planning and analysis throughout the executive branch. In a year in which a new President takes office, the outgoing President submits a budget. Usually, the new President proposes changes to that budget.

Formulation of the 1985 budget began in the spring of 1983, although general goals were set earlier. The budget is formulated in the context of a three-year budget planning and tracking system. The budget planning horizon covers the two years following the budget year and integrates long-range planning into the executive budget cycle. This multi-year budget planning system requires that broad fiscal goals and agency spending targets be established beyond the budget year.

During the period when a budget is being formulated in the executive branch, there is a continual exchange of information, proposals, evaluations, and policy decisions among the President, the Office of Management and Budget and other executive office units, and the various government agencies. Decision making in the budget process provides for in-depth evaluation of all proposed and existing programs and activities in conjunction with planning and budgeting.

In the spring, agency programs are evaluated, policy issues are identified, and budgetary projections are made, giving attention both to important modifications and innovations in programs and to alternative long-range program plans. These budgetary projections, including projections of estimated receipts prepared by the Department of the Treasury, are then presented to the President for his consideration, and the major issues are discussed. At about the same time, the President receives projections of the economic outlook that are prepared

EXHIBIT 30
Major Steps in the Budget Process

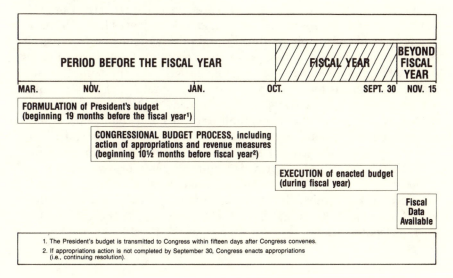

PERIOD BEFORE THE FISCAL YEAR   FISCAL YEAR   BEYOND FISCAL YEAR

MAR.   NOV.   JAN.   OCT.   SEPT. 30   NOV. 15

FORMULATION of President's budget
(beginning 19 months before the fiscal year[1])

CONGRESSIONAL BUDGET PROCESS, including
action of appropriations and revenue measures
(beginning 10½ months before fiscal year[2])

EXECUTION of enacted budget
(during fiscal year)

Fiscal
Data
Available

1. The President's budget is transmitted to Congress within fifteen days after Congress convenes.
2. If appropriations action is not completed by September 30, Congress enacts appropriations
   (i.e., continuing resolution).

jointly by the Council of Economic Advisers, OMB, and the Departments of Commerce, Labor, and the Treasury.

Following a review of these projections, the President establishes general budget and fiscal policy guidelines for both the fiscal year that will begin about 15 months later and for the two years beyond. General policy directions and planning ceilings are then given to the agencies to govern the preparation of their budget requests.

Throughout the fall and early winter the executive branch is involved in the development of the President's budget. The primary phase of the budget process involves the formulation and preparation of the President's budget for transmittal to the Congress. Budget determinations are developed after detailed reviews of agency budget requests and the government-wide OMB ranking of decision packages falling at the margin of approved agency totals. These determinations are then discussed with the agencies and revised as a result of later presidential decisions. Fiscal policy issues relating to total budget outlays and receipts are reexamined. Consistent with the multi-year budget planning system, the effects of budget decisions on budget authority and outlays in the years that follow are also considered and are explicitly taken into account. Thus, the budget formulation process involves the simultaneous consideration of the resource needs of individual programs and the total outlays and receipts that are appropriate in relation to current and prospective economic conditions. The budget reflects the results of both of these considerations.

Current services estimates are also prepared to provide the Congress with a basis for the review of the President's budget. These estimates are projections of budget authority and outlays required to continue federal programs and activities in the upcoming fiscal year without policy changes from the fiscal year in progress at the time the estimates are transmitted. The Congressional Budget Act of 1974 requires that these estimates be transmitted to provide the Congress with information on projected costs of current programs. For the first two years after the requirement became effective, they were transmitted in November. However, it was generally agreed that the estimates transmitted at that time did not provide a suitable basis for review since the underlying assumptions changed before the budget was transmitted. As a result, the comparability of the current services and the budget estimates was lessened significantly. Consequently, the current services estimates are now transmitted with the President's budget.

Congressional Action

Congress can act to approve, modify, or disapprove the President's budget proposals. It can change funding levels, eliminate proposals, or add programs not requested by the President. It also may act upon legislation determining taxes and other means of increasing or decreasing receipts.

In making appropriations, Congress does not normally vote on the level of outlays directly but rather on budget authority. Congress first enacts legislation that authorizes an agency to carry out a particular program and, in some cases, includes limits on the amount that can be appropriated for the program. Many programs are authorized for a specified number of years or indefinitely; other programs, such as most nuclear energy, space exploration, defense procurement, foreign affairs, and some construction programs, require annual authorizing legislation.

Provision of budget authority is usually a separate subsequent action. Generally, budget authority becomes available each year only as voted by the Congress in appropriations acts. However, in a number of cases the Congress has voted permanent budget authority, under which funds become available annually without further congressional action. Many trust fund appropriations are permanent, as are a number of federal fund appropriations, such as the appropriation to pay interest on the public debt.

Congressional review of the budget begins when the President transmits his budget estimates to Congress within 15 days after the start of each new session in January, as required by law. Under the procedures established by the Congressional Budget Act of 1974, Congress considers budget totals before completing action on individual appropriations. The Act requires that each standing committee of Congress submit reports on budget estimates to the House and Senate Budget Committees by March 15 and that the Congressional Budget Office submit a fiscal policy report to the two committees by April 1. Congress then adopts the first concurrent budget resolution to guide it in its subsequent consideration of appropriations and revenue measures. The first budget resolution, which is supposed to be adopted by May 15, sets targets for total receipts and for budget authority and outlays, in total and by functional category.

Congressional consideration of requests for appropriations and for changes in revenue laws occurs first in the House of Representatives. The Appropriations Committee, through its subcommittees, studies the proposals for appropriations and examines in detail each agency's performance. The Ways and Means Committee reviews proposed revenue measures. Each committee then recommends the action to be taken by the House.

When the appropriation and tax bills are approved by the House, they are forwarded to the Senate, where a similar review process is followed. In case of disagreement between the two Houses of Congress, a conference committee (consisting of members of both bodies) meets to resolve the differences. The report of the conference committee is returned to both Houses for approval. When the measure is agreed to in both Houses, it is ready to be transmitted to the President in the form of an enrolled bill for his approval or veto.

After action has been completed on all or most money bills, Congress adopts a second concurrent resolution containing a budget ceiling on total budget authority and outlays and a floor for budget receipts. This resolution, which is supposed to be adopted by September 15, may retain or revise the levels set earlier in the year. Either the first or second budget resolution can direct various committees to recommend reductions in budget authority and outlays or increases in budget receipts. Changes recommended by committees pursuant to the budget resolution are to be reported in a reconciliation bill.

After Congress completes action on the second resolution, it may not consider any spending or revenue legislation that would breach the totals specified in this resolution. Congress may, however, adopt a new budget resolution changing the levels set by the second resolution.

If action on appropriations is not completed by the beginning of the fiscal year, Congress enacts a continuing resolution to provide authority for the affected agencies to continue operations, usually until their regular appropriations are enacted.

Budget Execution and Control

Once approved, the President's budget, as modified by Congress, becomes the financial plan for the operations of each agency during the fiscal year. Under the law, most budget authority and other budgetary resources are made available to the agencies of the executive branch through an apportionment system. The director of OMB apportions appropriations and other budgetary resources to each agency by time periods (usually calendar quarters) or by activities. Obligations may not be incurred in excess of the amount apportioned. The objective of the apportionment system is to ensure the effective and orderly use of available resources and to preclude the need for additional or supplemental appropriations.

Nonetheless, changes in laws or other factors may indicate the need for additional appropriations during the year, and supplemental requests may have to be sent to Congress. On the other hand, reserves may be established under the Anti-deficiency Act to provide for contingencies or to effect savings made possible by changes in requirements or greater efficiency of operations. Amounts may also be withheld from obligation for policy or other reasons, but all amounts withheld must be reported for congressional review pursuant to the Impoundment Control Act of 1974.

Whenever the President determines that all or part of any budget authority provided by the Congress will not be required to carry out the full objectives or scope of a program for which it was provided, or that such budget authority should be rescinded for fiscal policy or other reasons, a special message is transmitted by the President to Congress requesting a rescission of the budget authority. The budget authority proposed for rescission by the President must be made available for obligation unless both the House and the Senate pass a rescission bill within 45 days of continuous session.

Whenever the President determines that the use of budget authority provided by Congress should be deferred (that is, temporarily withheld from obligation), the President transmits a special message to Congress on such deferrals. Either House may, at any time, pass a resolution disapproving this deferral of budget authority, thus requiring that the funds be made available for obligation. When no congressional action is taken, deferrals may remain in effect until, but not beyond the end of the fiscal year. If the funds remain available beyond the end of a fiscal year and continued deferral of their use is desired by the President, he must transmit a new special message to Congress.

Review and Audit

This is the final phase in the budget process. The individual agencies are responsible for assuring through their own review and control systems that the obligations they incur and the resulting outlays follow the provisions of the authorizing legislation and appropriations, as well as other laws and regulations relating to the obligation and expenditure of funds. Agencies are assisted in this responsibility by their audit staffs. In the case of 15 major departments and agencies, audit activities are directed by statutory inspectors general, appointed by the President. OMB reviews program and financial reports and keeps abreast of agency programs and the effort to attain program objectives.

In addition, the General Accounting Office, as an agent of the Congress, regularly audits, examines, and evaluates government programs. Its findings and recommendations are made to Congress, to OMB, and to the agencies concerned. The GAO also monitors the executive branch's reporting of special messages on proposed rescissions and deferrals. The GAO reports any items not reported by the executive branch and any differences that it may have with the classification (as a rescission or deferral) of withholdings included in special messages transmitted by the President. The GAO may bring civil action to obtain compliance should the President fail to report withholdings of budget authority in accordance with the Impoundment Control Act of 1974.

NOTES

1. Each agency's budget as sent to Congress is the subject of hearings in which the agency head appears personally before the given congressional committee to discuss his or her budget and submit to such questioning as may be necessary.

2. Instances where exceptions to the Anti-deficiency Act occur include the following: subsequent to receiving a duly authorized appropriation, an agency is permitted to incur expenditures in excess of its appropriation if the President declares that a state of emergency exists or if an agency clearly faces emergencies endangering human life or loss of property. Proceedings for relief from the provisions of the Anti-deficiency Act are generally initiated in anticipation of a deficiency of appropriation or as soon afterwards as is practicable with full documentation of the facts.

3. The amounts payable as interest on the public debt are authorized by Congress by the language of a permanent appropriation for the purpose: "Such amounts are appropriated as may be necessary to pay the interest each year on the public debt."

4. Similarly, Treasury is authorized to redeem matured debt principal by borrowing on new debt issues under the following permanent appropriation language: "Such accounts of new public debt may be issued as may be necessary to use the proceeds to pay for matured debt."

5. Source: Office of Management and Budget.

7.

FINANCIAL STATEMENTS OF A FEDERAL AGENCY

Each appropriated fund requires a separate set of financial statements. This chapter will illustrate and discuss a set of such financial statements for our example agency, NASB, the National Air Safety Board. It will be presented as a vehicle for considering the fundamentals of periodic financial reporting for the use of the financial managements to whom they are addressed.

The analysis is kept within the bounds of a single chapter and is thus in character with the study as a whole as a short treatment of the federal financial system. In light of these objectives, the content of the statements will be more like a simulation effort in which sufficient test conditions are presented to approximate actual operational conditions, rather than as a full-scale picture of current requirements as set forth in official documents. This approach is also useful in introducing concepts and procedures on their evident merit, rather than as agreements with or alternatives to current official federal financial practices. In sum, the financial statements of this chapter are fundamental models for study and consideration and are therefore not complete replicas of currently followed official financial reporting practices.

For readers who are interested in relating the content of the financial statements of this chapter to official documents, they will find equivalent or similar data, for the most part, in the official documents, as illustrated by the following:

OMB Documents. OMB Circular A-34, Instructions on Budget Execution, particularly the monthly report, SF 133; also monthly report on obligations, SF 225.

Treasury Department Documents. Monthly report on transactions, SF 224; year-end closing statement on report TF 2108; and annual statement of financial condition, SF 220.

Following is a list of the financial statements presented. Although these exhibits are not the only ones prepared periodically, they are the principal financial statements. The formats and content are the same regardless of whether they are issued monthly, quarterly, or annually. The main users of these statements, in addition to immediate agency managements at operating levels, are the agency's headquarters in Washington, OMB, and the Treasury Department. When the General Accounting Office conducts an audit of the agency for any reason, it also would use the statements and supporting details. Comparative and cumulative data fitting into the formats given also must be kept in mind in the discussions of the chapter. As a final reference, the agency's internal audit staffs verify the data and evaluate the procedures used to record and accumulate the information appearing in the statements.

Statement 15. Obligational authority received, obligations incurred, and unobligated balances—first quarter of fiscal year 19X9.

Statement 16. Costs, expenditures, and obligations incurred—first quarter of fiscal year 19X9.

Statement 17. Financial position—end of first quarter of fiscal year 19X9 (as of December 31, 19X8).

Since these statements are agency-wide in scope, they give effect to consolidation procedures involving all subdivisions of each fund within the agency. Statements 15 and 16 are period statements. They cover the first quarter of the fiscal year ended September 30, 19X9 (that is, October, November, and December, 19X8). Statement 17 presents the agency's financial position as of the end of the first quarter, December 31, 19X8.

STATEMENT OF OBLIGATIONAL AUTHORITY RECEIVED, OBLIGATIONS INCURRED, AND UNOBLIGATED BALANCE—FIRST QUARTER, FISCAL YEAR 19X9

Statement 15 consists of three sections. The upper portion sets forth the sources of receipts (resources) of appropriated funds (four funds in all). The middle part sets forth obligations incurred; an expanded version of this appears in Statement 16. The lower part gives the resulting balances of the appropriated funds. In equation form, the statement shows as to each fund: Resources received − obligations incurred = unobligated balances.

STATEMENT 15
National Air Safety Board—Appropriated Funds: Obligational Authority Received, Obligations Incurred, and Unobligated Balances, by Funds, First Quarter of Fiscal Year 19X9

Description	19X9 Fund	19X8 Fund	19X7 Fund	Prior Years' Funds	Combined Total
Obligational authority received					
Appropriations	$7,010,126	$	$	$	$7,010,126
Net transfers	6,540				6,540
Total new obligational authority	7,016,666				7,016,666
Net transfers--prior years	24				24
Deficiency appropriation		194,000			194,000
Reimbursements:					
Reimbursements earned	208,356				208,356
Unfilled orders	335,100				335,100
Anticipated orders	732,278				732,278
Total reimbursements	1,275,734				1,275,734
Net adjustments in reduction of prior years' obligations		7,928	1,430		9,358
Restoration of prior years' withdrawals				44	44
Unobligated balance brought forward (deficiency)		(192,530)			(192,530)
Total available	8,292,424	9,398	1,430	44	8,303,296
Obligations incurred					
Obligations incurred (Statement 16):					
Expenditures (accrued)	1,782,326	163,272	14,264	44	1,959,906
Net change in contracts and orders outstanding, excluding adjustments in reduction of prior years' contracts and orders	284,880	(163,272)	(14,264)		(107,344)
Total obligations incurred	2,067,206	--	--	44	2,067,250
Rescissions and other withdrawals (see note)	1,000	--	--	--	1,000
Total applied	2,068,206	--	--	44	2,068,250

STATEMENT 15 continued

Unobligated balances			
Currently available	180,326		180,326
Apportioned for subsequent quarters	5,306,614		5,306,614
Reserved for anticipated orders	732,278		732,278
Balance subject to future apportionment action	5,000		5,000
Balance in expired accounts		9,398	1,430	10,828
Total unobligated balances	$6,224,218	$ 9,398	$ 1,430	--	$6,235,046

Note:

Procedurally, rescissions are netted against appropriations as soon as related action is completed by Congress.

Life Cycle of a Fund

Generally, each appropriated fund is an expendable fund with a planned operating life of one year, after which the fund is exhausted. In theory, this would mean no assets, no liabilities, and no fund balance at the end of the year. However, in practice, the following realities intervene. If liabilities of a fund have not been fully liquidated, there should be enough assets to pay the liabilities when they become due. If, for any reason, not all of the obligational authority is obligated, the resulting unobligated fund balance is said to be expired, that is, it is no longer available for obligating. The equation of a fund with an expired fund balance is illustrated as follows, with assumptions of the data shown: resources, $1,000 − (liabilities, $700 + contracts and orders outstanding, $275) = expired balance of fund, $25.

A fund's expired balance cannot be used for any new obligating, but it may be used to absorb adjustments arising out of final settlements of liabilities and commitments on outstanding contracts and orders as of the end of the first year. Adjustments may of course increase or decrease an expired balance depending upon circumstances. The expired balance of a fund is continued in the accounts for years two and three, after which it is transferred to a merged fund of expired fund balances for prior years. An expired fund balance can be withdrawn by Treasury at any time. (The term "lapsed fund balance" is an alternative description to an expired fund balance.)

Receipts of Obligational Authority

Statement 15 shows several sources of obligational authority received. Following is an explanation of each source.

New Obligational Authority

For the fiscal year ending September 30, 19X9, our example agency was appropriated $7,010,126 for the purposes stated in the approved budget.

Also, the sum of $6,540 is received from the Office of the President as a supplementary emergency obligational authority (termed a "transfer") out of the appropriated fund that Congress made available to the President. (For purposes of budgeting, funding, and accounting, the Office of the President is treated as a separate agency.) The sum of $24, otherwise withdrawn from the agency by Treasury, is reappropriated by Congress to the agency under certain conditions spelled out in the law. The action is one of several kinds of appropriation transfers.

Deficiency Appropriation for Prior Year

The sum of $194,000 was appropriated in 19X9 in order to remove a deficiency in the appropriated fund for 19X8. Thus, deficiencies cannot be completely prevented even under the stringent provisions of the Anti-deficiency Act. In this case, the situation resulted from a period of crisis when one international incident after another, such as the shuttling of illegal residents to points of exit, unexpectedly became an acute problem of the national government.[1]

The 19X8 appropriated fund did in fact end up the year in a condition of overobligation. It required a new appropriation by Congress to provide the money to pay for the obligations incurred. Also, in the final settlements of some of the obligations, adjustments resulted in a net reduction of $7,928 of the book value of the outstanding obligations. During 19X9, the sum of the new appropriation, $194,000, plus the net adjustments of $7,928, or $201,928, more than offset the beginning of the year deficiency of $192,530, leaving the 19X8 fund with a positive fund balance of $9,398 at the end of the first quarter, which is not available for obligation.

Reimbursements

Reimbursements in Statement 15 are classified as earned if orders received are filled, as unfilled if orders received are waiting to be filled, and as anticipated if orders are yet to be received, though budgeted. Exhibit 29 (in chapter 6) will help explain the normal cycle of events involving reimbursements.

Assume that an agency budgets reimbursable orders totaling $100 (a); receives orders of $70 to be filled (b-1); provides for obligational authority for orders received (b-2); fills and bills orders of $55 (c-1); earns reimbursements on orders filled, $55 (c-2); and collects $42 from customers billed for work done. (d).

Omitted is the reference to the incurring of expenditures for work done on the reimbursable orders. This is the cost side of reimbursable orders, and it is assumed that adequate cost records are kept for later comparison of actual cost and budgeted cost. As expenditures are incurred, debit appropriate cost accounts, credit undisbursed Treasury balance (or accounts payable). Exhibit 31 illustrates entries that would be reflected in a Statement 15–type of report.

Year-End Closing Entries

At the end of the year, the following closing entries are necessary: the balance in anticipated orders is closed against the reserve for anticipated orders. The balance in unfilled orders is closed against a matching amount in unobligated balance, currently available. However, the

EXHIBIT 31
Journal Record

	Debit	Credit
(a)		
Anticipated reimbursable orders	100	
Reserve for anticipated reimbursable orders		100
Budget for reimbursable orders		
(b-1)		
Unfilled reimbursable orders	70	
Anticipated reimbursable orders		70
Receipt of reimbursable orders		
(b-2)		
Reserve for anticipated reimbursable orders	70	
Unobligated balance, currently available, unfilled reimbursable orders		70
Provide obligational authority		
(c-1)		
Accounts receivable, reimbursable orders	55	
Unfilled reimbursable orders		55
Bill for orders filled		
(c-2)		
Unobligated balance, currently available, unfilled reimbursable orders	55	
Unobligated balance, currently available, earned reimbursable orders		55
Earn reimbursements on orders filled		
(d)		
Undisbursed Treasury balance	42	
Accounts receivable, reimbursable orders		42
Collect from customers for work done		

amount of unfilled orders is reinstated at the beginning of the next year: debit unfilled orders and credit a matching amount to unobligated balance, currently available. The reinstated amount is, of course, assumed to cover orders still valid; that is, not cancelled and still wanted by the ordering organization.

Obligations Incurred

Accrued Expenditures

Accrued expenditures, amounting to $1,782,326 in the 19X9 fund, measure the cost of goods and services received.[2] In a different concept, accrued expenditures include only the cost of goods and services used or consumed, commonly observed in the measurement of expenses. Inventories of consumable materials and supplies account for the difference between the two methods. In Statement 15, accrued expenditures include such inventories. Following the other method, which is common in state and local governmental accounting, inventories are considered a fund resource of an expendable fund until drawn for use or consumption, an anomaly that has been traditional practice in that field.[3]

Accrued expenditures under prior years' appropriated funds reflect goods and services that have been received in fulfillment of contracts and orders issued in prior years. Thus, in the first quarter of 19X9, accrued expenditures of $163,272 were incurred in fulfillment of 19X8 contracts and orders outstanding at September 30, 19X8. The $44 item in the merged category of appropriated funds applies to years prior to 19X7. It arose probably from settlements of unrecorded liabilities for those years; apparently, the related contracts were assumed to be completely liquidated. To meet the settlements, it was necessary to restore obligational authority in the sum of $44. Unlike the other adjustments, the $44 item is in the nature of upward adjustments of obligations recorded in the years prior to 19X9.

Changes in Contracts and Orders Issued in Current Year

In the first quarter covered in Statement 15, contracts and orders were issued that remained unfilled by the end of that quarter in the amount of $284,880.[4] This situation is described as a net change, although it is really a net increase inasmuch as the quarter began with no balance in the contracts and orders outstanding account. As goods and services are received, the corresponding amounts are debited to accrued expenditures and credited to accounts payable. Obligations are incurred as soon as contracts and orders are issued. When deliveries (or performance) are received, outstanding contracts and orders are reduced and replaced with accrued expenditures and accounts payable for the costs incurred. The replacements are dollar for dollar except when actual costs are not the same as contracted costs.[5]

Changes in Contracts and Orders Issued in Prior Years

For goods and services received in the current year on contracts and orders issued in prior years, the transactions affect only the accounts of

EXHIBIT 32
Prior Year Expenditures

When goods and services are received:

Accrued expenditures, 19X8 fund	163,272	
Accounts payable, 19X8 fund		163,272

End-of-period closing:

Contracts and orders outstanding, 19X8 fund	163,272	
Accrued expenditures, 19X8 fund		163,272

the applicable prior year fund. The fact that the goods and services received benefit current year operations, though the expenditures are treated as those of an earlier year, does not match costs with benefits received in ways the federal government accounts for expendable funds. In Statement 15, as an example, expenditures accounted for in this manner amount to $163,272 for the 19X8 fund. The entries for any prior year are illustrated in Exhibit 32.

Adjustments of Prior Years' Obligations

Statement 15 shows that adjustments of this nature totaled $7,928 under the 19X8 fund and $1,430 under the 19X7 fund. In addition to the reasons for adjustments previously noted, are contract terminations before contracts are completed, price changes, and other allowable adjustments written in the contracts. In Statement 15, the adjustments referred to reduced the book value of contracts and orders outstanding. However, the $44 adjustment increased the recorded obligation.[6]

Rescissions and Other Withdrawals

The item of $1,000 is another type of adjustment more or less normal to the operating experience of a federal agency. The life cycle of an appropriation may be cut short by congressional action to rescind a stated amount of an appropriation. Rescinded appropriations are added back to the unappropriated balance of the government's General Fund. Further, Treasury may withdraw an apportionment to an agency, if legally empowered to take such action "for cause," and add the withdrawn amount to the unapportioned balance to be disposed of in a manner provided for in the related appropriation law.

Unobligated Balances—Current Year

Statement 15 shows a total of $6,224,218 of unobligated balances as of the end of the first quarter of the current year. But only $180,326 of this total is currently available as of the end of the first quarter. The remaining amounts are reserved.

By far, the largest of the reserves is for apportionments that go into effect in the second, third, and fourth quarters in accordance with OMB directions. (The amount apportioned for a given quarter becomes available at the beginning of the quarter.) The next item in the statement, a sum of $732,278 described as "reserved for anticipated orders," will become available for obligating only as reimbursable orders are received later in the year. The last reserve, balance subject to future apportionment action, $5,000, is for program elements that are in suspense, pending further discussions with OMB even though they were incorporated in the budget of the agency as approved by Congress. This sometimes happens when OMB exercises its right to withhold, delay, or reduce apportionment action in the interest of adjusting to unforeseen conditions.

Unobligated Balances—Prior Years

As already noted, prior years' unobligated balances are not available for any new obligating. Any such balances expire and are automatically not available for obligating. Expired balances can be withdrawn by Treasury at any time and usually by the end of the year. (The 19X8 treatment is used for purposes of discussion.) Some or all of such withdrawn amounts can be restored at a later time, as in the case of the $44 item. If adjustments of outstanding contracts and orders throw a prior year's appropriated fund into a state of deficiency, Congress must make a deficiency appropriation to correct the condition. An example of this in the amount of $194,000 is also found in Statement 15.

FUNDAMENTAL MULTI-CONCEPT STATEMENT OF OPERATIONS

Statement 16 displays the linkage of important financial, accounting, and legal concepts. These concepts are introduced below before discussing Statement 16. The content and scope of Statement 16 will be more readily understood by this approach.

Fundamental Model

Four concepts are involved and marked a, b, c, and d in Exhibit 33: In this model (and also in Statement 16), the data cover, from left to

STATEMENT 16

National Air Safety Board—Appropriated Funds: Costs, Expenditures, and Obligations Incurred, Statement of Interrelationships, First Quarter of Fiscal Year 19X9

	Actual First Q	Budget First Q	Budget FY 19X9
Program			
Air traffic safety	$ 749,742	$ 787,432	$3,043,586
Airport safety	569,732	590,576	2,320,190
Safety research laboratory	284,886	295,287	1,160,095
Administrative services	189,924	190,858	773,397
International relations	94,962	94,429	386,698
Total expenses (a)	1,889,246	1,958,582	7,683,966
Consumable materials transferred to others			
Cost of materials sold	30,680	29,640	88,668
Cost of materials transferred without reimbursement	7,860	10,460	63,630
Total cost of materials transferred to others	38,540	40,100	152,298
Costs applicable to prior years			
Inventory losses, etc., as adjustments of beginning inventories	12,586	9,300	32,070
Changes in inventories during current year			
Materials purchased	521,640	534,208	1,901,968
Materials received without charge	8,460	9,000	36,216
Materials issued for use or consumption (charged to program expenses)	(465,780)	(469,126)	(1,848,104)
Transfers to others (as above)	(38,540)	(40,100)	(152,298)
Adjustments of inventories			
Inventory losses and adjustments	(9,432)	(9,300)	(32,070)
Standard price adjustments of purchases	(642)		
Revision of standard prices	2,288		
Net change in inventories	17,994	24,682	(94,288)
Equipment purchases	10,000	10,000	50,000
Total costs	1,968,366	2,042,684	7,824,046
Deduct: unfunded costs of materials received	8,460	9,000	36,216
Total Expenditures (accrued)	1,959,906	2,033,684	7,787,830
Changes in contracts and orders outstanding at end of period			
New contracts and orders outstanding, end of period	284,880	236,884	388,944
Deduct: expenditures under contracts and orders outstanding at beginning of period	177,536	160,592	354,562
Net change in contracts and orders	107,344	75,932	34,382
Provision for contingencies (unprogrammed)			270,212
Obligations incurred	$2,067,250	$2,109,596	$8,092,424 (b)

Notes: (a) Typical expense classes are illustrated as follows: personal services (payroll), materials and supplies used, official travel, transportation of things, rent, communication, utilities, printing, in-house reproduction of forms and messages, and subscriptions.

(b) Total budgeted obligations for fiscal year 19X9 appearing above in the amount of $8,092,424 are $200,000 less than total available funds per Statement 15 because of allowance for estimated unearned reimbursements on unfilled orders when the year ends on September 30, 19X9, as projected.

EXHIBIT 33
Fundamental Model Concepts

Concept	Actual for First Quarter	Budget for First Quarter	Budget for Year
Expenses (costs incurred and expired)	$100	$108	$400 (a)
Costs incurred, not expired	7	8	32 (b)
Accrued expenditures	107	116	432 (c)
Increase in contracts and orders outstanding	9	12	18
Obligations incurred	$116	$128	$450 (d)

right, actuals for the first quarter, budget estimates for the first quarter, and budget estimates for the year as a whole. Differences between the two budget columns represent projected amounts for the remaining quarters of the year, but neither this model nor Statement 16 shows these amounts although an additional column could be provided for this purpose.

Value of Cost Information

Costs move through a process of conversions and transfers in time within an activity. Costs initially measure the prices paid for resources. When resources are used or used up, the related costs are said to have expired. Costs that have expired become the measure of resources gone and are reclassified in the reporting as expenses. It follows that unexpired costs are the measure of resources waiting to be used or used up.

Tracking resources in this manner from the time they are acquired to the time they are used or used up facilitates the management and control of resources in a number of important ways. It assures that all resources acquired are accounted for, it serves to measure expense as such, it identifies expense with the operating program that is budgeted for it, and it shows where, when, and how much resources were employed as planned in budgets and as actually experienced in operation for each given aspect of the data. Some comparisons are an undoubted stimulus that motivate decision makers to take an action or, perhaps wisely, no action at all. Useful information is superior to cursory knowledge because it reduces uncertainty about the state of things. Useful information reinforces the decision-making art because it gives guidance to those responsible for making decisions. Today, the power of computers to melt mountains of data in a fraction of a minute into desired cost elements clearly must be a boon in gathering and disseminating this information.

EXPANDED MULTI-CONCEPT STATEMENT OF OPERATIONS

In this model (Exhibit 34) the interrelationships found in the fundamental model above are now expanded to reveal the elements more specifically. Assume that the data considered are for the year as a whole and that actuals for the year are the same as budget estimates for the year.

Expenses. The cost of goods and services used or consumed, labeled as expenses (or operating expenses), is $400 for the year. The relative size of expenses in the model is realistic here inasmuch as the principal cost of operation and maintenance of a typical federal agency is cost of payroll and ordinary utilities, rent, travel, communication, and the like.

Changes in Inventories of Materials and Supplies. Inventories of materials and supplies increased $15. This represents costs incurred but not expired. It is added to the period's beginning inventory of resources waiting to be used or consumed. Cost of issues, $56, is transferred to expenses as used.

Purchases of Equipment. The next item in the model shows that equipment is purchased at a total cost of $22, probably on contracts previously issued.

Total Costs Incurred. It is now possible to take a measurement of total costs incurred during the year, $437. Recapitulating, expenses of $400 were incurred for goods and services used, purchased materials and supplies of $15 were added to inventories for use in the future, and equipment was purchased at a cost of $22 and placed in service, all for an aggregate cost of $437.

Free Materials and Supplies. The total costs incurred is $437, as noted above, but this includes $5 of "free materials" received from another unit that is financed by a different appropriated fund.[7] Transfers of this nature are usually acts of accommodation by the supplying unit and generally are not supposed to be repetitive. (The recommended arrangement is that the sending unit be reimbursed by the receiving unit.)

Expenditures Incurred. To arrive at expenditures incurred, it is necessary to deduct the cost of free materials and supplies received, $5. In the model, the result is expenditures totaling $432.[8]

Changes in Contracts and Orders Outstanding. Because budgeting

EXHIBIT 34
Expanded Model Concepts

EXPENSES

Cost of goods and services used		$400
Changes in inventories of materials and supplies:		
Receipts of materials and supplies purchased	$ 66	
Receipts of free materials and supplies	5	
Issues of materials and supplies	(56)	
Net change in inventories	15	
Purchases of equipment	22	
Costs incurred, not expired		37
Total costs incurred		437
Deduct: materials and supplies received free of charge, at cost to furnisher, being unfunded costs		5
Accrued expenditures		432
Changes in contracts and orders outstanding:		
Current year contracts and orders:		
Issued and still outstanding at end of year	$ 22	
Prior year contracts and orders:		
Decrease since beginning of year	(4)	
Net change in contracts and orders outstanding		18
OBLIGATIONS INCURRED		$450

and funding is in terms of obligations to be incurred, one more link is necessary in the chain of accountability. In the current year, contracts and orders were issued, of which $22 is still outstanding, thus obligating the agency for this amount. Shouldn't the $22 be added to expenditures of $432 to determine the amount obligated, namely, $454? Not in the illustration used because one more factor must be considered. The year began with contracts and orders issued under prior years appropriated funds. In the first quarter of the present year, performance on the prior years commitments totaled $4. The resulting expenditures of $4 are charged against prior years' contracts and orders, not the current year's. To put this in other words, the current year benefitted from expenditures of $4 that were charged against prior years' commitments and therefore are interpreted as not affecting obligations incurred this year.

In the logic used, the sum of $4 is subtracted from obligations otherwise charged against the current year. Obligations charged to the current year to date are accordingly not $454 ($432 + $22), but $450 ($432 + $22 − $4).

Value of Model

Our expanded model (and Statement 16 structure) explains the logic of the methodology followed. It shows how to integrate all of the important financial, accounting, and legal concepts into a complete reporting of what happened over a period of time. Setting up the several links separately permits visibility of the data for different users.

Thus, operating expenses are segregated to assist management plan and control day-to-day operations. Then the data on costs incurred are presented, which are useful to managers responsible for procurement planning and control. This data also should be of interest to expenditures watchers; however, unfunded costs, if any, are excluded before expenditures are determined. In the final part, the data are reconciled to the legally established budget and funding by Congress by considering the net change in contracts and orders outstanding. The last step ends up with the amount of obligations incurred, which is primarily a legal concept.

Special Problems in Measurement of Expenses

Expenses measure expired costs, but physical facilities are not expensed through depreciation and materials and supplies are treated as unexpired costs until used or consumed. Inventories of materials and supplies are not, however, fund assets because they are charged off as purchased in fund accounts. Inventories are accordingly treated as nonfund assets; they are accounted for through a supplementary cost system that keeps track of increases and decreases. Only issues from inventories are treated as expenses. Thus, in the above model, materials and supplies used, $56, is included in the expense total of $400.

If issues from inventories exceeded current purchases, expenses would include all currently purchased materials and supplies plus amounts drawn from beginning inventories. Thus, if in the model issues totaled $80 instead of $56, the measure of expired costs would be

EXHIBIT 35
Abbreviated Operating Statement

<u>Expenses</u>		$424
Change in inventories of materials and supplies:		
Receipts of materials and supplies purchased	$ 66	
Receipts of free materials and supplies	5	
Issues of materials and supplies	(80)	
Net change in inventories (decrease)	(9)	
Purchases of equipment	22	
Cost incurred, not expired		13
Total costs incurred		437
Deduct cost of free materials		5
Accrued expenditures		$432

$80 (as compared to costs incurred of $71), representing a difference of $24 ($80 − $56). With the new assumption, an abbreviated operating statement would show the data in Exhibit 35.

Should depreciation of physical facilities be ignored in determining expired costs? Costs are incurred when physical facilities are purchased, but the acquired items are treated as nonfund assets and do

EXHIBIT 36
Operating Statement Including Depreciation

<u>Expenses (including depreciation)</u>		$427
Net decrease in inventories (detail omitted)	$(9)	
Purchases of equipment	22	
Costs incurred, not expired		13
Total costs incurred		440
Cost of free materials	5	
Depreciation provision included in costs	3	
Total unfunded costs		8
Accrued expenditures		$432

not reenter the flow as expired costs in the form of depreciation expense. The reasoning is that the inclusion of depreciation expense in expired costs would have little or no managerial value because they are more or less noncontrollable. Advocates of full costing are inclined to disagree with this logic, even in the management of expendable funds, which is the type of fund represented in the model statement.

Procedurally, the handling of depreciation as an expired cost would be similar to the handling of materials and supplies in the above model statement. To illustrate this, assume that depreciation expense of $3 is added to $424, resulting in total expense of $427. The display of the data would now appear as shown in Exhibit 36.

STATEMENT OF COSTS, EXPENDITURES, AND OBLIGATIONS INCURRED

With the discussion of Exhibits 33 and 34 as an introduction, comments on Statement 16 itself can be briefer.

Expenses by Programs

Statement 16 lists the major programs or functions for which the illustrative agency is responsible. All work of the agency comes under one of those programs. Subprograms under each major program are provided as necessary. Expenses are accounted for by program and subprogram. The same program categories are utilized throughout the agency. This approach makes it possible to develop combined financial statements for the agency as a whole.

Each organizational unit of the agency carries out a stated program or subprogram, supported by an approved budget and a corresponding set of expense accounts, which permit comparison between actual and budgeted expenses. Sometimes, for various reasons, a program or subprogram may be conducted at a given time and place through more than one organizational unit; however, the program identity must be preserved.

The authors believe that the cost of goods and services used or consumed, the heart of the expense concept demonstrated in this discussion, is the most accurate measure of cost of performance. It should be used both in preparing budgets and in after-the-fact reporting so planned costs can be compared with actual costs. In the example case, the object of the costing is each program of the agency: air traffic safety, airport safety, safety research, administrative services, and international relations. Depreciation of facilities and equipment is excluded because appropriations and supporting appropriation budgets include no allowance for this cost. In short, the operating environment does not permit including depreciation as a cost, in view of current laws and legislative practices. However, as shown earlier, accounting method has no difficulty in adding depreciation as an operating expense, should the information be managerially useful and still reconcile with the concept of appropriation.

Change in Inventories

In Statement 16, program expenses include the cost of materials and supplies used or consumed in the amount of $465,780 for the first quarter. The excess of increases of inventories (mainly from purchases) over decreases (mainly from issues) is $17,994 and measures the net increase in inventories. To put this in other words, the sum of $17,994 is the amount of costs incurred but not expired, to be added to inventory assets for future use. Being nonfund assets, they are not included among fund assets in Statement 17, which is a report of financial position of the fund. The data on inventories are presented in the supplement to Statement 17.

The problem of distinguishing between used and unused materials and supplies arises from the necessity of reconciling the funding or appropriation process based on purchases and the managerially useful process of accountability based on use or consumption. The appropriation process is legally required, and until or unless it is changed the reconciliation is achieved through the multi-concept reporting demonstrated in Statement 16 and appropriate procedures in underlying accounts.

Enter Revolving Fund; Exit Inventory Problems of User

If an agency—any agency—has convenient access to a revolving fund, the accounting for materials and supplies can be greatly simplified. Buying, stocking, and issuing functions are taken over by a revolving fund which is operated similar to a commercial-type enterprise except that sales are priced at cost. A user agency would buy from the revolving fund on an "as needed" basis, thereby enabling it to operate with a relatively small inventory. A user agency would charge purchases to expense from the revolving fund, and, in the agency's budget, the amount funded for materials and supplies would approximate the amount used or consumed. If this approach were adopted, the section in the model (and in Statement 16) showing changes in inventories would be eliminated and the report greatly simplified, as would the user agency's managerial and accounting problems.

Purchases of Equipment

In Statement 16, the sum of $10,000 is shown as expended for equipment, delivered and put in service. Costs incurred are increased by $10,000 and so are nonfund assets of this class. Supplementary property accounts keep track of items until they are no longer useful. When a property item is removed from service, the event is recorded by a debit to government's investment and a credit to property for purchase cost. This assumes that the supplementary records are kept in accordance with the double-entry principle.

Cost of Free Materials (Unfunded Costs)

The item that prevents total cost of $1,968,366 from measuring expenditures is the free materials received from other appropriated funds. (It is necessary to send along with a shipment of free materials a memorandum invoice stating the price information to be used to account for the value of the materials in the manner shown in Statement 16 and in the nonfund inventory records of the recipient.)

Adding receipts of free materials to costs incurred achieves a more accurate measure of cost flow. After all, the materials did cost the government the price paid, and this cost is identified and traced in the accounts until the materials are drawn from inventory for use or other disposition. At the same time, the treatment of free materials received as an item of cost need not interfere with accounting for actual expenditures. Thus, in Statement 16, total costs of $1,968,366 less unfunded costs of $8,460 equals accrued expenditures of $1,959,906, creating another link to the chain of accountability presented in this report.

Changes in Contracts and Orders Outstanding

To complete the operating story, one more section is needed to arrive at the amount of obligations incurred, which is the focus of control by Congress. This is provided by changes in contracts and orders outstanding as shown in Exhibit 37.

STATEMENT OF FINANCIAL POSITION

Statement 17 gives the financial position of our agency's several appropriated funds. The date of the statement is December 31, 19X8, which is the end of the first quarter of the year ending September 30, 19X9. Most of the items in this statement are either self-explanatory or they have been discussed already, especially in relation to Statement 15. However, several items require comment.

STATEMENT 17
National Air Safety Board—Appropriated Funds: Financial Position, by Fund, End of First Quarter, December 31, 19X8

	19X9 Fund	19X8 Fund	19X7 Fund	Prior Years' Funds	Combined Total
Fund resources					
Undisbursed Treasury balance	$5,540,188	$332,196	$37,258	$78,960	$5,988,602
Accounts receivable	246,084	44,572	4,638		295,294
Anticipated reimbursements:					
Unfilled orders	335,100				335,100
Anticipated orders	732,278				732,278
Travel advances	212				212
Undistributed charges (net)	482		206		688
	6,854,344	376,768	42,102	78,960	7,352,174
Obligations (unpaid)					
Accounts payable	207,148	152,694	40,672	78,960	479,474
Accrued liabilities	138,098				138,098
Total liabilities	345,246	152,694	40,672	78,960	617,572
Contract and orders outstanding	284,880	207,440			492,320
Undistributed credits (net)		7,236			7,236
Total obligations	630,126	367,370	40,672	78,960	1,117,128
Unobligated balances					
Currently available	180,326				180,326
Apportioned for subsequent quarters	5,306,614				5,306,614
Reserved for anticipated reimbursable earnings	732,278				732,278
Balance subject to future apportionment action (of OMB)	5,000				5,000
Balance in expired accounts		9,398	1,430		10,828
Total unobligated balances	$6,224,218	$9,398	$1,430	$ --	$6,235,046

STATEMENT 17 continued

Summary of Property Acquired from and Related to the Appropriated
Funds of This Agency, End of First Quarter, December 31, 19X8

Inventory of consumable materials:
Government's investment:

At beginning of fiscal year 19X9	$436,648
Increase for first quarter (per Statement 16)	17,994
At end of first quarter of fiscal year 19X9	$454,652

Equipment in active use, at cost
Government's investment:

At beginning of fiscal year 19X9	$240,000
Additions for first quarter (per Statement 16)	10,000
At end of first quarter of fiscal year 19X9	$250,000

EXHIBIT 37
Changes in Contracts and Orders Outstanding

Accrued expenditures		$1,959,906
Add: this year's contracts and orders placed but not filled as of the end of the quarter	$284,880	
Deduct: expenditures under prior years' contracts and orders (orders filled)	(177,536)	
Net change in contracts and orders		107,344
Obligations incurred		$2,067,250

Undisbursed Treasury Balance

This item, stated separately for each appropriated fund, is the reciprocal of the credit in the central accounts kept by the Treasury Department. The relationship here is much like that existing between a depositor and the bank holding the deposit in the commercial environment. In Statement 17, the item is a measure of the amount that may be drawn through issuance of checks. In both the agency's and Treasury's accounts, it is stated separately for each appropriated fund until the end of year three. After year three, a given undisbursed Treasury balance is transferred into a merged balance for all prior years. It remains in this state until it is withdrawn by Treasury or put to some other legal use. As a clarification, the merged balance for prior years represents only the total undisbursed Treasury balances required to satisfy unpaid obligations less accounts receivable, if any.

In considering the changes in contracts and orders, the purpose of Statement 16 should be kept in mind: to end up the report with the amount of obligations incurred under the current year's fund. If only the current year's contracts and orders were involved, adding the amount still outstanding, $284,880, to expenditures would arrive at obligations incurred. But some of the expenditures were financed under contracts and orders issued under prior years' appropriated funds. The amount of such expenditures, $177,536, must therefore be deducted to arrive at obligations incurred under the current year's funding. The deduction is shown as an element of change in contracts and orders outstanding because the decrease in these contracts and orders outstanding led to expenditures charged to prior years' funding, not

EXHIBIT 38
Undisbursed Treasury Balance

Appropriation for current year, per Statement 15		$7,015,690
Reimbursements collected		--
Expenditures, per Statement 15	$1,782,326	
Less unpaid liabilities, per Statement 17	345,246	
Payments on expenditures		(1,437,080)
Payments for work done on reimbursable orders in progress (charged to accounts receivable) (Note)		(37,728)
Other payments: per Statement 17 outstanding		
Travel advances	212	
Undistributed charges, pending further data	482	(694)
Undisbursed Treasury balance, per Statement 17		$5,540,188

Note

In Statement 17, accounts receivable of $246,084 represents reimbursements earned on completed orders, $208,357, per Statement 15, plus $37,728 charged to accounts receivable as explained above for work done on orders in progress, which will not generate revenue until completed.

the current year's. Of course, the expenditures of $177,536 represent goods and services received in the current year that benefitted from the receipts without incurring the expenditures.

Changes in Undisbursed Treasury Balance

Procedurally, the undisbursed Treasury balance for a given appropriated fund is subject to change in accordance with the following factors: appropriation received + reimbursements collected − checks drawn = undisbursed balance. Exhibit 38 shows the relevant factors for this case.

Undistributed Charges and Credits

These are items held in suspense, pending clarification for proper disposition. They normally arise at the end of a period when there is insufficient time to determine proper accounting treatment and thereby hold up preparation of the financial statements in accordance with established time tables.

To illustrate, a debit is made to undistributed charges with a corresponding credit to accounts payable if a vendor's invoice, otherwise valid, does not identify which program expense is to be charged for the cost incurred. As soon as the necessary clarification is made, the proper program expense is debited and undistributed charges is credited.

Or, a credit is made to undistributed credits, with a corresponding debit to undisbursed Treasury balance if a remittance of a refund from a vendor does not identify which program expense is to be credited. As soon as the information is obtained, the appropriate program expense is credited, and undistributed credits is debited.

In Statement 17, undistributed charges and credits are netted. The item appears as a net debit under the 19X9 fund, but it is a net credit under the 19X8 fund.

Nonfund Assets

National Air Safety Board, our example agency, owns and uses two classes of nonfund assets that were financed from appropriations received. Expenditures for acquiring the assets were charged off in the fund accounts of the given appropriated fund, but the assets are nevertheless accounted for satisfactorily through supplementary cost accounts. The status of these assets is reported in the supplement to Statement 17. In the case of materials and supplies, purchases and other receipts are added to inventories; issues and other dispositions are deducted. Perpetual inventory records are recommended with information on status available at any time, especially if the records are computerized. Activity in the case of property items is relatively low: additions are made as received, and deductions are made as items are removed from service. Physical inventories should be taken at least once a year to check the accuracy of book balances. Applying the double-entry principle, each nonfund asset ledger is composed of a self-balancing group of accounts.

Interrelations between Statements 15 and 17

Considerable cross referencing of data is possible between Statements 15 and 17. Thus, for 19X9, obligational authority received of

$8,292,424 minus obligations incurred of $2,068,206 per Statement 15 plus unpaid obligations of $630,126 per Statement 17 agrees with total fund resources of $6,854,344 per Statement 17. Unobligated balances of $6,224,218 are the same in Statements 15 and 17 under the 19X9 fund.

RELATION TO GOVERNMENT-WIDE FINANCIAL STATEMENTS

Although the National Air Safety Board is relatively small, its financial statements enter into the totals of government-wide financial summaries discussed and illustrated in earlier chapters. Thus, government-wide financial statements are consolidated statements. They are prepared, for example, by combining Statement 17s of all federal agencies financed under the General Fund to arrive at Statement 7, which is the combined statement of financial position of the General Fund of the government as a whole.

As in any consolidation procedure, consistency of classifications of data in individual reports is difficult to achieve, especially in the case of the federal government since there are hundreds of reporting federal agencies. However, to minimize crude and arbitrary combining steps, consistency of classification of data and other appropriate standards in the consolidation procedure, too technical to discuss here, are to be encouraged. Quality control of data reported must be balanced against the constraints of the time and cost of the consolidation procedure.

TREASURY'S NETWORK OF DISBURSEMENT OFFICES

To handle the government's cashiering functions, the Treasury Department maintains a network of disbursement offices that issue checks and receive cash. All agencies wishing to draw checks against their Treasury balances must do this through disbursement offices nearest their operating locations because only authorized disbursement officers may issue the checks. Likewise, agencies receiving remittances from any source must take or send the remittances to the nearest disbursement office for deposit. (A disbursement office is administratively divided for purposes of internal control into disbursing and collecting functions.)

Rules of documentation, supported by audited papers, must be strictly observed in any agency's requests for issuing checks or accepting remittances. These are the papers that initiate the transactions of cash receipts and disbursements and later generate the related records kept at all levels of the federal government. Of particular interest here is that field disbursement offices regularly compile and transmit to the Treasury summaries as well as detailed documents supporting cash disbursements made and cash receipts accepted for a period of time. Only by this procedure is it possible for Treasury to stay abreast of transactions of individual agencies involving cash disbursed and received and at the same time build summaries of the data for the government as a whole.

EACH AGENCY IS RESPONSIBLE FOR ITS ACCOUNTING SYSTEM

The financial statements of a federal agency illustrated and espoused in this chapter can serve as a model for any agency that is financed by appropriated funds, which are subdivisions of the government's General Fund. The National Air Safety Board, for example, though a relatively small agency, is intended as a good prototype organization and related financial system in the federal government. Even the larger agencies, including the great executive departments such as State, Labor, or Commerce, conduct the bulk of their operations through bureaus and other subdivisions similar in organizational structure and financial system illustrated and discussed in this chapter. Of course, record and report formats may vary, but the essentials of their data content and scope should be expected to be similar.

SYSTEM MANUAL OF AN AGENCY

Every federal agency uses its own design of a financial management system manual, reflecting its stage of development and stated goals. Some do no more than is necessary to meet the reporting requirements laid down in official report forms by the three central authorities: Treasury, OMB, and GAO. Other accounting systems (or financial management systems, as they are called) provide additional management information for use at agency level depending upon those who manage the agency.

The exhibits discussed and illustrated in this chapter are intended to conform to the information standards of the three central authorities. The exhibits also suggest how managerially useful additional data for the use of agency management can be reported. In this connection, data for purposes of variable expense budgeting possess the greatest significance. Overall, the problem is to generate information that will assist managers to run an agency, assist Congress and OMB to evaluate the role played by an agency and provide it with the needed financing, and conform to the budgeting, accounting, auditing, and internal control principles required by law, as set forth in the directives of Treasury, OMB, and GAO. An agency's information system should help answer these questions: Were resources received, safeguarded, and applied in conformance with covering laws and directives? Were resources used efficiently? Did the results justify the costs; that is, were the results cost effective?

NOTES

1. The deficiency was given advance approval by OMB and the concerned standing committees of Congress upon the request and required documentation by our example agency. Budgetary control, in other words, was at work.

2. Within the federal government, the term "accrued expenditures" is preferred over the shorter term "expenditures," so as to avoid confusion with usage of the latter term as synonymous with disbursements.

3. Physical facilities such as equipment, buildings, and so on are treated as accrued expenditures when received under the expendable fund that financed the purchases or construction, not as fund assets. Such charge-offs are uniformly followed in state and local governments as well as consistent with the character of expendable funds.

4. This sum is net of progress payments to vendor contractors. Progress payments, as distinguished from advances, are accrued expenditures, the same as if goods and services are received. In the current year, the entries are debit accrued expenditures and credit accounts payable; debit contracts and orders outstanding and credit commitments (or contracts and orders issued) as progress payments are made.

5. Under fixed-price contracts, departures from contracted costs must be covered in explicit language in the contracts, such as allowance for inflation, penalty for late deliveries or performance, or allowable changes in contract specifications. Contract accounting and reporting concepts observed by the federal government are beyond the scope of this book. Besides fixed-price contracts are cost reimbursable contracts, further identified as cost plus fixed fee, cost plus incentive fee, and straight cost reimbursement, common in contracts with nonprofit institutions.

6. The treatment of the reductions of $7,928 and $1,430 as receipts of obligational authority for the funds concerned may appear a bit strange, but the alternative may prove confusing. These amounts could be added to the $163,272 and $14,264 items lower down in the statement, representing net change in contracts and orders outstanding and making the latter amounts larger. Under this treatment, there would be negative amounts on the line described as obligations incurred; for example, $7,928 in the 19X8 column, which could be confusing.

7. Transfers of free goods and services within the same appropriated fund at lower levels are eliminated in consolidation of data for an agency as a whole.

Transfers of free goods and services in the context of the present discussion are an important practice in the military departments, though by no means limited to them.

8. The sum of $432 is the total of expenditures incurred during the current year, financed by the agency's appropriated funds, current and prior years together. The underlying accounts are, of course, separated by year of appropriation because under the law each appropriation is accounted for by a separate appropriated fund throughout its legal existence.

8.

COMPLETE BUDGETING, ACCOUNTING, AND REPORTING CYCLE OF A FEDERAL AGENCY: A CASE STUDY _____

This chapter presents a case study of a federal agency financed by appropriated funds of the government's General Fund.[1] The procedures, charts of accounts, record formats, and report formats, and the resulting total financial system, including the form and content of the financial statements, are intended to serve as a model of the better ideas found in federal financial management today. A different sample agency is presented in this chapter to provide comments and illustrations that would not be available if the NASB case was continued.

ORGANIZATION OF SAMPLE AGENCY

Sample Agency is a regulatory commission operating in the field of communications. Its mission is to oversee this field as it applies to interstate and foreign commerce utilizing television programs.

Sample Agency was created by the Sample Act of 19X2 to administer the provisions of this Act. Like other federal laws, the provisions of the Act are amended by Congress from time to time as new conditions appear. Exhibit 39 is a condensed chart of organization.

The members of the commission are responsible for policy matters. The office of the commissioners is treated as a separate program for purposes of budgeting, accounting, and reporting. The executive director is responsible for executing the commission's policies and general management of the agency on behalf of the commission. The agency uses three operating programs as shown in the chart. The manager of each operating program is under the supervision of the executive director.

EXHIBIT 39
Condensed Organizational Chart

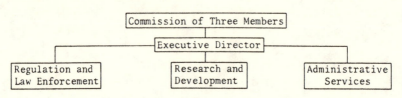

HOW THE AGENCY IS FINANCED

Sample Agency is financed by annual appropriation from Congress out of the General Fund. Any unused (unobligated) appropriation expires at the end of the year for which the appropriation is received.

An expired appropriation balance for a given year remains open to absorb changes in amounts obligated for that year for two additional years. After two years, an expired balance of a given year is transferred to a merged account for all prior years' expired balances. Congress reserves the right, of course, to withdraw any or all of such expired balances; if this happens, the amounts withdrawn are added to the unappropriated balance of the General Fund (discussed in Chapter 4).

As with any federal appropriation of this nature, the appropriation is based upon an approved budget that specifies the purposes for which the appropriation is made. Generally, each such annual appropriation covers the money required to meet operating expenses, purchase materials and supplies, and acquire capital items. In the case of Sample Agency, for the time being, only equipment is necessary as a capital item because the agency rents the physical facilities it requires.

EXHIBIT 40
Trial Balances of Fund Accounts

Account Name	19X7 FUND		19X8 FUND	
	Debit	Credit	Debit	Credit
Undisbursed Treasury balance	$667		$15,500	
Vouchers payable		--		$ 4,000
Contracts and orders outstanding		$167		9,000
Expired balance		500		2,500
	$667	$667	$15,500	$15,500

YEARS COVERED IN SAMPLE CASE

The transactions and events assumed occur in the year ended September 30, 19X9 as the current year. Some of the transactions affect appropriated funds of prior years because goods and services received in the current year were contracted under prior years' appropriated funds and financed by those funds.

Fund accounts are separated by the appropriated fund with which they are identified. Each appropriation is accounted for by a separate appropriated fund, a requirement that has been discussed in earlier chapters.

TRIAL BALANCES—BEGINNING OF CURRENT FISCAL YEAR

Trial Balances of Fund Accounts

Exhibit 40 shows the trial balances of the two funds, which take their names from the year for which they were established. (Note: The merged fund for years prior to 19X7 has completed its transactions and has been dissolved.)

Trial Balances of Nonfund Asset Accounts

Sample Agency has two categories of nonfund assets: materials and supplies and items of equipment. As already stated, for the time being operating quarters are rented, so there is no requirement for land and buildings. The trial balance of the nonfund asset accounts is shown in Exhibit 41.

EXHIBIT 41
Trial Balances on Nonfund Asset Accounts

Account Names	Debit	Credit
Materials and supplies (classified)[a]	$ 4,500	
Items of equipment (classified)	200,000	
Government's investment in materials and supplies		$ 4,500
Government's investment in equipment		200,000
	$204,500	$204,500

[a]Relates to program for administrative services.

EXHIBIT 42
Sample Agency's Chart of Accounts

Fund ledgers (three separate ledgers)	19X9 Fund Ledger	19X8 Fund Ledger	19X7 Fund Ledger
Resources:			
Undisbursed Treasury balance	x	x	x
Receivables from other agencies	x		
Anticipated reimbursements	x		
Refunds receivable	x		
Advances for travel	x		
Liabilities:			
Vouchers payable	x	x	x
Payable to other agencies	x		
Payable to U.S. Treasury	x		
Contracts and orders outstanding	x	x	x
Unobligated balance:			
Appropriations	x		
Anticipated reimbursements	x		
Unfilled orders	x		
Reimbursements earned	x		
Expired balance	x	x	x
Obligations incurred:			
Programs			
Office of commissioners	x		
Regulation and law enforcement	x		
Research and development	x		
Administrative services	x		

Expense ledger (all funds)	
Program: office of the commissioners	dr
Program: regulation and law enforcement	dr
Program: research and development	dr
Program: administrative services	dr
Control account: all programs	cr

Nonfund asset ledger for material and supplies	
Classified assets	dr
Investment in material/supplies	cr

Nonfund asset ledger for equipment	
Classified assets	dr
Investment in equipment	cr

CHART OF ACCOUNTS

Sample Agency's chart of accounts appears in Exhibit 42.

RECORD-KEEPING PROCESS

The next sections and exhibits consist of Sample Agency's transactions presented in the summary segments, journal record of the transactions, year-end closing procedure, ledger records, year-end work sheet for the 19X9 fund ledger, trial balances, and six principal financial statements appropriate to the financial system of Sample Agency. Postings to the several ledger records are in some instances made directly from the journal record in order to avoid excessive journalizing. Note particularly the account formats in the 19X9 fund ledger. Where columnarizing is used, as in the case of the accounts for obligations incurred for each program, the subcolumns are readily replaced by separate subsidiary accounts in order to avoid excessive subcolumns in the given program obligation account.

TRANSACTION SUMMARIES

Approval of Agency Budget

The approved budget of Sample Agency is $1,714,000.[2] The budget resulted from a long succession of preparations, reviews, and changes spread over the customary months. Initially, the budget involved Sample Agency's management. Later, higher levels participated in the budget-making process, including OMB, the appropriate committees of Congress, Treasury, and OMB (again), in the order indicated. It is to be financed by congressional appropriation for the year ended September 30, 19X9 totaling $1,701,500 and anticipated reimbursements for work to be done for others of $12,500.[3]

Transactions Related to 19X8 Fund

The transactions related to the 19X8 fund include receipt of $9,100 on contracts and orders outstanding under the 19X8 fund, broken down as follows: received final performance of services, $6,000; final delivery of equipment, $2,500; and received delivery of materials and services, $600. The amounts exceeded the related and recorded contract prices by $100. All of the events described affect only the program for regulation and law enforcement. Payments totaling $13,100 were made on account.

EXHIBIT 43
Budget by Operating Programs

19X9 APPROPRIATED FUND

By Object \ By Program	Office of the Commissioners	Regulation and Law Enforcement	Research and Development	Administrative Services	Combined
Salaries	$50,500	$ 750,000	$354,000	$142,500	$1,297,000
Outside services	3,500	195,000	30,500	17,000	246,000
Rentals of offices	6,000	50,000	15,000	49,000	120,000
Purchases of materials and supplies	2,500	5,000	2,000	17,500	27,000
Purchases of equipment	500	6,500	2,500	14,500	24,000
	$63,000	$1,006,500	$404,000	$240,500	$1,714,000

Note: To avoid lengthy journalizing, detail budget data are entered directly on the budget line in the obligation account provided for each program (see 19X9 fund ledger).

EXHIBIT 44
Summary of Expenditures and Obligations

By Object \ By Program	Office of the Commissioners	Regulation and Law Enforcement	Research and Development	Administrative Services	Combined
Expenditures					
Salaries	$50,500	$ 747,500	$351,000	$142,500	$1,291,500
Outside services	500	44,500	5,500	10,500	61,000
Rentals of offices	4,000	21,000	4,500	45,500	75,000
Purchases of equipment	--	--	--	--	--
Purchases of materials and supplies	2,000	5,000	1,500	17,500	26,000
Total expenditures	$57,000	818,000	362,500	216,000	1,453,500
Contracts					
Total Contracts	3,000	184,500	37,500	25,000	250,000
Total Obligations	$60,000	$1,002,500	$400,000	$241,000	$1,703,500

Transactions Related to the 19X7 Fund

The transactions related to the 19X7 fund are as follows: receive final performance of services, $165; vendors are paid in full. The services affect only the program for regulation and law enforcement.

19X9 Fund: Expenditures and Issuance of Contracts and Orders

Presented in Exhibit 44 is the summary of expenditures and obligations aggregating $1,703,500, identified by program, and in the case of expenditures, also by object of the expenditures. An adequate file on contracts and orders is assumed here as in every agency organization. If the file is computerized, the data content of each contract or order can be as comprehensive as procurement managers think necessary, and data can be called up and displayed instantly on computer terminals for any reason, such as for referencing and updating.

To avoid lengthy journalizing, the following details were posted directly to the indicated accounts (see the respective ledgers for postings made):

• Expenditures to program accounts in the 19X9 fund ledger;
• Operating expenses to the expense ledger;
• Delivered equipment to the equipment ledger; and
• Delivered materials/supplies to the materials and supplies ledger.

19X9 Fund: Usage of Materials and Supplies

During the year, requisitions were filled resulting in the withdrawals of materials and supplies from inventory, as shown in Exhibit 45.

EXHIBIT 45
Requisitions

For Program	Amount
Office of the Commissioners	$ 1,500
Regulation and law enforcement	3,750
Research and development	900
Administrative services	16,500
	$22,650

EXHIBIT 46
Performance Data

By Object / By Program Description	Office of the Commissioners	Regulation and Law Enforcement	Research and Development	Administrative Services	Combined
Initial Amounts	$3,000	$184,500	$37,500	$25,000	$250,000
Outside services	800	148,000	25,000	7,000	
Rentals of offices	1,200	17,000	9,500	3,500	
Materials/supplies (a)	500	1,000	500	--	
Equipment (a)	500	6,500 (b)	500	13,000	
Total reductions	$3,000	$172,500	$35,500	$23,500	$234,500
Balance	--	12,000	2,000	1,500	$ 15,500

Notes: (a) Deliveries from vendors.
(b) Bill received is for $7,000, compared with contracted amount of $6,500. All other bills were the same as amounts contracted. ($172,500 + $500 = $173,000)

The changes required by the entries in Exhibit 45, when posted, affect the subcolumns of accrued expenditures, not the total of expenditure, in each program account for obligations incurred. (See the respective ledgers for postings made.)

To avoid lengthy journalizing, the following details were posted directly to the indicated accounts: expenses for materials and supplies used to the expense ledger and reduction of inventory to the materials and supplies ledger.

19X9 Fund: Performance on Contracts and Orders

Issuance of contracts and orders were presented under an earlier summary. The performance data on the contracts and orders appear in Exhibit 46.

To avoid lengthy journalizing, the following details were posted directly to the indicated accounts (see the respective ledgers for postings made):

- Expenditures to the program accounts in the 19X9 fund ledger;
- Operating expenses to the expense ledger;
- Delivered equipment to the equipment ledger; and
- Delivered materials/supplies to the materials and supplies ledger.

19X9 Fund: Payments of Vouchered Bills, including Payroll

During the year, payments totaling $1,630,000 were made on vouchered bills, including payrolls; also, payments totaling $47,000 were made on account to other federal agencies.

19X9 Fund: Earnings and Collections on Reimbursable Work

During the year, earnings of $12,000 were made on reimbursable work done for other federal agencies. Collections on this work totaled $11,250. There were no unfilled orders at the end of the year. (Reimbursable work is done under the research and development program.) Considering the way the facts are stated, processing the orders through the unfilled stage is optional, though this is the treatment used here. A shortcut would be a debit to unobligated balance—anticipated reimbursements and a credit to unobligated balance—obligational authority—reimbursements earned, thereby omitting the unfilled orders recording stages.

19X9 Fund: Post-Purchase Adjustments of Materials and Supplies

Materials and supplies were returned to vendors in the amount of $300. Also, price reductions were made in the amount of $400, which was accepted by the vendors as a result of errors in pricing goods received and was discovered in audits of transaction papers. The two adjustments relate only to the program for administrative services. Finally, 90% of the foregoing claims against vendors was collected by the end of the fiscal year. For items returned, both costs and quantities are reduced in the materials and supplies inventory; for items over-priced, costs only are reduced.

19X9 Fund: Removal of Obsolete Equipment from Service

Purchased equipment for $9,500 is declared obsolete and removed from service. It is sold for salvage for a cash price of $1,000. The amount received is payable to the U.S. Treasury and is paid in a timely manner. (The amount received by Treasury is credited to miscellaneous revenues of the General Fund.)

19X9 Fund: Advances for Official Travel and Subsequent Settlement

In accordance with general practice, employees were advanced $5,000 for official travel. All but $1,500 of this sum represents completed travel relating to the program for office of the commissioners (60%) and the program for regulation and law enforcement (40%).

Adjustments of Materials/Supplies Inventories Due to Shortages and Damage

Semi-annual physical inventories of materials and supplies resulted in disclosures of inventory shortages and damaged items totaling $50. The program affected is administrative services.

The changes required, when posted, affect the subcolumns of accrued expenditure, not the total of expenditures, in the administrative services account for obligations incurred. To avoid lengthy journalizing, the $50 item was posted directly to the following accounts: expenses for materials and supplies used to the expense ledger and reduction of inventory to the materials and supplies ledger.

CLOSING PROCEDURES

At the end of each fiscal year, temporary accounts of each ledger are formally closed, and existing balances are transferred to the parent or primary account for which the closed accounts served as an amplification or detail support. Considerable flexibility is involved in the closing procedure because the number and kinds of temporary accounts depend on the detailed accounts provided in the chart of accounts designed in a particular situation. The charts of accounts in this case are typical of those found in federal practice, but the reader should expect some differences from one agency to another due, for example, to size and complexity of the activities carried out. Exhibit 47 shows the compound closing procedure used in this case. Exhibits 48 through 55 show Sample Agency's journal records, ledgers, trial balances, and work sheet.

FINANCIAL STATEMENTS

Sample Agency's annual financial statements consist of the six listed below:

Statement 18. Obligational Authority Received, Obligations Incurred, and Unobligated Balance by Funds, Year Ended September 30, 19X9

Statement 19. Summary of Cash Transactions by Funds, Year Ended September 30, 19X9

Statement 20. Costs, Expenditures, and Obligations Incurred by Programs for Each Fund, Year Ended September 30, 19X9

Statement 21. Operating Expenses by Program for All Funds, Year Ended September 30, 19X9

Statement 22. Financial Position by Funds, September 30, 19X9

Statement 23. Changes in Nonfund Assets, Combined Funds, Year Ended September 30, 19X9

NOTES

1. Not considered are the problems associated with the government's other types of funds, namely, special funds, revolving funds, trust funds, and deposit funds.

2. The record and report formats, as distinguished from matters of content, used in this chapter are subject to computer and other machine mandates for more effective procedures. The record and report formats are accordingly flexible to writing, storing, and reproducing practices in a given work environment.

3. Reimbursement work is done under the research and development program.

EXHIBIT 47
Journal Record: Closing Entry

19X9 Fund Ledger	Debit	Credit
Unobligated balance--appropriations	1,701,500	
Unobligated balance--reimbursements	12,000	
Unobligated balance--anticipated reimbursements	500	
Anticipated reimbursements		500
Obligations incurred--office of the commissioners		62,100
Obligations incurred--regulation/law enforcement		1,004,400
Obligations incurred--research and development		400,000
Obligations incurred--administrative services		240,300
Expired balance		6,700

Year-end closing of temporary accounts in the 19X9
    fund ledger.

19X8 and 19X7 Fund Ledgers

No temporary accounts were used in these ledgers.

Expense Ledger

This is a cumulative ledger for one year at a time. The data are not
transferred or closed into other accounts.

Nonfund Asset Ledgers

The accounts in these ledgers are not subject to year-end transfers or
closings to other accounts.

EXHIBIT 48
Journal Record of Transactions

Ledgers: 1) 19X9 Fund Ledger   3) 19X7 Fund Ledger   5) Nonfund
            2) 19X8 Fund Ledger   4) Expense Ledger   Asset Ledger

Ref.		Debit	Credit
	(A) APPROVAL OF BUDGET		
1	Anticipated reimbursements	12,500	
	Undisbursed Treasury balance	1,701,500	
	Unobligated balance--appropriation		1,701,500
	Unobligated balance--anticipated		
	reimbursements		12,500
	Per budget approved for 19X9 fund		
	(B) TRANSACTIONS RELATED TO 19X8 FUND		
2	Contracts and orders outstanding	9,000	
	Expired balance (after approval)	100	
	Vouchers payable		9,100
4	Outside services--regulation/law enforcement		
	program	6,000	
	Expense ledger control		6,000
	(Financed by 19X8 fund)		
5	Equipment	2,500	
	Investment in property--equipment		2,500
	(Financed by 19X8 fund)		
5	Materials and supplies	600	
	Investment in property--materials and		
	supplies		600
2	Vouchers payable	13,100	
	Undisbursed Treasury balance		13,100
	(C) TRANSACTIONS RELATED TO 19X7 FUND		
3	Contracts and orders outstanding	167	
	Vouchers payable		165
	Expired balance (after approval)		2
3	Vouchers payable	165	
	Undisbursed Treasury balance		165

EXHIBIT 48 continued

Ref.		Debit	Credit

(C) continued

4 Outside services--regulation/law enforcement
program   165 (a)

    Expense ledger control   165

(Financed by 19X7 fund)

(D) EXPENDITURES AND ISSUANCE OF CONTRACTS
AND ORDERS

1 Obligations incurred:

    Office of commissioners program   57,000
    Regulation/law enforcement program   818,000
    Research and development program   362,500
    Administrative services program   216,000

    Vouchers payable   1,403,500

    Payable to other federal agencies   50,000

Accrued expenditures

1 Obligations incurred (contracts and orders
issued):

    Office of commissioners program   3,000
    Regulation/law enforcement program   184,500
    Research and development program   37,500
    Administrative services program   25,000

    Contracts and orders outstanding   250,000

Issues of contracts and orders

(E) USAGE OF MATERIALS AND SUPPLIES

1 Materials and supplies used   1,500

    Decrease in materials and supplies   1,500
    Office of commissioners program

1 Materials and supplies used   3,750

    Decrease in materials and supplies   3,750
    Regulation/law enforcement program

1 Materials and supplies used   900

    Decrease in materials and supplies   900
    Research and development program

1 Materials and supplies used   16,500

    Decrease in materials and supplies   16,500
    Administrative services program

EXHIBIT 48 continued

Ref.		Debit	Credit
	(F) PERFORMANCE ON CONTRACTS AND ORDERS		
1	Contracts and orders outstanding:	234,500	
	Contracts and orders issued:		
	Office of commissioners program		3,000
	Regulation/law enforcement program		172,500
	Research and development program		35,500
	Administrative services program		23,500
	Performance on outstanding contracts and orders		
1	Obligations incurred:		
	Office of commissioners program	3,000	
	Regulation/law enforcement program	173,000	
	Research and development program	35,500	
	Administrative services program	23,500	
	Vouchers payable		235,000
	Receipts of goods and services		
	(G) PAYMENT OF VOUCHERED BILLS		
1	Vouchers payable	1,630,000	
	Payable to other federal agencies	47,000	
	Undisbursed Treasury balance		1,677,000
	(H) EARNINGS AND COLLECTIONS ON REIMBURSABLE WORK		
1	Receivable from other agencies	12,000	
	Anticipated reimbursements		12,000
1	Undisbursed Treasury balance	11,250	
	Receivable from other agencies		11,250
1	Unobligated balance--anticipated reimbursements	12,000	
	Unobligated balance--obligational authority (unfilled orders)		12,000
1	Unobligated balance--obligational authority (unfilled orders)	12,000	
	Unobligated balance--obligational authority (reimbursements earned)		12,000

EXHIBIT 48 continued

Ref.		Debit	Credit
	(I) ADJUSTMENTS OF MATERIALS AND SUPPLIES		
1	Refunds receivable	700	
	Obligations incurred--materials/supplies Administrative services program		700
1	Undisbursed Treasury balance	630	
	Refunds receivable		630
5	Investment in property--materials/supplies	700	
	Materials and supplies		700
	(J) REMOVAL OF OBSOLETE EQUIPMENT FROM SERVICE		
1	Undisbursed Treasury balance	1,000	
	Payable to U.S. Treasury		1,000
1	Payable to U.S. Treasury	1,000	
	Undisbursed Treasury balance		1,000
5	Investment in property	9,500	
	Equipment		9,500
	(K) ADVANCES FOR OFFICIAL TRAVEL		
1	Advances for travel	5,000	
	Undisbursed Treasury balance		5,000
1	Obligations incurred--outside services		
	Office of commissioners program Regulation/law enforcement program	2,100 1,400	
	Advances for travel		3,500
4	Outside services--office of commissioners program	2,100	
	Expense ledger control		2,100
4	Outside services--regulation/law enforcement program	1,400	
	Expense ledger control		1,400

EXHIBIT 48 continued

Ref.		Debit	Credit
	(L) ADJUSTMENTS OF MATERIALS AND SUPPLIES		
1	Materials and supplies used	50	
	Decrease in materials and supplies		50
	Administrative services program		

Note: If desired, the following items can also be recorded in expenditures accounts under the 19X8 and 19X7 funds and closed at the end of the year as an additional step in budgetary control: outside services-- regulation/law enforcement, investment in property--equipment, and materials and supplies.

In each program's obligations incurred account, in the contracts and orders column, issues are posted as increases and represent debits; performances are posted as decreases and represent credits.

19X9 Fund Ledger

Undisbursed Treasury Balance

	Debit	Credit	Balance
A	1,701,500		1,701,500
G		1,677,000	24,500
H	11,250		35,750
I	630		36,380
J	1,000		37,380
J		1,000	36,380
K		5,000	31,380

Anticipated Reimbursements

	Debit	Credit	Balance
A	12,500		12,500
H		12,000	500

Receivables from Other Agencies

	Debit	Credit	Balance
H	12,000		12,000
H		11,250	750

Refunds Receivable

	Debit	Credit	Balance
I	700		700
I		630	70

Advances for Travel

	Debit	Credit	Balance
K	5,000		5,000
K		3,500	1,500

Vouchers Payable

	Debit	Credit	Balance
D		1,403,500	1,403,500
F		235,000	1,638,500
G	1,630,000		8,500

Payable to Other Federal Agencies

	Debit	Credit	Balance
D		50,000	50,000
G	47,000		3,000

Payable to U.S. Treasury

	Debit	Credit	Balance
J		1,000	1,000
J	1,000		--

Contracts and Orders Outstanding

	Debit	Credit	Balance
D		250,000	250,000
F	234,500		15,500

Unobligated Balances

OBLIGATIONAL AUTHORITY

Ref.	Anticipated Reimburse-ments	Reimbursements Unfilled Orders	Earned	Appro-priation	Expired Balance	Total	Control
A	12,500			1,701,500		1,701,500	1,714,000
H	(12,000)	12,000				1,713,500	1,714,000
H		(12,000)	12,000			1,713,500	1,714,000
Totals	500	--	12,000	1,701,500		1,713,500	1,714,000
X*	(500)		(12,000)	(1,694,800)		(1,706,800)	6,700
Y*				(6,700)	6,700	6,700	6,700

Note: *Year-end closing entries. X and Y are merged in the formal journal record.

EXHIBIT 49 continued

Federal Sample Agency — Record of Obligations Incurred--Programs — Office of Commissioners 21

ACCRUED EXPENDITURES

19X9 Trans.	Operating Expenses — Salaries	Outside Services	Rentals Offices	Material/Supplies Used	Total	MEMO Material/Supply Inventories	Material/Supply Increase or Decrease	Purchase of Equipment	Total	Contracts and Orders	Obligations Incurred
Budget	50,500	3,500	6,000	1,500	61,500		2,500 (1,500)	500	63,000	3,000 (3,000)	63,000
D	50,500	500	4,000		55,000	2,000	2,000		57,000		57,000
D										3,000	60,000
E				1,500	1,500	500	(1,500)				60,000
F		800	1,200		2,000	1,000	500	500	3,000	(3,000)	60,000
K		2,100			2,100				2,100		62,100
	50,500	3,400	5,200	1,500	60,600	1,000	1,000	500	62,100	--	62,100

Federal Sample Agency — Record of Obligations Incurred--Programs — Regulation and Law Enforcement 22

ACCRUED EXPENDITURES

19X9 Trans.	Operating Expenses — Salaries	Outside Services	Rentals Offices	Material/Supplies Used	Total	MEMO Material/Supply Inventories	Material/Supply Increase or Decrease	Purchase of Equipment	Total	Contracts and Orders	Obligations Incurred
Budget	750,000	195,000	38,000	3,750	986,750		5,000 (3,750)	6,500	994,500	184,500 (172,500)	1,006,500
E						600					
D	747,500	44,500	21,000		813,000	5,600	5,000		818,000		818,000
D										184,500	1,002,500
E				3,750	3,750	1,850	(3,750)				1,002,500
F		148,000	17,000		165,000	2,850	1,000	7,000	173,000	(172,500)	1,003,000
		1,400			1,400				1,400		1,004,400
K										12,000	1,004,400
	747,500	193,900	38,000	3,750	983,150	2,850	2,250	7,000	992,400	12,000	1,004,400

EXHIBIT 49 continued

Federal Sample Agency   Record of Obligations Incurred--Programs   Research and Development 23

ACCRUED EXPENDITURES

19X9

Trans.	Salaries	Outside Services	Rentals Offices	Material/ Supplies Used	Total	MEMO Material/ Supply Inventories	Material/ Supply Increase or Decrease	Purchase of Equipment	Total	Contracts and Orders	Obliga- tions Incurred
		Operating Expenses									
Budget	354,000	30,500	15,000	900	400,400	2,000	(900)	500	402,000	37,500 (35,500)	404,000
D	351,000	5,500	4,500		361,000	1,500	1,500		362,500	37,500	362,500
D				900	900	600	(900)				400,000
E						1,100	500	500	35,500	(35,500)	400,000
F		25,000	9,500		34,500					2,000	400,000
	351,000	30,500	14,000	900	396,400	1,100	1,100	500	398,000	2,000	400,000

Federal Sample Agency   Record of Obligations Incurred--Programs   Administrative Services 24

ACCRUED EXPENDITURES

19X9

Trans.	Salaries	Outside Services	Rentals Offices	Material/ Supplies Used	Total	MEMO Material/ Supply Inventories	Material/ Supply Increase or Decrease	Purchase of Equipment	Total	Contracts and Orders	Obliga- tions Incurred
		Operating Expenses									
Budget	142,500	17,000	49,000	16,500	225,000		17,500	13,000	239,000	25,000 (23,500)	240,500
Beg.						4,500	(16,500)				
D	142,500	10,500	45,500		198,500	22,000	17,500		216,000	25,000	216,000
D				16,500	16,500	5,500	(16,500)				241,000
E		7,000	3,500		10,500			13,000	23,000	(23,500)	241,000
F						4,800	(700)		(700)		241,000
I				50	50	4,750	(50)				240,300
L											
	142,500	17,500	49,000	16,550	225,550	4,750	250	13,000	238,800	1,500	240,300

EXHIBIT 50
19X8 Fund Ledger

Undisbursed Treasury Balance	Debit	Credit	Balance
Bal.			15,500
B		13,100	2,400

Contracts and Orders Outstanding	Debit	Credit	Balance
Bal.			9,000
B	9,000		--

Vouchers Payable	Debit	Credit	Balance
Bal.			4,000
B		9,100	13,100
B	13,100		

Expired Balance	Debit	Credit	Balance
Bal.			2,500
B	100		2,400

EXHIBIT 51
19X7 Fund Ledger

Undisbursed Treasury Balance	Debit	Credit	Balance
Bal.			667
C		165	502

Contracts and Orders Outstanding	Debit	Credit	Balance
Bal.			167
C	167		--

Vouchers Payable	Debit	Credit	Balance
Bal.			--
C		165	165
C	165		--

Expired Balance	Debit	Credit	Balance
Bal.			500
C		2	502

EXHIBIT 52
Expense Ledger

Control Account (Credit)

	19X9 Fund	19X8 Fund	19X7 Fund	Prior Years	Total
B		6,000			6,000
C			165		165
D	55,000				55,000
D	813,000				813,000
D	361,000				361,000
D	198,500				198,500
	1,427,500	6,000	165		1,433,665
E	1,500				1,500
E	3,750				3,750
E	900				900
E	16,500				16,500
	22,650				22,650
F	2,000				2,000
F	165,000				165,000
F	34,500				34,500
F	10,500				10,500
	212,000				212,000
K	2,100				2,100
K	1,400				1,400
	3,500				3,500
L	50				50
	1,665,700	6,000	165		1,671,865

EXHIBIT 52 continued

Expense (debit) 1   Program: Office of the Commissioners

	Salaries	Outside Services	Rent of Offices	Materials and Supplies Used	Cumulative Total
D	50,500	500	4,000		55,000
E				1,500	56,500
F		800	1,200		58,500
K		2,100			60,600

Expense (debit) 2   Program: Regulation and Law Enforcement

	Salaries	Outside Services	Rent of Offices	Materials and Supplies Used	Cumulative Total
B		6,000			6,000
C		165			6,165
D	747,500	44,500	21,000		819,165
E				3,750	822,915
F		148,000	17,000		987,915
K		1,400			989,315

Expense (debit) 3   Program: Research and Development

	Salaries	Outside Services	Rent of Offices	Materials and Supplies Used	Cumulative Total
D	351,000	5,500	4,500		361,000
E				900	361,900
F		25,000	9,500		396,400

Expense (debit) 4   Program: Administrative Services

	Salaries	Outside Services	Rent of Offices	Materials and Supplies Used	Cumulative Total
D	142,500	10,500	45,500		198,500
E				16,500	215,000
F		7,000	3,500		225,500
L				50	225,550

Memo: proof of control: Program expense

1	60,600	
2	989,315	
3	396,400	
4	225,550	1,671,865

EXHIBIT 53
Nonfund Asset Ledgers

Materials and Supplies (Itemized)

	Debit	Credit	Balance
Bal.			4,500
B	600		5,100
D	26,000		31,100
E		22,650	8,450
F	2,000		10,450
I		700	9,750
L		50	9,700

Investment in Material/Supply Control Account

	Debit	Credit	Balance
Bal.			4,500
B		600	5,100
D		26,000	31,100
E	22,650		8,450
F		2,000	10,450
I	700		9,750
L	50		9,700

Equipment (Itemized)

	Debit	Credit	Balance
Bal.			200,000
B	2,500		202,500
F	21,000		223,500
J		9,500	214,000

Investment in Equipment Control Account

	Debit	Credit	Balance
Bal.			200,000
B		2,500	202,500
F		21,000	223,500
J	9,500		214,000

EXHIBIT 54
Work Sheet

Description	Preclosing Trial Balance	Statement of Obligational Authority, Obligations Incurred, and Unobligated Balance	Statement of Financial Position
(Debits)			
Undisbursed Treasury balance	31,380		31,380
Anticipated reimbursements	500	500	
Receivables from other agencies	750		750
Refunds receivable	70		70
Advances for travel	1,500		1,500
Obligations incurred--office of the commissioners	62,100	62,100	
Obligations incurred--regulation and law enforcement	1,004,400	1,004,400	
Obligations incurred--research/ development	400,000	400,000	
Obligations incurred--administrative services	240,300	240,300	
	1,741,000	1,707,300	33,700
(Credits)			
Vouchers payable	8,500		8,500
Payable to other agencies	3,000		3,000
Contracts and orders outstanding	15,500		15,500
Unobligated balance--appropriations	1,701,500	1,701,500	
Unobligated balance--reimbursements	12,000	12,000	
Unobligated balance--anticipated reimbursements	500	500	
	1,741,000	1,714,000	
Excess of obligational authority available over obligations incurred: expired balance		6,700	6,700
			33,700

EXHIBIT 55
Trial Balances: September 30, 19X9, 19X8, and 19X7

APPROPRIATED FUND(S)

Debits	19X9 Fund	19X8 Fund	19X7 Fund
Undisbursed Treasury balance	31,380	2,400	502
Anticipated reimbursements	500		
Receivables from other agencies	750		
Refunds receivable	70		
Advances for travel	1,500		
Obligations incurred--program total			
Office of the commissioners	62,100		
Regulation and law enforcement	1,004,400		
Research and development	400,000		
Administrative services	240,300		
	1,741,000	2,400	502

Credits			
Vouchers payable	8,500		
Payable to other agencies	3,000		
Contracts and orders outstanding	15,500		
Unobligated balance:			
Appropriation(s)	1,701,500		
Reimbursements	12,000		
Anticipated reimbursements	500		
Expired fund balance		2,400	502
	1,741,000	2,400	502

OTHER ACCOUNT GROUPS

Debits	Expense Ledger	Materials and Supplies Ledger	Equipment Ledger
Program total			
Office of the commissioners	60,600		
Regulation and law enforcement	989,315		
Research and development	396,400		
Administrative services	225,550		
Materials and supplies inventories (total)		9,700	
Equipment (Total)			214,000
	1,671,865	9,700	214,000

Credits			
Expense control	1,671,856		
Government's investment in materials/ supplies		9,700	
Government's investment in equipment			214,000

STATEMENT 18
Sample Agency—Obligational Authority Received, Obligations Incurred, and Unobligated Balance, by Funds, Year Ended September 30, 19X9

Description	19X9 Fund	19X8 Fund	19X7 Fund	Prior Years' Fund	Total
Obligational authority received:					
Appropriations	$1,701,500	$ --	$ --	$ --	$1,701,500
Reimbursements	12,000				12,000
Adjustments in prior years' obligations: (increase)		(100)			(100)
decrease			2		2
Prior years' expired balances brought forward		2,500	500		3,000
Total	1,713,500	2,400	502	--	1,716,402
Obligations incurred:					
Accrued expenditures	1,691,300	9,100	165		1,700,565
Net change in contracts and orders outstanding*	15,500	(9,100)	(165)		6,235
Total obligations incurred	1,706,800	--	--	--	1,706,800
Unobligated balance (expired)	$ 6,700	$2,400	$ 502	$ --	$ 9,602

Note: *Including adjustments in prior years' contracts and orders shown.

STATEMENT 19
Sample Agency—Summary of Cash Transactions, by Funds, Year Ended September 30, 19X9

Description	19X9 Fund	19X8 Fund	19X7 Fund	Prior Years' Fund	Total
Undisbursed Treasury balance, October 1, 19X8	$	$15,500	$667		$ 16,167
Appropriation received	1,701,500				1,701,500
Reimbursements collected	11,250				11,250
Total	1,712,750	15,500	667		1,728,917
Disbursements (normally categorized), less refunds	1,681,370	13,100	165		1,694,635
Undisbursed Treasury balance, September 30, 19X9	$ 31,380	$ 2,400	$502		$ 34,282

STATEMENT 20
Sample Agency—Costs, Expenditures, and Obligations Incurred, by Programs for Each Fund, Year Ended September 30, 19X9

Description	19X9 Fund	19X8 Fund	19X7 Fund	Prior Years' Fund	Total
Office of the commissioners					
Operating expenses	$60,600	$ --	$ --	$ --	$60,600
Equipment	500				500
Changes in material/ supply inventory	1,000				1,000
Accrued expenditures	62,100	--	--	--	62,100
Obligations incurred	$62,100	$ --	$ --	$ --	$62,100

Note:
A similar presentation is made for each program.

STATEMENT 21
Sample Agency—Operating Expenses by Programs—All Funds, Year Ended September 30, 19X9

Office of the commissioners	Budget	Actual	Actual (Over) Under Budget
Salaries	$ 50,500	$ 50,500	$ --
Outside services	3,500	3,400	100
Rent of offices	6,000	5,200	800
Materials and supplies used	1,500	1,500	--
Total expenses	$ 61,500	$ 60,600	(900)
Total--all programs			
Salaries	$1,297,000	$1,291,500	$5,500
Outside services	252,165	251,465	(700)
Rent of offices	108,000	106,200	1,800
Materials and supplies used	22,700	22,700	--
Total expenses	$1,679,865	$1,671,865	$8,000

Note:
The budget data represent managerial cost targets (or standards) for purposes of control of performance; the budget data here do not represent limitations on cost in terms of obligations to be incurred under a particular year's appropriation. To shorten presentation, the budgeted expenses shown in the first column to the left were not furnished earlier in the case.

STATEMENT 22
Sample Agency—Financial Position, by Funds, September 30, 19X9

Description	19X9 Fund	19X8 Fund	19X7 Fund	Prior Years' Fund	Total
Resources					
Undisbursed Treasury balances	$31,380	$2,400	$502		$34,282
Receivable from other agencies	750				750
Refunds receivable	70				70
Advances for travel	1,500				1,500
	$33,700	$2,400	$502	--	$36,602
Obligations and fund balance					
Vouchers payable	$ 8,500	$	$	$	$ 8,500
Payable to other agencies	3,000				3,000
Total liabilities	11,500				11,500
Contracts and orders outstanding	15,500				15,500
Total obligations	27,000				27,000
Fund balance:					
Balance in expired accounts	6,700	2,400	502		9,602
	$33,700	$2,400	$502	$--	$36,602

STATEMENT 23
Sample Agency—Changes in Nonfund Assets—Combined Funds, Year Ended September 30, 19X9

Description	19X8	Additions	Deductions	19X9
Materials and supplies, at cost	$ 4,500	$28,600	$23,400	$ 9,700
Equipment, at cost	200,000	23,500	9,500	214,000
Total nonfund assets	204,500	52,100	32,900	223,700
Government's investment in nonfund assets	204,500	52,100	32,900	223,700

Note:
Depreciation provision is not made for purposes of financial accounting. The property account for each item of equipment states historical cost, estimated useful life in years, accumulated depreciation based on such estimated useful life, and annual repairs and maintenance expense incurred to keep the item in satisfactory working condition. (This information was not furnished in order to shorten the case.)

Appendix A
TERMS USED IN THE FEDERAL BUDGET AND FINANCIAL MANAGEMENT SYSTEM _____

Budget Terms and Definitions _____

ACCRUED EXPENDITURES

Charges during a given period that reflect liabilities incurred and the need to pay for: (a) services performed by employees, contractors, other Government accounts, vendors, carriers, grantees, lessors, and other payees; (b) goods and other tangible property received; and (c) amounts becoming owed under programs for which no current service or performance is required (such as annuities, insurance claims, other benefit payments, and some cash grants, but excluding the repayment of debt, which is considered neither an obligation nor an expenditure). Expenditures accrue regardless of when cash payments are made, whether invoices have been rendered, or, in some cases, whether goods or other tangible property have been physically delivered. (*See also* Accrual Basis of Accounting and Liabilities defined in the Accounting Terms section of this glossary.)

ACTIVITY

A specific and distinguishable line of work performed by one or more organizational components of a governmental unit for the purpose of discharging a function or subfunction for which the governmental unit is responsible. For example, food inspection is an activity performed in the discharge of the health function. (*See also* Budget Activity; Functional Classification.)

ADVANCE APPROPRIATION

Budget authority provided in an appropriation act to become available in a fiscal year, or more, beyond the fiscal year for which the appropriation act is passed. The amount is not included in the budget totals of the year in which the appropriation bill is enacted but it is included in the budget totals for the fiscal year in which the amount will become available for obligation. For examples and further discussion of this term, see Part V of *The Budget of the United States Government, Appendix.* (For distinction, *see* Advance Funding; Forward Funding *under* Budget Authority.)

ADVANCE FUNDING

Budget authority provided in an appropriation act to obligate and disburse funds during a fiscal year from a succeeding year's appropriation. The funds so obligated increase the budget authority for the fiscal year in which obligated and reduce the budget authority of the succeeding fiscal year. Advance funding is a device for avoiding supplemental requests late in the fiscal year for certain entitlement programs should the appropriations for the current year prove to be too low. For examples and further discussion of this term, see Part V of *The Budget of the United States Government, Appendix.* (For distinction, *see* Advance Appropriation; Forward Funding *under* Budget Authority.)

ADVANCES

Amounts of money prepaid pursuant to budget authority in contemplation of the later receipt of goods, services, or other assets. Advances are ordinarily made only to payees to whom an agency has an obligation, and not in excess of the amount of the obligation. A common example is travel advances which are amounts made available to employees prior to the beginning of a trip for costs incurred in accordance with the Travel Expense Act of 1949 and·in accordance with standardized Government travel regulations. (*See also* Undelivered Orders.)

AGENCY

There is no single definition of the term agency. Any given definition usually relates to specific legislation. Generally, executive agency means any executive branch department, independent commission, board, bureau, office or other establishment of the Federal Government, including independent regulatory commissions and boards. (The term sometimes includes the municipal government of the District of Columbia.) Federal agency is a broader term, encompassing executive agencies and establishments in the judicial and legislative branches (except the Senate, the House of Representatives, and activities under the direction of the Architect of the Capitol).

AGENCY MISSIONS

Responsibilities assigned to a specific agency for meeting national needs.

Agency missions are expressed in terms of the purpose to be served by the programs authorized to carry out functions or subfunctions which, by law, are the responsibility of that agency and its component organizations. In contrast to national needs, generally described in the context of major functions, agency missions are generally described in the context of subfunctions. (*See also* Functional Classification; Mission Budgeting; National Needs.)

ALLOCATIONS

For purposes of Government accounting, an allocation is the amount of obligational authority transferred from one agency, bureau, or account that is set aside in a transfer appropriation account to carry out the purposes of the parent appropriation or fund. (The account to which the appropriation is made is called the parent account.) For example, allocations are made when one or more agencies share the administration of a program for which appropriations are made to only one of the agencies or to the President. Transactions involving allocation accounts appear in the Object Classification Schedule with the corresponding Program and Financing Schedule in *The Budget of the United States*

Government, Appendix. (For detailed discussion on the treatment of Object Classification—with Allocation Accounts, *see* OMB Circular No. A-11, revised.)

For purposes of section 302(a) of the Congressional Budget and Impoundment Control Act of 1974 (P.L. 93-344; 31 U.S.C. 1323), an allocation is the distribution of total budget outlays or total new budget authority in a concurrent resolution on the budget to the various committees having spending responsibilities. (*See also* Crosswalk; Object Classification; Transfer Appropriation Accounts *under* Appropriation (Expenditure), Receipt, and Fund Accounts; Transfer Between Appropriation/Fund Accounts; Transfer of Funds.)

ALLOTMENT

An authorization by the head (or other authorized employee) of an agency to his/her subordinates to incur obligations within a specified amount. An agency makes allotments pursuant to the requirements stated in OMB Circular No. A-34. The amount allotted by an agency cannot exceed the amount apportioned by the Office of Management and Budget. (*See also* Apportionment; Reapportionment.)

ALLOWANCES

Amounts included in the President's budget request or projections to cover possible additional proposals, such as statutory pay increases and contingencies for relatively uncontrollable programs and other requirements. As used by Congress in the concurrent resolutions on the budget, allowances represent a special functional classification designed to include amounts to cover possible requirements, such as civilian pay raises and contingencies. Allowances remain undistributed until they occur or become firm, then they are distributed to the appropriate functional classification(s). For a more detailed discussion, see Part 5, Meeting National Needs: The Federal Program by Function, *The Budget of the United States Government.* (*See also* Controllability.)

ANTIDEFICIENCY ACT

Legislation enacted by Congress to prevent the incurring of obligations or the making of expenditures (outlays) in excess of amounts available in appropriations or funds; to fix responsibility within an agency for the creation of any obligation or the making of any expenditure in excess of an apportionment or reapportionment or in excess of other subdivisions established pursuant to 31 U.S.C. 665(g); and to assist in bringing about the most effective and economical use of appropriations and funds. The Act is sometimes known as Section 3679 of the Revised Statutes, as amended. (*See also* Apportionment; Budgetary Reserves; Deferral of Budget Authority; Deficiency Apportionment; Deficiency Appropriation; Fund Accounting defined in the Accounting Terms section of this glossary; Supplemental Appropriation.)

APPLIED COSTS

The financial measure of resources consumed or applied within a given period of time to accomplish a specific purpose, such as performing a service, carrying out an activity, or completing a unit of work or a specific project, regardless of when ordered, received, or paid for. (For further discussion of this term, as it applies to the budgetary process and to particular types of transactions, see OMB Circular No. A-34.)

APPORTIONMENT

A distribution made by the Office of Management and Budget of amounts available for obligation, including budgetary reserves established pursuant to law, in an appropriation or fund account. Apportionments divide amounts available for obligation by specific time periods (usually quarters), activities, projects, objects, or a combination thereof. The amounts so apportioned limit the amount of obligations that may be incurred. In apportioning any account, some funds may be reserved to provide for contingencies or to effect savings, pursuant to the Antideficiency Act; or may be proposed for deferral or rescission pursuant to the Impoundment Control Act of 1974 (Title X of the Congressional Budget and Impoundment Control Act, P.L. 93-344, 31 U.S.C. 1400, et seq.).

The apportionment process is intended to prevent obligation of amounts available within an appropriation or fund account in a manner that would require deficiency or supplemental appropriations and to acheve the most effective and economical use of amounts made available for obligation. In this regard, Federal agency obligations may not be incurred in excess of the amount of budget authority apportioned. (*See also* Allotment; Antideficiency Act; Budgetary Reserves; Deferral of Budget Authority; Deficiency Apportionment; Deficiency Appropriation; Reapportionment; Rescission; Supplemental Appropriation.)

APPROPRIATION ACCOUNT/FUND ACCOUNT

A summary account established in the Treasury for each appropriation and/or fund showing transactions to such accounts. Each such account provides the framework for establishing a set of balanced accounts on the books of the agency concerned.

APPROPRIATION ACT

A statute, under the jurisdiction of the House and Senate Committees on Appropriations, that generally provides authorization for Federal agencies to incur obligations and to make payments out of the Treasury for specified purposes. An appropriation act, the most common means of providing budget authority, generally follows enactment of authorizing legislation unless the authorizing legislation itself provides the budget authority.

Currently, there are 13 regular appropriation acts enacted annually. From time to time, Congress also enacts supplemental appropriation acts. (*See also* Budget Authority; Supplemental Appropriation.)

APPROPRIATION (EXPENDITURE), RECEIPT, AND FUND ACCOUNTS

Expenditure and Receipt Accounts

There are a number of expenditure, receipt, and other accounts used by the Federal Government. The expenditure and receipt accounts used for budget and accounting purposes are those that record the Federal and trust fund amounts. (*See also under* Collections.)

In addition to the above, some accounts are used only for accounting purposes. These include transfer appropriation accounts, foreign currency accounts, receipt clearing accounts, and deposit fund accounts.

The Federal and trust fund amounts (except those specifically excluded by law) comprise the President's budget.

Federal Fund Accounts

General Fund Receipt Accounts. Those accounts credited with all collections that are not earmarked by law for a specific purpose. These collections are presented in *The Budget of the United States Government* as either budget (governmental) receipts or offsetting collections.

General Fund Expenditure Accounts. Appropriation accounts established to record amounts appropriated by Congress to be expended for the general support of the Federal Government.

Public Enterprise Revolving Fund Accounts

Expenditure accounts authorized by Congress to be credited with collections, primarily from the public, that are generated by, and earmarked to finance, a continuing cycle of business-type operations.

Intragovernmental Fund Accounts

Expenditure accounts specifically authorized by law to facilitate financing transactions within and between Federal agencies.

Intragovernmental Revolving Fund Accounts. Authorized by law to carry out a cycle of intragovernmental business-type operations. They are similar to public enterprise revolving fund accounts except they are credited with offsetting collections primarily from other Federal agencies and accounts. Some examples are working capital fund, stock fund, industrial fund, and supply fund.

Management Fund Accounts. Authorized by law to credit collections from two or more appropriations to finance activity not involving a continuing cycle of business-type operations. Such accounts do not generally own a significant amount of assets (e.g., supplies, equipment, loans, etc.), nor do they have a specified amount of capital provided (a corpus of the fund).

Consolidated Working Fund Accounts. Included under management fund accounts, these are special working funds established under the authority of Section 601 of the Economy Act (31 U.S.C. 686) to receive advance payments from other agencies or accounts. Consolidated working funds are not used to finance the work directly, but only to reimburse the appropriation or fund account that will finance the work to be performed. Amounts in consolidated working fund accounts are available for the same periods as those of the accounts advancing the funds.

Special Fund Accounts

Special Fund Receipt Accounts. Those accounts credited with collections from specific sources that are earmarked by law for a specific purpose. These collections are presented in *The Budget of the United States Government* as either budget (governmental) receipts or offsetting collections.

Special Fund Expenditure Accounts. Appropriation accounts established to record appropriated amounts of special fund receipts to be expended for special programs in accordance with specific provisions of law.

Trust Fund Accounts

Usually recorded in separate receipt and expenditure accounts. In a few cases, namely trust revolving funds, collections are authorized to be credited to an expenditure account.

Trust Fund Receipt Accounts. Credited with collections generated by the terms of a trust agreement or statute. These collections are presented in *The Budget of the United States Government* either as budget (governmental) receipts or offsetting collections.

Trust Fund Expenditure Accounts. Appropriation accounts established to record appropriated amounts of trust fund receipts to be used to finance specific purposes or programs under a trust agreement or statute.

Trust Revolving Fund Accounts. Expenditure accounts used to carry out a cycle of business-type operations (e.g., the Federal Deposit Insurance Corporation) in accordance with a trust agreement or statute. They are authorized to be credited with offsetting collections.

In addition to the Federal and trust funds, there exist the following kinds of accounts for purposes other than budget presentation:

Foreign Currency Fund Accounts

Established in the Treasury for foreign currency that is acquired without payment of United States dollars, primarily in payment for commodities (such as through the Agricultural Trade Development Assistance Act, P.L. 83-480). (For distinction, *see* Special Foreign Currency Program Appropriation.)

Receipt Clearing Accounts

Set up to hold general, special, or trust fund receipts temporarily, pending credit to the applicable Federal or trust fund receipt accounts.

Deposit Fund Accounts

Expenditure accounts established to account for collections that are either (a) held temporarily and later refunded or paid upon administrative or legal determination as to the proper disposition thereof, or (b) held by the Government as banker or agent for others and paid out at the direction of the depositor. (For example, savings accounts for military personnel; Federal, State, and local income taxes withheld from Federal employees' salaries; and payroll deductions for the purchase of savings bonds by civilian employees of the Government. Deposit funds are accounted for as liabilities of the Federal Government. These accounts are not included in the budget totals because the amounts are not available for Government purposes. However, since the cash in the accounts is used by the Treasury to satisfy immediate cash requirements of the Government, deposit fund balances are shown as a means of financing the deficit in the budget.

Transfer Appropriation Accounts

Established to receive and disburse allocations. Such allocations and transfers are not adjustments to budget authority or balances of budget authority. Rather, the transactions (including any adjustments therein) are treated as nonexpenditure transactions at the time the allocation is made. The accounts carry symbols that identify the original appropriation from which monies were advanced. Transfer appropriation accounts are symbolized by adding the receiving agency's department prefix to the original appropriation or fund account symbol. In some cases a bureau suffix is added to show that the transfer is being made to a particular bureau within the receiving department. For budget purposes, transactions in the transfer accounts are reported with the transactions in the parent accounts. (See also Allocations; Nonexpenditure Transactions.)

APPROPRIATION LIMITATION

A statutory restriction in appropriation acts that establishes the maximum or minimum amount that may be obligated or expended for specified purposes.

AUTHORIZING COMMITTEE

A standing committee of the House or Senate with legislative jurisdiction over the subject matter of those laws, or parts of laws, that set up or continue the legal operations of Federal programs or agencies. An authorizing committee also has jurisdiction in those instances where backdoor authority is provided in the substantive legislation. (See also Oversight Committee; Spending Committee.)

AUTHORIZING LEGISLATION

Substantive legislation enacted by Congress that sets up or continues the legal operation of a Federal program or agency either indefinitely or for a specific period of time or sanctions a particular type of obligation or expenditure within a program.

Authorizing legislation is normally a prerequisite for appropriations. It may place a limit on the amount of budget authority to be included in appropriation acts or it may authorize the appropriation of "such sums as may be necessary." In some instances authorizing legislation may provide authority to incur debts or to mandate payment to particular persons or political subdivisions of the country. (See also Backdoor Authority; Entitlements; Spending Legislation; Substantive Law.)

BACKDOOR AUTHORITY

Budget authority provided in legislation outside the normal (appropriations committees) appropriations process. The most common forms of backdoor authority are authority to borrow (also called borrowing authority or authority to spend debt receipts) and contract authority. In other cases (e.g., interest on the public debt), a permanent appropriation is provided that becomes available without any current action by Congress. Section 401 of the Congressional Budget and Impoundment Control Act of 1974 (31 U.S.C. 1351) specifies certain limits on the use of backdoor authority. (*See also* Authorizing Legislation; Appropriations *under* Budget Authority; Spending Authority; Spending Committees; Spending Legislation.)

BALANCED BUDGET

A budget in which receipts are equal to or greater than outlays. (*See also* Budget Deficit; Budget Surplus.)

BALANCES OF BUDGET AUTHORITY

Balances of budget authority result from the fact that not all budget authority enacted in a fiscal year is obligated and paid out in that same year. Balances are classified as follows:

Obligated Balance

The amount of obligations already incurred for which payment has not yet been made. This balance can be carried forward indefinitely until the obligations are paid. (*See also* "M" Account.)

Unobligated Balance

The portion of budget authority that has not yet been obligated. In 1-year accounts the unobligated balance expires (ceases to be available for obligation) at the end of the fiscal year. In multiple-year accounts the unobligated balance may be carried forward and remain available for obligation for the period specified. In no-year accounts the unobligated balance is carried forward indefinitely until (1) specifically rescinded by law, or (2) until the purposes for which it was provided have been accomplished, or (3), in any event, whenever disbursements have not been made against the appropriation for 2 full consecutive years. (*See also* Merged Surplus Accounts.)

Unexpended Balance

The sum of the obligated and unobligated balances.

BUDGET ACTIVITY

Categories within most accounts that identify the purposes, projects, or types of activities financed. They are presented in the Program by Activities section in the Program and Financing schedule of *The Budget of the United States Government, Appendix. (See also* Activity.)

BUDGET AMENDMENT

A revision to some aspect of a previous budget request, submitted to Congress by the President before Congress completes appropriation action. (*See also* Presidential Statement of Budgetary Amendments or Revisions.)

BUDGET AUTHORITY

Authority provided by law to enter into obligations that will result in immediate or future outlays involving Federal Government funds, except that budget authority does not include authority to insure or guarantee the repayment of indebtedness incurred by another person or government. The basic forms of budget authority are appropriations, authority to borrow, and contract authority. Budget authority may be classified by the period of availability (1-year, multiple-year, no-year), by the timing of congressional action (current or permanent), or by the manner of determining the amount available (definite or indefinite).

Forms of Budget Authority

Appropriations. An authorization by an act of Congress that permits Federal agencies to incur obligations and to make payments out of the Treasury for specified purposes. An appropriation usually follows enactment of authorizing legislation. An appropriation act is the most common means of providing budget authority, but in some cases the authorizing legislation itself provides the budget authority. (*See* Backdoor Authority.) Appropriations do not represent cash actually set aside in the Treasury for purposes specified in the appropriation act: they represent limitations of amounts that agencies may obligate during the period of time specified in the respective appropriation acts. Several types of appropriations are not counted as budget authority, since they do not provide authority to incur additional obligations. Examples of these include:

—Appropriations to liquidate contract authority—congressional action to provide funds to pay obligations incurred against contract authority;

—Appropriations to reduce outstanding debt—congressional action to provide funds for debt retirement; and,

—Appropriations for refunds of receipts. (*See also* Refunds.)

Authority To Borrow. Also called borrowing authority or authority to spend debt receipts. Statutory authority that permits a Federal agency to incur obligations and to make payments for specified purposes out of borrowed monies. (*See also* Debt, Federal.)

Contract Authority. Statutory authority that permits obligations to be incurred in advance of appropriations or in anticipation of receipts to be credited to a revolving fund or other account. (By definition, contract authority is unfunded and must subsequently be funded by an appropriation to liquidate obligations incurred under the contract authority, or by the collection and use of receipts.) (*See also* Backdoor Authority.)

Determination of Amount

Definite Authority. Authority which is stated as a specific sum at the time the authority is granted. This includes authority stated as "not to exceed" a specified amount.

Indefinite Authority. Authority for which a specific sum is not stated but is determined by other factors, such as the receipts from a certain source or obligations incurred. (Authority to borrow that is limited to a specified amount that may be outstanding at any time, i.e., revolving debt authority is considered to be indefinite budget authority.)

Period of Availability

One-Year (Annual) Authority. Budget authority that is available for obligation only during a specified fiscal year and expires at the end of that time.

Multiple-Year Authority. Budget authority that is available for a specified period of time in excess of one fiscal year. This authority generally takes the form of 2-year, 3-year, etc., availability, but may cover periods that do not coincide with the start or end of a fiscal year. For example, the authority may be available from July 1 of one year through September 30 of the following fiscal year (15 months). This type of multiple-year authority is sometimes referred to as "forward funding." (For distinction, *see* Advance Appropriation and Advance Funding. *See also* Full Funding; Multi-Year Budget Planning.)

No-Year Authority. Budget authority that remains available for obligation for an indefinite period of time, usually until the objectives for which the authority was made available are attained.

Extensions of Budget Authority

Reappropriations. Congressional action to continue the obligational availability, whether for the same or different purposes, of all or part of the unobligated portion of budget authority that has expired or would otherwise expire. Reappropriations are counted as budget authority in the year for which the availability is extended. (For distinction, *see* Restoration.)

Continuing Resolution. Legislation enacted by Congress to provide budget authority for Federal agencies and/or specific activities to continue in operation until the regular appropriations are enacted. Continuing resolutions are enacted when action on appropriations is not completed by the beginning of a fiscal year. The continuing resolution usually specifies a maximum rate at which the obligations may be incurred, based on the rate of the prior year, the President's budget request, or an appropriation bill passed by either or both Houses of the Congress.

Timing of Congressional Action

Current Authority. Budget authority enacted by Congress in or immediately preceding the fiscal year in which it becomes available.

Permanent Authority. Budget authority that becomes available as the result of previously enacted legislation (substantive legislation or prior appropriation act) and does not require current action by Congress. Authority created by such legislation is considered to be "current" in the first year in which it is provided and "permanent" in succeeding years. (*See also* Controllability.)

BUDGET DEFICIT

The amount by which the Government's budget outlays exceed its budget receipts for a given fiscal year. (*See also* Balanced Budget; Budget Surplus.)

BUDGET ESTIMATES

Estimates of budget authority, outlays, receipts, or other budget measures that cover the current and budget years, as reflected in the President's budget and budget updates. (*See also* Budget Updates; President's Budget; Projections.)

BUDGET SURPLUS

The amount by which the Government's budget receipts exceed its budget outlays for a given budget/fiscal year. (*See also* Balanced Budget; Budget Deficit.)

BUDGET UPDATES

Amendments to, or revisions in, budget authority requested, estimated outlays, and estimated receipts for the ensuing fiscal year. The President is required by the Congressional Budget and Impoundment Control Act of 1974 (P.L. 93-344, 31 U.S.C. 11(g)) to transmit such statements to Congress by April 10 and July 15 of each year; however, the President may also submit budget updates at other times during the fiscal year. (*See also* Budget Estimates; President's Budget; Presidential Statement of Budgetary Amendments or Revisions.)

BUDGETARY RESERVES

Portions of budgetary resources set aside (withheld from apportionment) by the Office of Management and Budget by authority of the Antideficiency Act (31 U.S.C. 665) to (a) provide for contingencies, or (b) effect saving whenever savings are made possible by, or through changes in, requirements or greater efficiency of operations. Budgetary resources may also be set aside as specified by particular appropriation acts or other laws.

Except as specifically provided by law, no reserves shall be established other than as authorized under the Antideficiency Act (31 U.S.C. 665). Reserves established are reported to Congress in accordance with the Congressional Budget and Impoundment Control Act of 1974 (31 U.S.C. 1401 et seq.). (*See also* Antideficiency Act; Apportionment; Deferral of Budget Authority; Rescission.)

CAPITAL BUDGET

A divided budget with investment in capital assets excluded from calculations of the budget surplus or deficit, is often referred to as a capital budget. A capital budget provides for separating financing of capital or investment expenditures from current or operating expenditures.

The Federal Government has never had a capital budget in the sense of financing capital or investment-type programs separately from current expenditures. However, Federal expenditures of an investment nature are presented in Special Analysis D of the *Special Analyses, Budget of the United States Government*. (*See also* Capital defined in the Economic Terms section of this glossary.)

CHANGE IN SELECTED RESOURCES

An adjustment representing the bridge between program costs and obligations. It represents an increase or decrease in (a) those assets and liabilities that have been recorded as obligations but have not yet been consumed (e.g., inventories), and (b) those assets and liabilities which have become costs but have not yet become obligations (e.g., accrued annual leave).

This measure is shown as an entry in the Program and Financing Schedule of *The Budget of the United States Government, Appendix*. Details for computing change in selected resources are explained in section 32.3 of OMB Circular No. A-11. (*See also* Cost-Based Budgeting.)

COLLECTIONS

Amounts received by the Federal Government during the fiscal year. (*See also* Appropriation (Expenditure), Receipt, and Fund Accounts.) Collections are classified into two major categories:

Budget Receipts

Collections from the public (based on the Government's exercise of its sovereign powers) and from payments by participants in certain voluntary Federal social insurance programs. These collections, also called governmental receipts, consist primarily of tax receipts and social insurance premiums, but also include receipts from court fines, certain licenses, and deposits of earnings by the Federal Reserve System. Gifts and contributions (as distinguished from payments for services or cost-sharing deposits by State and local governments) are also counted as budget receipts. Budget receipts are compared with total outlays in calculating the budget surplus or deficit.

Offsetting Collections

Collections from Government accounts or from transactions with the public that are of a business-type or market-oriented nature. They are classified into two major categories: (a) collections credited to appropriation or fund accounts, and (b) offsetting receipts (i.e., amounts deposited in receipt accounts). In general, the distinction between these two major categories is that "collections credited to appropriation or fund accounts" normally can be used without appropriation action by Congress, whereas funds in "receipt accounts" cannot be used without being appropriated. Offsetting collections are deducted from disbursements in calculating total outlays. Corresponding offsets are made in arriving at total budget authority and net obligations incurred. The two categories of offsetting collections are defined as follows:

Collections Credited to Appropriation or Fund Accounts. These occur in two circumstances:

Reimbursements. When authorized by law, amounts collected for materials or services furnished are treated as reimbursements to appropriations. For accounting purposes, earned reimbursements are also known as *revenues*. These collections are netted in determining outlays from such appropriations. (For distinction, *see* Refunds. *See also* Unfilled Customers' Orders.)

Revolving Funds. In the three types of revolving funds—public enterprise, intragovernmental, and trust revolving—collections are netted against spending and outlays are reported as the net amount.

Offsetting Receipts. Amounts deposited in receipt accounts (i.e., general funds, special funds, or trust funds). These receipts generally are deducted from budget authority and outlays by function and/or subfunction, and by agency. Offsetting receipts are subdivided as follows:

Proprietary Receipts from the Public. Collections from the public deposited in receipt accounts of the general fund, special funds, or trust funds as a result of the Government's business-type or market-oriented activities (e.g., loan repayment, interest, sale of property and products, charges for nonregulatory services, and rents and royalties). Such collections are not counted as budget receipts, and with one exception, are offset against total budget authority and outlays by agency and by function. The exception consists of receipts from rents and royalties from Outer Continental Shelf lands that are deducted from total budget authority and outlays for the Government as a whole rather than from any single agency or function. (*See also* Undistributed Offsetting Receipts.)

Intragovernmental Transactions. Payments into receipt accounts from Federal appropriations or fund accounts. They are treated as an offset to budget authority and outlays, rather than as a budget receipt. Intragovernmental transactions may be intrabudgetary (where both the payment and receipt occur within the budgetary universe) or they may result from the payment by an off-budget Federal entity whose funds are excluded from the budget totals. Normally, intragovernmental transactions are deducted from both the outlays and the budget authority for the agency receiving the payment. However, in two cases, these transactions are not deducted from the figures of any agency or function. Instead, intragovernmental transactions that involve agencies' payments (including payments by off-budget Federal entities) as employers into employee retirement trust funds and the payment of interest to nonrevolving trust funds appear as special deduct lines in computing total budget authority and outlays for the Government.

Intrabudgetary transactions are further subdivided into three categories: (1) inter-fund transactions, where the payment is from one fund group (either Federal funds or trust funds) to a receipt account in the other fund group; (2) Federal intrafund transactions, where the payment and receipt both occur within the Federal fund group; and (3) trust intrafund transactions, where the payment and receipt both occur within the trust fund group.

CONCURRENT RESOLUTION ON THE BUDGET

A resolution passed by both Houses of Congress, but not requiring the signature of the President, setting forth, reaffirming, or revising the congressional budget for the United States Government for a fiscal year.

Two such resolutions are required before the start of a fiscal year. The first, due by May 15, establishes the congressional budget targets for the next fiscal year; the second, scheduled to be passed by September 15, sets a ceiling on budget authority and outlays and a floor on receipts. Additional concurrent resolutions revising the previously established budget levels may be passed by Congress at any time. (*See also* Congressional Budget; First Concurrent Resolution on the Budget; Second Concurrent Resolution on the Budget.)

CONGRESSIONAL BUDGET

The budget as set forth by Congress in a concurrent resolution on the budget. By law the resolution includes:

—the appropriate level of total budget outlays and of total new budget authority;

—an estimate of budget outlays and new budget authority for each major functional cate-gory, for undistributed intergovernmental transactions, and for such other matters relating to the budget as may be appropriate to carry out the purposes of the 1974 Con-gressional Budget and Impoundment Control Act;

—the amount, if any, of the surplus or deficit in the budget;

—the recommended level of Federal receipts; and

—the appropriate level of the public debt.

(*See also* Concurrent Resolution on the Budget; President's Budget.)

CONSOLIDATED DECISION PACKAGES

Packages prepared at higher organizational and program levels that summarize and sup-plement information contained in decision packages received from subordinate units in an agency. Consolidated packages may reflect different priorities, including the addition of new programs or the abolition of existing ones. (*See also* Decision Package; Zero-Base Budgeting.)

CONTROLLABILITY

The ability of Congress and the President to increase and decrease budget outlays or budget authority in the year in question, generally the current or budget year. Relatively uncontrollable refers to spending that the Federal Government cannot increase or decrease without changing existing substantive law. For example, outlays in any one year are considered to be relatively uncontrollable when the program level is determined by existing statute or by contract or other obligations. (*See* Permanent Authority *under* Budget Authority.)

Controllability, as exercised by Congress and the President, is determined by statute. In the case of Congress, all permanent budget authority is uncontrollable. For example, most trust fund appropriations are permanent, as are a number of Federal fund appropriations, and interest on the public debt, for which budget authority is automatically provided under a permanent appropriation enacted in 1847. In the case of the President, .relatively uncontrollable spending is usually the result of open-ended programs and fixed costs (e.g., social security, medical care, veterans benefits—outlays generally mandated by law), but also includes payments coming due resulting from budget authority enacted in prior years, such as entering into contracts. (*See also* Allowances; Contract Authority; Entitlements.)

COOPERATIVE AGREEMENT

A form of assistance award from the Federal Government to a State or local government or other recipient to support and stimulate an activity or venture to accomplish a public purpose, and in which the Federal Government will be substantially involved during the performance of the contemplated activity. (*See also* Grants; Grants-in-Aid.)

COST-BASED BUDGETING

Budgeting in terms of costs to be incurred, that is, the resources to be consumed in carrying out a program, regardless of when the funds to acquire the resources were obligated or paid, and without regard to the source of funds (i.e., appropriation). For example, inventory items become costs when they are withdrawn from inventory, and the cost of buildings is distributed over time, through periodic depreciation charges, rather than in a lump sum when the buildings are acquired.

Cost-based budgeting, in lieu of reflecting the obligational requirements for programs, reflects costs expected to be incurred during the budget year. When the program and financing schedules in the appendix to the President's budget are stated in terms of cost, additional entries are used to present the obligations required for inventories and other items that are not costed in the period. (*See also* Change in Selected Resources. For distinction, *see* Obligation-Based Budgeting.)

CROSS AGENCY RANKING

A process of ranking, on a Government-wide basis, the decision packages that fall within a specified margin of the President's budget total. The purpose of cross agency ranking is to help assure that diverse programs of the same priority are considered for inclusion within the budget total recommended by the President. (*See also* Decision Package; Ranking; Zero-Base Budgeting.)

CROSSWALK

Any procedure for expressing the relationship between budgetary data from one set of classifications to another, such as between appropriation accounts and authorizing legislation or between the budget functional structure and the congressional committee spending jurisdictions. (*See also* Allocations.)

CURRENT SERVICES ESTIMATES

Presidential estimates of budget authority and outlays for the ensuing fiscal year based on continuation of existing levels of service. These estimates reflect the anticipated costs of continuing Federal programs and activities at present spending levels without policy changes, that is, ignoring all new initiatives, presidential or congressional, that are not yet law.

These estimates of budget authority and outlays, accompanied by the underlying economic and programmatic assumptions upon which they are based (such as the rate of inflation, the rate of real economic growth, the unemployment rate, program caseloads, and pay increases) are required to be transmitted by the President to the Congress with the President's budget. (For a more detailed discussion of this term, see Special Analysis A of the *Special Analyses, Budget of the United States Government.*)

DEBT, FEDERAL

There are three basic tabulations of Federal debt: gross Federal debt, debt held by the public, and debt subject to statutory limit. (*See also* Authority To Borrow *under* Budget Authority.)

Gross Federal Debt

Consists of public debt and agency debt and includes all public and agency debt issues outstanding.

Public Debt. That portion of the Federal debt incurred when the Treasury or the Federal Financing Bank (FFB) borrows funds directly from the public or another fund or account. To avoid double counting, FFB borrowing from the Treasury is not included in the public debt. (The Treasury borrowing required to obtain the money to lend to the FFB is already part of the public debt.)

Agency Debt. That portion of the Federal debt incurred when a Federal agency, other than the Treasury or the Federal Financing Bank, is authorized by law to borrow funds directly from the public or another fund or account. To avoid double counting, agency borrowing from Treasury or the FFB and Federal fund advances to trust funds are not included in the Federal debt. (The Treasury or FFB borrowing required to obtain the money to lend to the agency is already part of the public debt.) Agency debt may be incurred by agencies within the Federal budget (such as the Tennessee Valley Authority) or by off-budget Federal entities (such as the Postal Service). Debt of Government-sponsored, privately owned enterprises (such as the Federal National Mortgage Association) is not included in the Federal debt.

Debt Held by the Public

Part of the gross Federal debt held by the public. (The Federal Reserve System is included in "the public" for this purpose.) Debt held by Government trust funds (e.g., Social Security Trust Fund), revolving funds, and off-budget Federal entities is excluded from debt held by the public.

Debt Subject to Statutory Limit

As defined by the Second Liberty Bond Act of 1917, as amended, it currently includes virtually all public debt. However, only a small portion of agency debt is included in this tabulation of Federal debt.

Under Public Law 96-78, approved September 29, 1979, an amendment to the Rules of the House of Representatives makes possible the establishment of the public debt limit as a part of the congressional budget process.

DEBT MANAGEMENT

Operations of the U.S. Treasury Department that determine the composition of the Federal debt. Debt management involves determining the amounts, maturities, other terms and conditions, and schedule of offerings of Federal debt securities and raising new cash to finance the Government's operations. The objective of debt management is to raise the money necessary for the Government's operations at least cost to the taxpayer· and in a manner that will minimize the effect of Government operations on financial markets and on the economy.

DECISION PACKAGE

In zero-base budgeting, a brief justification document containing the information managers need to judge program or activity levels and resource requirements. Each decision package presents a level of request for a decision unit, stating the costs and performance associated with that level. Separate decision packages are prepared for incremental spending levels:

—Minimum Level—performance below which it is not feasible for the decision unit to continue because no constructive contribution could be made toward fulfilling the unit's objectives.

—Intermediate Level—performance between the minimum and current levels. There may be more than one intermediate level.

—Current Level—performance that would be reflected if activities for the budget year were carried on at current year service or output levels without major policy changes. This level permits internal realignments of activities within existing statutory authorizations.

—Enhancement Level—where increased output or service are consistent with major objectives and where sufficient benefits are expected to warrant the serious review of higher authorities.

A series of decision packages are prepared for each decision unit. Cumulatively, the packages represent the total budget request for that unit. (*See also* Consolidated Decision Packages; Cross Agency Ranking; Decision Package Set; Decision Unit; Decision Unit Overview; Ranking; Zero-Base Budgeting.)

DECISION PACKAGE SET

Consists of decision unit overview and the decision packages for the decision unit. (*See also* Decision Package; Decision Unit; Decision Unit Overview; Zero-Base Budgeting.)

DECISION UNIT

In zero-base budgeting, that part (or component) of the basic program or organizational entity for which budget requests are prepared and for which managers make significant decisions on the amount of spending and the scope or quality of work to be performed. (*See also* Decision Package; Decision Package Set; Zero-Base Budgeting.)

DECISION UNIT OVERVIEW

The part of a decision package set that provides information necessary to evaluate and make budget decisions on each of the decision packages, without repeating the same information in each package. (*See also* Decision Package; Decision Package Set; Zero-Base Budgeting.)

DEFERRAL OF BUDGET AUTHORITY

Any action or inaction by an officer or employee of the United States Government that temporarily withholds, delays, or effectively precludes the obligation or expenditure of budget authority, including authority to obligate by contract in advance of appropriations as specifically authorized by law. Deferrals consist of (a) amounts reserved for contingencies pursuant to the Antideficiency Act (31 U.S.C. 665), and (b) amounts temporarily withheld for other reasons pursuant to the Congressional Budget and Impoundment Control Act of 1974 (P.L. 93-344; 31 U.S.C. 1403).

Deferrals may not extend beyond the end of the fiscal year in which the message reporting the deferral is transmitted and may be overturned by the passage of an impoundment resolution by either House of Congress. (*See also* Antideficiency Act; Apportionment; Budgetary Reserves; Impoundment; Impoundment Resolution; Rescission.)

DEFICIENCY APPORTIONMENT

A distribution by the Office of Management and Budget of available budgetary resources for the fiscal year that anticipates the need for supplemental budget authority. Such apportionments may only be made under certain specified conditions provided for in law (Antideficiency Act, 31 U.S.C. 665(e)). In such instances, the need for additional budget authority is usually reflected by making the amount apportioned for the fourth quarter less than the amount that will actually be required. Approval of requests for deficiency apportionment does not authorize agencies to exceed available resources within an account. (*See also* Antideficiency Act; Apportionment; Deficiency Appropriation; Supplemental Appropriation.)

DEFICIENCY APPROPRIATION

An appropriation made to an expired account to cover obligations that have been incurred in excess of available funds.

Deficiency appropriations are rare since obligating in excess of available funds generally is prohibited by law. Deficiency appropriation is sometimes erroneously used as a synonym for supplemental appropriation. (*See also* Antideficiency Act; Apportionment; Deficiency Apportionment; Supplemental Appropriation.)

DEFICIT FINANCING

A situation in which the Federal Government's excess of outlays over receipts for a given period is financed primarily by borrowing from the public.

DEOBLIGATION

A downward adjustment of previously recorded obligations. This may be attributable to the cancellation of a project or contract, price revisions, or corrections of estimates previously recorded as obligations.

DIRECT LOANS

A direct loan is a disbursement of funds (not in exchange for goods or services) that is contracted to be repaid—with or without interest—on any of the following transactions:

—direct Federal participation in loans privately made or held;

—purchase of private loans through secondary market operations; and,

—acquisition of guaranteed private loans or collateral in satisfaction of default or other guarantee claims.

For informational purposes, transactions similar to direct loans are sometimes displayed in the budget. For example:

—sale of Federal assets on credit terms for more than 90 days duration;

—investments in obligations or preferred stock of any privately owned enterprises; and,

—deferred or delinquent interest that is capitalized.

Direct loans, unlike loan guarantees, are included (net of repayments) as outlays in the budget. For a more detailed discussion, see Federal Credit Programs in Special Analysis F of the *Special Analyses, Budget of the United States Government. (See also* Loan Guarantee; Loan Insurance.)

ENTITLEMENTS

Legislation that requires the payment of benefits (or entitlements) to any person or unit of government that meets the eligibility requirements established by such law. Authorizations for entitlements constitute a binding obligation on the part of the Federal Government, and eligible recipients have legal recourse if the obligation is not fulfilled. Budget authority for such payments is not necessarily provided in advance, and thus entitlement legislation requires the subsequent enactment of appropriations unless the existing appropriation is permanent. Examples of entitlement programs are social security benefits and veterans compensation or pensions. Section 401(b) of the Congressional Budget and Impoundment Control Act of 1974 (P.L. 93-344, 31 U.S.C. 1351(b)) imposes certain limits on the use of entitlements. (*See also* Authorizing Legislation; Controllability; Spending Authority; Spending Legislation.)

EXCHANGE OF ASSETS

The movement of money between the International Monetary Fund (IMF), or similar organizations, and the Department of Treasury.

The Government's deposits with the IMF are considered to be assets. Therefore, the movement of money between the IMF and the Department of the Treasury is not in itself considered a receipt or an outlay, borrowing or lending. Changes in these holdings are outlays only to the extent that there is a realized loss, and are offsetting collections only to the extent that there is a realized profit on the exchange.

EXPENDED APPROPRIATION

The amount of expenditures (outlays) during the current fiscal year net of refunds to the appropriation made from general funds, special funds, and trust funds.

EXPENDITURES

With respect to provisions of the Antideficiency Act (31 U.S.C. 665) and the Congressional Budget and Impoundment Control Act of 1974 (P.L. 93-344, 31 U.S.C. 1301, note), the term expenditures has the same definition as outlays. (*See also* Outlays. For distinction, *see* Accrued Expenditures.)

EXPENDITURE TRANSACTIONS

For accounting and reporting purposes, transactions between appropriation and fund accounts which represent payments, repayments, or receipts for goods or services furnished or to be furnished. Expenditure transactions are recorded as obligations/outlays of the transferring accounts and as reimbursements/receipts of the receiving accounts. (*See also* Nonexpenditure Transactions; Transfer Between Appropriation Accounts; Transfer of Funds.)

EXPIRED ACCOUNT

An account in which authority to incur obligations has lapsed but from which outlays may be made to pay existing obligations and liabilities previously incurred, as well as valid adjustments thereto. This includes successor accounts established pursuant to 31 U.S.C. 701-708. (*See also* "M" Account.)

FEEDER ACCOUNT

Certain appropriation and revolving fund accounts whose resources are available only for transfer to other specified appropriation or revolving fund accounts.

FIRST CONCURRENT RESOLUTION ON THE BUDGET

The resolution, containing Government-wide budget targets of receipts, budget authority, and outlays that guides Congress in its subsequent consideration of appropriations and revenue measures. It is required to be adopted by both Houses of Congress no later than May 15, pursuant to the Congressional Budget and Impoundment Control Act of 1974 (P.L. 93-344, 31 U.S.C. 1324). (*See also* Concurrent Resolution on the Budget; Second Concurrent Resolution on the Budget.)

FISCAL POLICY

Federal Government policies with respect to taxes, spending and debt management, intended to promote the nation's macroeconomic goals, particularly with respect to employment, gross national product, price level stability, and equilibrium in balance of payments. The budget process is a major vehicle for determining and implementing Federal fiscal policy. The other major component of Federal macroeconomic policy is monetary policy. (*See also* Monetary Policy defined in the Economic Terms section of this glossary.)

FISCAL YEAR

Any yearly accounting period, without regard to its relationship to a calendar year.

The fiscal year for the Federal Government begins on October 1 and ends on September 30. The fiscal year is designated by the calendar year in which it ends; for example, fiscal year 1980 is the year beginning October 1, 1979, and ending September 30, 1980. (Prior to fiscal year 1977, the Federal fiscal year began on July 1 and ended on June 30.)

Budget Year

The fiscal year for which the budget is being considered; the fiscal year following the current year.

Current Year

The fiscal year in progress.

Prior Year

The fiscal year immediately preceding the current year.

FULL EMPLOYMENT BUDGET

The estimated receipts, outlays, and surplus or deficit that would occur if the U.S. economy were continually operating at full capacity (traditionally defined as a certain percentage of the unemployment rate of the civilian labor force). (*See also* Employment and Labor Force defined in the Economic Terms section of this glossary.)

FULL FUNDING

Provides budgetary resources to cover the total cost of a program or project at the time it is undertaken.

Full funding differs from incremental funding, where budget authority is provided or recorded for only a portion of total estimated obligations expected to be incurred during a single fiscal year. Full funding is generally discussed in terms of multi-year programs, whether or not obligations for the entire program are made in the first year. For further discussion of this term, see U.S. General Accounting Office, *Further Implementation of Full Funding in the Federal Government,* PAD-78-80, September 7, 1978. (For distinction, *see* Incremental Funding. *See also* Multiple-Year Authority *under* Budget Authority; Multi-Year Budget Planning.)

FUNCTIONAL CLASSIFICATION

A system of classifying budget resources by function so that budget authority and outlays of budget and off-budget Federal entities, loan guarantees, and tax expenditures can be related in terms of the national needs being addressed.

Budget accounts are generally placed in the single budget function (e.g., national defense, health) that best reflects its major end purpose addressed to an important national need, regardless of the agency administering the program. A function may be divided into two or more subfunctions, depending upon the complexity of the national need addressed by that function.

For budget presentation purposes, each budget function is described in the context of national needs being served, and the subfunctions are described in the context of the major missions devoted to meeting national needs. For a presentation of the budget in terms of functional classification, see Appendix B in this glossary. (For distinction, *see* Object Classification. *See also* Activity; Agency Missions; National Needs.)

GOVERNMENT-SPONSORED ENTERPRISES

Enterprises established and chartered by the Federal Government to perform specific functions under the supervision of a Government agency. Since they are private corporations, they are excluded from the budget totals. Detailed budgets and explanatory statements of these enterprises are presented in Part VI of *The Budget of the United States Government, Appendix.* (For distinction, *see* Mixed-Ownership Government Corporation and Wholly-Owned Government Corporation. *See also* Off-Budget Federal Entities.)

GRANTS

Assistance awards in which substantial involvement is not anticipated between the Federal Government and the State or local government or other recipient during the performance of the contemplated activity. Such assistance is not limited to a State or local government as in the case of grants-in-aid. (See P.L. 95-224, Federal Grant and Cooperative Agreement Act of 1977.)

The two major forms of Federal grants are block and categorical. Block grants are given primarily to general purpose governmental units in accordance with a statutory formula. Such grants can be used for a variety of activities within a broad functional area. Examples of Federal block-grant programs are Omnibus Crime Control and Safe Streets Act of 1968, Comprehensive Employment and training Act of 1973, Housing and Community Development Act of 1974, and the 1974 Amendments to the Social Security Act of 1935 (Title XX).

Categorical grants can be used only for a specific program and are usually limited to narrowly defined activities. Categorical grants consist of formula, project, and formula-project grants.

Formula grants allocate Federal funds to States or their subdivisions in accordance with a distribution formula prescribed by law or administrative regulation.

Project grants provide Federal funding for fixed or known periods for specific projects or the delivery of specific services or products. (*See also* Cooperative Agreement; Grants-in-Aid.)

GRANTS-IN-AID

For purposes of the budget, grants-in-aid consist of budget outlays by the Federal Government to support State or local programs of governmental service to the public. Grants-in-aid do not include purchases from State or local governments or assistance awards to other classes of recipients (e.g., outlays for research or support of Federal prisoners). (*See also* Cooperative Agreement; Grants; Revenue Sharing.)

IDENTIFICATION CODE

Each appropriation or fund account in *The Budget of the United States Government* carries an 11-digit code that identifies: (a) the agency, (b) the account, (c) the timing of the transmittal to Congress, (d) the type of fund, and (e) the account's functional classification. For a detailed explanation of the account identification code, *see* Appendix C in this glossary.

IMPOUNDMENT

Any action or inaction by an officer or employee of the United States Government that precludes the obligation or expenditure of budget authority provided by Congress. (*See also* Deferral of Budget Authority; Impoundment Resolution; Rescission.)

IMPOUNDMENT RESOLUTION

A resolution by either the House of Representatives or the Senate that expresses disapproval of a proposed deferral of budget authority set forth in a special message transmitted by the President as required under Sec. 1013(a) of the Impoundment Control Act of 1974 (P.L. 93-344, 31 U.S.C. 1403).

Whenever all or part of any budget authority provided by Congress is deferred, the President is required to transmit a special message to Congress describing the deferrals. Either House may, at any time, pass a resolution disapproving this deferral of budget authority, thus requiring that the funds be made available for obligation. When no congressional action is taken, deferrals may remain in effect until, but not beyond, the end of the fiscal year. If the funds remain available beyond the end of a fiscal year and continued deferral of their use is desired, the President must transmit a new special message to Congress. (*See also* Deferral of Budget Authority; Impoundment.)

INCREMENTAL FUNDING

The provision (or recording) of budgetary resources for a program or project based on obligations estimated to be incurred within a fiscal year when such budgetary resources will cover only a portion of the obligations to be incurred in completing the program or project as programmed. This differs from full funding, where budgetary resources are provided or recorded for the total estimated obligations for a program or project in the initial year of funding. (For distinction, *see* Full Funding.)

JOINT RESOLUTION

A joint resolution requires the approval of both Houses of Congress and the signature of the President, just as a bill does, and has the force of law if approved. There is no real difference between a bill and a joint resolution. The latter is generally used in dealing with limited matters, such as a single appropriation for a specific purpose.

Joint resolutions also are used to propose amendments to the U.S. Constitution. These do not require presidential signature, but become a part of the Constitution when three-fourths of the States have ratified them.

LOAN GUARANTEE

A loan guarantee is an agreement by which the Government pledges to pay part or all of the loan principal and interest to a lender or holder of a security, in the event of default by a third party borrower. If it becomes necessary for the Government to pay part or all of the loan principal or interest, the payment is a direct outlay. Otherwise, the guarantee does not directly affect Federal budget outlays. For a more detailed discussion, see Federal Credit Programs in Special Analysis F, of the *Special Analyses, Budget of the United States Government. (See also* Direct Loans; Loan Insurance.)

LOAN INSURANCE

A type of loan guarantee whereby a Government agency operates a program of pooled risks, pledging the use of accumulated insurance premiums to secure a lender against default on the part of the borrower. (*See also* Direct Loans; Loan Guarantee.)

"M" ACCOUNT

A successor account into which obligated balances under an appropriation are transferred (merged) at the end of the second full fiscal year following expiration. The "M" account remains available for the payment of obligations and liabilities charged or chargeable to various year appropriation accounts. (*See also* Expired Account; Merged Surplus Accounts; Obligated Balance *under* Balances of Budget Authority.)

MEANS OF FINANCING

Ways in which a budget deficit is financed or a budget surplus is used.

A budget deficit may be financed by Treasury (or agency) borrowing, by reducing Treasury cash balances, by allowing unpaid liabilities to increase, or by certain equivalent transactions. Conversely, a budget surplus may be used to repay borrowings or to build up cash balances.

MERGED SURPLUS ACCOUNTS

Accounts that are part of the Treasury's general fund. They represent undisbursed and unobligated balances of previously appropriated monies for prior fiscal years which can be made available (restored) for disbursements under certain circumstances. The accounts are maintained by appropriation type (i.e., salaries and expenses for X agency) without regard to the fiscal year in which the appropriation was made. Restorations are made once each year and represent amounts needed to pay obligations contained in the "M" accounts. (*See also* "M" Account; Unobligated Balance *under* Balances of Budget Authority; Restoration; Withdrawal.)

MISSION BUDGETING

A budget approach that focuses on output rather than input and directs attention to how well an agency is meeting its responsibilities. By grouping programs and activities according to an agency's mission or end purposes, mission budgeting makes it easier to identify similar programs. Missions at the highest level in the budget structure represent basic end-purpose responsibilities assigned to an agency. Descending levels in the budget structure then focus more sharply on the specific components of the mission and the programs needed to satisfy them. At the lowest levels are line items—that is—the supporting activities necessary to satisfy the missions. For further discussion of this term, see U.S. General Accounting Office, *A Mission Budget Structure for the Department of Agriculture—A Feasibility Study, PAD-80-08. (See Also* Agency Missions.)

MIXED-OWNERSHIP GOVERNMENT CORPORATION

A federally chartered enterprise or business activity designated by statute (31 U.S.C. 856) as a mixed ownership government corporation. Mixed-ownership government corporations are subject to audits by the General Accounting Office as required by the Government Corporation Control Act, as amended (31 U.S.C. 857). They are also required to submit annual business-type budget statements to the Treasury and to the Office of Management and Budget in accordance with the Treasury Fiscal Requirements Manual, I-2-4100 and OMB Circular A-11, Sec. 37.1.

Although off-budget entities are excluded from the budget, some of the outlays related to their operations are included. The Rural Telephone Bank is an example of a mixed-ownership corporation and an off-budget Federal entity whose fiscal activities appear in the budget documents. (*See also* Government Sponsored Enterprises; Wholly-Owned Government Corporations; Off-Budget Federal Entities.)

MONTHLY TREASURY STATEMENT (MTS)

A summary statement prepared from agency accounting reports and issued by the Department of Treasury. The MTS presents the receipts, outlays, and resulting budget surplus or deficit for the month and the fiscal year to date. (*See also* Treasury Combined Statement.)

MULTI-YEAR BUDGET PLANNING

A budget planning process designed to make sure that the long-range consequences of budget decisions are identified and reflected in the budget totals. Currently, multi-year budget planning in the executive branch encompasses a policy review for a 3-year period beginning with the budget year, plus projections for the subsequent 2 years. This process provides a structure for the review and analysis of long-term program and tax policy choices. (*See also* Forward Funding *under* Budget Authority; Full Funding; Projections.)

NATIONAL NEEDS

Broad areas established to provide a coherent and comprehensive basis for analyzing and understanding the budget, in terms of the end purposes being served, without regard to the means that may be chosen to meet those purposes. The budget resources devoted to meeting national needs are classified by budget functions so that budget authority and outlays of budget and off-budget Federal entities, loan guarantees, and tax expenditures can be grouped in terms of the national needs being addressed. National needs are generally described in the context of major functions, whereas agency missions devoted to serving national needs are generally described as subfunctions. (*See also* Agency Missions; Functional Classification.)

NEW SPENDING AUTHORITY

Spending authority not provided by law on the effective date (January 19, 1976) of Section 401 of the Congressional Budget and Impoundment Control Act of 1974 (P.L. 93-344, 31 U.S.C. 1351), including any increase in or addition to spending authority provided by law on such date. However, this term does not apply to insured or guaranteed loan programs. (*See also* Spending Authority.)

NONEXPENDITURE TRANSACTIONS

For accounting and reporting purposes, transactions between appropriation and fund accounts that do not represent payments for goods and services received or to be received but serve only to adjust the amounts available in the accounts for making payments, except that transactions between accounts within the budget and deposit funds (which are outside the budget) will always be treated as expenditure transactions. Nonexpenditure transactions may not properly be recorded as obligations or outlays of the transferring accounts or as reimbursements or receipts of the receiving accounts.

The statutory restrictions on the purpose, availability, and use of appropriated funds by administrative agencies require that no change be made in the availability of funds by agencies through the use of nonexpenditure transactions unless specifically authorized by law. (*See also* Expenditure Transactions; Transfer Appropriation Accounts *under* Appropriation (Expenditure), Receipt, and Fund Accounts; Transfer Between Appropriation/Fund Accounts; Transfer of Funds.)

OBJECT CLASSIFICATION

A uniform classification identifying the transactions of the Federal Government by the nature of the goods or services purchased (such as personnel compensation, supplies and materials, and equipment), without regard to the agency involved or the purpose of the programs for which they are used. Data according to object classification are provided in the Object Classification Schedule along with the corresponding Program and Financing Schedule, in *The Budget of the United States Government, Appendix. See* Explanation of Estimates in Part I of the *Budget Appendix* for detailed discussion. General instructions are provided in OMB Circular No. A-12, revised. (*See also under* Allocations. For distinction, *see* Functional Classification.)

OBLIGATIONAL AUTHORITY

The sum of (a) budget authority provided for a given fiscal year, (b) balances of amounts brought forward from prior years that remain available for obligation, and (c) amounts authorized to be credited to a specific fund or account during that year, including transfers between funds or accounts.

OBLIGATION-BASED BUDGETING

Financial transactions involving the use of funds are recorded in the accounts primarily when obligations are incurred, regardless of when the resources acquired are to be consumed. (For distinction, *see* Cost-Based Budgeting.)

OBLIGATIONS INCURRED

Amounts of orders placed, contracts awarded, services received, and similar transactions during a given period that will require payments during the same or a future period. Such amounts will include outlays for which obligations had not been previously recorded and will reflect adjustments for differences between obligations previously recorded and actual outlays to liquidate those obligations. (For legal basis of Obligations Incurred, *see* 31 U.S.C. 200. *See also* OMB Circular A-34.)

OFF-BUDGET FEDERAL ENTITIES

Certain federally owned and controlled entities whose transactions (e.g., budget authority or outlays) have been excluded from budget totals under provisions of law. The fiscal activities of these entities, therefore, are not reflected in either budget authority or budget outlay totals. However, the outlays of off-budget Federal entities are added to the budget deficit to derive the total Government deficit that has to be financed by borrowing from the public or by other means. Off-budget Federal entities are discussed in Part 6, Perspectives on the Budget, of *The Budget of the United States Government.* Schedules and financial statements are presented in Part IV of *The Budget of the United States Government, Appendix. (See also* Government-Sponsored Enterprises; Mixed-Ownership Government Corporation; Off-Budget Outlays; Wholly-Owned Government Corporation.)

OFF-BUDGET OUTLAYS

Outlays of off-budget Federal entities whose transactions have been excluded from the budget totals under provisions of law, even though these outlays are part of total Government spending. (*See also* Off-Budget Federal Entities; Outlays.)

OUTLAYS

Obligations are generally liquidated when checks are issued or cash disbursed. Such payments are called outlays. In lieu of issuing checks, obligations may also be liquidated (and outlays occur) by the maturing of interest coupons in the case of some bonds, or by the issuance of bonds or notes (or increases in the redemption value of bonds outstanding).

Outlays during a fiscal year may be for payment of obligations incurred in prior years (prior-year outlays) or in the same year. Outlays, therefore, flow in part from unexpended balances of prior-year budget authority and in part from budget authority provided for the year in which the money is spent.

Total budget outlays are stated net of offsetting collections, and exclude outlays of off-budget Federal entities. (*See under* Collections.)

The terms expenditure and net disbursement are frequently used interchangeably with the term outlays. (*See also* Off-Budget Outlays.)

OVERSIGHT COMMITTEE

The congressional committee charged with general oversight of the operation of an agency or program. In most cases, but not all, the oversight committee for an agency is also the authorizing committee for that agency's programs. (*See also* Authorizing Committee.)

PERSONAL SERVICES AND BENEFITS

Personnel Compensation

Comprises gross compensation (before deduction for taxes and other purposes) for services of individuals, including terminal leave payments. This classification covers all payments (salaries, wages, fees) for personal services rendered to the Government by its officers or employees, either civil or military, and compensation for special services rendered by consultants or others.

Personnel Benefits

Comprises cash allowances paid to civilian and military employees incident to their employment and payment to other funds for the benefit of employees. Prerequisites provided in kind, such as uniforms or quarters, and payments to veterans and former employees resulting from their employment are excluded.

Benefits to Former Personnel

Pensions, annuities, or other benefits due to former employees or their survivors based (at least in part) on the length of their services to the Government, other than benefits paid from funds financed from employer and/or employees contributions and premiums. Includes Federal payments to funds that provide benefits to former employees. Excludes benefits provided in kind, such as hospital and medical care, and indemnities for disability or death of former employees. (*See also* Wages and Salaries defined in the Economic Terms section of this glossary.)

PRESIDENTIAL STATEMENT OF BUDGETARY AMENDMENTS OR REVISIONS

A statement of all amendments to or revisions in the budget authority requested, the estimated outlays, and the estimated receipts for the ensuing fiscal year as set forth in the President's budget transmitted to Congress pursuant to the Budget and Accounting Act of 1921, as amended (31 U.S.C. 11(a)). The presidential statement is required on or before April 10 and July 15 pursuant to 31 U.S.C. 11(g), and may include any previous amendments or revisions proposed on behalf of the executive branch that the President deems necessary and appropriate.

The presidential statement transmitted on or before July 15 of any year may be included in the supplemental summary required to be transmitted during such year pursuant to the Budget and Accounting Act of 1921, as amended (31 U.S.C. 11(b)). The budget transmitted to Congress pursuant to 31 U.S.C. 11(a) for any fiscal year, or the supporting detail transmitted in connection therewith, must also include a statement of all such amendments and revisions with respect to the fiscal year in progress made before the date of transmission of such budget. (*See also* Budget Amendment; Budget Updates; President's Budget; Supplemental Summary of the Budget.)

PRESIDENT'S BUDGET

The document sent to Congress by the President in January of each year in accordance with the Budget and Accounting Act of 1921, as amended, estimating Government receipts and outlays for the ensuing fiscal year and recommending appropriations in detail. Estimates for the legislative and judicial branches of the Federal Government are "transmitted without revision" (31 U.S.C. 11). (*See also* Budget Estimates; Budget Updates; Congressional Budget; Presidential Statement of Budgetary Amendments and Revisions; Tax Expenditures Budget defined in the Tax Terms section of this glossary.)

PROGRAM

Generally defined as an organized set of activities directed toward a common purpose, or goal, undertaken or proposed by an agency in order to carry out its responsibilities. In practice, however, the term program has many uses and thus does not have a well-defined, standard meaning in the legislative process. Program is used to describe an agency's mission, programs, functions, activities, services, projects, and processes.

PROGRAM EVALUATION

In general, the process of assessing program alternatives, including research and results, and the options for meeting program objectives and future expectations. Specifically, program evaluation is the process of appraising the manner and extent to which programs

—achieve their stated objectives,

—meet the performance perceptions and expectations of responsible Federal officials and other interested groups,

—produce other significant effects of either a desirable or undesirable character.

PROJECTIONS

Estimates of budget authority, outlays, receipts, or other budget amounts that extend several years into the future. Projections generally are intended to indicate the budgetary implications of continuing or proposed programs and legislation for an indefinite period of time. These include alternative program and policy strategies and ranges of possible budget amounts. Projections usually are not firm estimates of what will occur in future years, nor are they intended to be recommendations for future budget decisions. The third and fourth years beyond the current budget year (BY + 3 and BY + 4) are considered projections in the President's Budget.

The statutory basis for preparing and submitting projections are spelled out in the Congressional Budget and Impoundment Control Act of 1974 (P.L. 93-344), section 603 for the President's projections, and sections 308 and 403 for Congress' and the Congressional Budget Office's projections. (*See also* Budget Estimates; Multi-Year Budget Planning.)

RANKING

In zero-base budgeting, the process by which higher level managers evaluate and array program or activity levels (as shown in decision packages) in decreasing order of priority. The ranking process results in a relative priority assigned to each decision package in the budget request. (*See also* Cross-Agency Ranking; Decision Package; Zero-Base Budgeting.)

REAPPORTIONMENT

A revision by the Office of Management and Budget of a previous apportionment of budgetary resources for an appropriation or fund account. Agency requests for reapportionment are usually submitted to OMB as soon as a change in previous apportionment becomes necessary due to changes in amounts available, program requirements, or cost factors. (For exceptions, see OMB Circular A-34, sec. 44.4.) A reapportionment would ordinarily cover the same period, project, or activity covered in the original apportionment. (*See also* Allotment; Apportionment.)

RECONCILIATION PROCESS

A process used by Congress to reconcile amounts determined by tax, spending, and debt legislation for a given fiscal year with the ceilings enacted in the second required concurrent resolution on the budget for that year. Section 310 of the Congressional Budget and

Impoundment Control Act of 1974 (31 U.S.C. 1331) provides that the second concurrent resolution on the budget, which sets binding totals for the budget, may direct committees to determine and recommend changes to laws, bills, and resolutions, as required to conform with the binding totals for budget authority, revenues, and the public debt. Such changes are incorporated into either a reconciliation resolution or a reconciliation bill. (*See also* Concurrent Resolution on the Budget.)

Reconciliation Bill

A bill, requiring enactment by both Houses of Congress and approval by the President, making changes to legislation that has been enacted or enrolled.

Reconciliation Resolution

A concurrent resolution, requiring passage by both Houses of Congress but not the approval of the President, directing the Clerk of the House or the Secretary of the Senate to make specified changes in bills or resolutions that have not yet reached the stage of enrollment.

RECOVERIES OF PRIOR-YEAR OBLIGATIONS

Amounts made available in no-year and unexpired multi-year accounts through (a) downward adjustments of prior-year obligations, including amounts returned from prior-year advances to consolidated working funds; (b) downward adjustment for the difference between obligations previously recorded and outlays made in payment thereof; and (c) refunds due to the recovery of erroneous payments or accounting adjustments.

REFUNDS

Returns of advances or recoveries of erroneous disbursements from appropriation or fund accounts that are directly related to, and reductions of, previously recorded payments from the accounts. Also considered refunds are returns to the taxpayers of receipt collections in excess of liabilities (i.e., tax refunds). These refunds are recorded only if the cash is actually disbursed to the taxpayer. If the taxpayer chooses to apply credits for tax refunds to succeeding tax liabilities, the transaction is not recorded as a refund. In certain cases, payments are made under refund authority that exceed tax liabilities. Such excesses over liabilities are treated as budget outlays rather than refund of receipts. (For distinction, *see* Reimbursements. *See also* Appropriations *under* Budget Authority; Refundable Tax Credits and Tax Credits defined in the Tax Terms section of this glossary.)

REIMBURSEMENTS

Sums received by the Federal Government as a repayment for commodities sold or services furnished either to the public or to another Government account that are authorized by law to be credited directly to specific appropriation and fund accounts. These amounts are deducted from the total obligations incurred (and outlays) in determining net obligations (and outlays) for such accounts.

Anticipated reimbursements are, in the case of transactions with the public, estimated collections comprising advances expected to be received and reimbursements expected to be earned. In transactions between Government accounts, anticipated reimbursements consist of orders expected to be received but for which no orders have been accepted. (For distinction, *see* Refunds. *See also* Offsetting Collections *under* Collections; Unfilled Customers' Orders.)

REPROGRAMMING

Utilization of funds in an appropriation account for purposes other than those contemplated at the time of appropriation.

Reprogramming is generally preceded by consultation between the Federal agencies and the appropriate congressional committees. It involves formal notification and, in some instances, opportunity for disapproval by congressional committees.

RESCISSION

The consequence of enacted legislation that cancels budget authority previously provided by Congress before the time when the authority would otherwise lapse (i.e., cease to be available for obligation).

The Congressional Budget and Impoundment Control Act of 1974 (P.L. 93-344; 31 U.S.C. 1402) specifies that whenever the President determines that all or part of any budget authority will not be needed to carry out the full objectives or scope of programs for which the authority was provided, the President will propose to Congress that the funds be rescinded. Likewise, if all or part of any budget authority limited to a fiscal year—that is, annual appropriations or budget authority of a multiple-year appropriation in the last year of availability—is to be reserved from obligation for the entire fiscal year, a rescission will be proposed. Budget authority may also be proposed for rescission for fiscal policy or other reasons. Generally, amounts proposed for rescission are withheld for up to 45 legislative days while the proposals are being considered by Congress.

All funds proposed for rescission, including those withheld, must be reported to Congress in a special message. If both Houses have not completed action on a rescission proposed by the President within 45 calendar days of continuous session, any funds being withheld must be made available for obligation. (*See also* Apportionment; Budgetary Reserves; Deferral of Budget Authority; Impoundment; Rescission Bill.)

RESCISSION BILL

A bill or joint resolution that cancels, in whole or in part, budget authority previously granted by Congress.

Rescissions proposed by the President must be transmitted in a special message to Congress. Under section 1012 of the Congressional Budget and Impoundment Control Act of 1974 (P.L. 93-344), unless both Houses of Congress complete action on a rescission bill within 45 days of continuous session after receipt of the proposal, the budget authority must be made available for obligation. (*See also* Rescission.)

RESEARCH AND DEVELOPMENT

Research is systematic, intensive study directed toward fuller scientific knowledge or understanding of the subject studied. Development is the systematic use of the knowledge and understanding gained from research, directed toward the production of useful materials, devices, systems or methods, including the design and development of prototypes and processes.

Research and development is a broad term that embraces the work performed by Federal Government agencies and private individuals or organizations under contractual or grant arrangements with the Government. It includes all fields—education and the social sciences, as well as the physical sciences and engineering.

Research and development excludes routine product testing, quality control, mapping, collection of general purpose statistics, experimental production, routine evaluation of an operational program, and the training of scientific and technical personnel.

RESTORATION

An unobligated amount previously withdrawn by administrative action that is again made available for obligation and outlay. (For distinction, *see* Reappropriations *under* Budget Authority. *See also* Merged Surplus Accounts.)

REVENUE SHARING

Federal funds distributed by formula to States and general-purpose local governments with few or no limits on the purposes for which the funds may be used and few restrictions on the procedures which must be followed in spending the funds. (*See also* Grants-in-Aid.)

SCOREKEEPING

Procedures for tracking the status of congressional budgetary actions. Examples of score-keeping information include up-to-date tabulations and reports on congressional actions affecting budget authority, receipts, outlays, surplus or deficit, and the public debt limit, as well as outlay and receipt estimates and reestimates.

Scorekeeping data published by the Congressional Budget Office (CBO) include, but are not limited to, status reports on the effects of congressional actions (and in the case of scorekeeping reports prepared for the Senate Budget Committee, the budget effects of potential congressional actions), and comparisons of these actions to targets and ceilings set by Congress in the budget resolutions. Periodic scorekeeping reports are required to be produced by the CBO pursuant to section 308(b) of the Congressional Budget and Impoundment Control Act of 1974 (P.L. 93-344, 31 U.S.C. 1329).

SECOND CONCURRENT RESOLUTION ON THE BUDGET

The resolution adopted by Congress containing budget ceilings classified by function for budget authority and outlays and a floor for budget receipts. This resolution may retain or revise the levels set earlier in the year, and can include directives to the appropriations committees and to other committees with jurisdiction over budget authority or entitlement authority. The second resolution may also direct the appropriate committees to recommend changes in budget receipts or in the statutory limit on the public debt.

Changes recommended by various committees pursuant to the second budget resolution are to be reported in a reconciliation bill (resolution, in some cases) on which Congress must complete action by September 25, a few days before the new fiscal year commences on October 1. (*See also* Concurrent Resolution on the Budget; First Concurrent Resolution on the Budget; Reconciliation Process.)

SEIGNIORAGE

The difference between the face value of minted coins and the cost of their production. Seigniorage arises from the exercise of the Government's monetary powers and differs from receipts coming from the public, since there is no corresponding payment by another party. Therefore, seigniorage is excluded from budget receipts and treated as a means of financing a budget deficit, or as a supplementary amount to be applied to reduce debt or to increase the cash in the Treasury in the years of a budget surplus.

SPECIAL FOREIGN CURRENCY PROGRAM APPROPRIATION

An appropriation made available to incur obligations for which payments must be made only in U.S.-owned foreign currencies that are declared in excess of the normal requirements of the United States by the Secretary of the Treasury. The appropriation is made in general fund dollar amounts credited to the account or fund generating the currency, or to miscellaneous receipts of the Treasury, as appropriate. The appropriated dollars are thereby exchanged for excess foreign currency (held in Treasury foreign currency fund accounts) that is used to make the necessary payments. (For distinction, *see* Foreign Currency Fund Accounts *under* Appropriation (Expenditure), Receipt, and Fund Accounts.)

SPENDING AUTHORITY

As defined by the Congressional Budget and Impoundment Control Act of 1974 (P.L. 93-344, 31 U.S.C. 1323), a collective designation for appropriations, borrowing authority, contract authority, and entitlement authority for which the budget authority is not provided in advance by appropriation acts. The latter three are also commonly referred to as backdoor authority. (*See also* Backdoor Authority; Entitlements; New Spending Authority; Spending Committees; Spending Legislation.)

SPENDING COMMITTEES

The standing committees of the House and Senate with jurisdiction over legislation that permits the obligation of funds. For most programs, the House and Senate Appropriations Committees are the spending committees. For other programs, the authorizing legislation itself permits the obligation of funds (backdoor authority). When this is the case, the authorizing committees are then the committees with spending responsibility. (*See also* Authorizing Committee; Backdoor Authority; Spending Authority; Spending Legislation.)

SPENDING LEGISLATION (SPENDING BILL)

A term used in the budget scorekeeping of the Congressional Budget Office to indicate legislation that directly provides budget authority or outlays. Spending legislation includes (1) appropriations legislation, (2) legislation that provides budget authority directly without the need for subsequent appropriations action, and (3) entitlement legislation which, while requiring subsequent appropriations action, essentially "locks in" budget authority at the time of authorization (except legislation that establishes conditional entitlements, where recipients are entitled to payments only to the extent that funds are made available in subsequent appropriations legislation). (*See also* Authorizing Legislation; Backdoor Authority; Entitlements; Spending Authority; Spending Committees.)

SUBFUNCTION

Subdivisions of a budget function. For example, health care services and health research are subfunctions of the function Health. For a presentation of the budget in terms of subfunctions, see Appendix B in this glossary. (*See also* Functional Classification.)

SUBSIDY

Generally, a payment or benefit made by the Federal Government for which there is no current charge. Subsidies are designed to support the conduct of an economic enterprise or activity, such as ship operations. They may also refer to provisions in the tax laws that provide certain tax expenditures and to the provisions of loans, goods, and services to the public at prices lower than market value, such as interest subsidies. (*See also* Tax Expenditures defined in the Tax Terms section of this glossary.)

SUBSTANTIVE LAW

Statutory public law other than appropriation law; sometimes referred to as basic law. Substantive law usually authorizes, in broad general terms, the executive branch to carry out a program of work. Annual determination as to the amount of the work to be done is usually thereafter embodied in appropriation law. (*See also* Authorizing Legislation.)

SUPPLEMENTAL APPROPRIATION

An act appropriating funds in addition to those in an annual appropriation act. Supplemental appropriations provide additional budget authority beyond the original estimates for programs or activities (including new programs authorized after the date of the original appropriation act) in cases where the need for funds is too urgent to be postponed until enactment of the next regular appropriation bill. Supplementals may sometime include items not appropriated in the regular bills for lack of timely authorizations. (*See also* Antideficiency Act; Apportionment; Appropriation Act; Deficiency Apportionment; Deficiency Appropriation.)

SUPPLEMENTAL SUMMARY OF THE BUDGET
(MID-YEAR OR MID-SESSION REVIEW)

A supplemental summary of the budget for the ensuing fiscal year transmitted to Congress by the President on or before July 15 of each year pursuant to the Budget and Accounting Act of 1921, as amended (31 U.S.C. 11(b)). With respect to that ensuing fiscal year, the summary reflects (a) all substantial alterations in or reappraisals of the estimates of expenditures and receipts, (b) all substantial obligations imposed on that budget after its transmission to Congress, (c) the actual or proposed appropriations made during the fiscal year in progress, and (d) the estimated condition of the Treasury at the end of the fiscal year if the financial proposals contained in the budget are adopted. The summary also contains any information the President considers necessary or advisable to provide the Congress and a complete and current estimate of the functions, obligations, requirements, and financial condition of the Government for that ensuing fiscal year. (*See also* Presidential Statement of Budgetary Amendments or Revisions.)

TRANSFER BETWEEN APPROPRIATION/FUND ACCOUNTS

A transaction that, pursuant to law, withdraws budget authority or balances from one appropriation account for credit to another.

Withdrawals that are adjustments to obligational authority are treated as "adjustments of budgetary resources" rather than as payments. Payments to other accounts for goods or services received, or to be received, are not transfers but are outlay transactions. (*See also* Allocations; Expenditure Transactions; Nonexpenditure Transactions; Transfer Appropriation Accounts *under* Appropriation (Expenditure), Receipt, and Fund Accounts; Transfer of Funds.)

TRANSFER OF FUNDS

When specifically authorized in law, all or part of the budget authority in one account may be transferred to another account. Depending upon the nature of the transfer, these charges and credits will be treated as either expenditure transfers or nonexpenditure transfers. (*See also* Allocations; Expenditure Transactions; Nonexpenditure Transactions; Transfer Appropriation Accounts *under* Appropriation (Expenditure), Receipt, and Fund Accounts; Transfer Between Appropriation/Fund Accounts.)

TRANSITION QUARTER (TQ)

The 3-month period (July 1 to September 30, 1976) between the end of fiscal year 1976 and the beginning of fiscal year 1977 resulting from the change from a July 1 through June 30 fiscal year to an October 1 through September 30 fiscal year beginning with fiscal year 1977.

TREASURY COMBINED STATEMENT

An annual statement of budgetary results on a cash basis presented at the individual receipt and appropriation account level. It supports in detail the fiscal year-end results published in the *Monthly Treasury Statement.* (*See also* Monthly Treasury Statement.)

UNDELIVERED ORDERS

The value of goods and services ordered and obligated, but which have not been received. This amount includes any orders for which advance payment has been made but for which delivery or performance has not yet occurred. This term is synonymous with unliquidated obligations. (*See also* Advances; Withdrawal.)

UNDISTRIBUTED OFFSETTING RECEIPTS

Composed of (a) payments to trust funds by Government agencies, as employer, for their employees' retirement; (b) interest paid to trust funds on their investments in Government securities; and (c) proprietary receipts from rents and royalties on the Outer Continental Shelf lands. Undistributed offsetting receipts are included as a separate category in the Functional Classification. (See Appendix B in this glossary.) For a more detailed discussion, *see* Part 5, Meeting National Needs, The Federal Program by Function, *The Budget of the United States Government.* (*See also* Offsetting Receipts *under* Collections.)

UNFILLED CUSTOMERS' ORDERS

The amount of orders accepted from other accounts within the Government for goods and services to be furnished on a reimbursable basis. In the case of transactions with the public, amounts advanced or collected for which the account or fund has not yet performed the service or incurred its own obligations for that purpose. (*See also* Reimbursements.)

UNIFIED BUDGET

The present form of the budget of the Federal Government adopted beginning with the 1969 budget, in which receipts and outlays from Federal funds and trust funds are consolidated. When these fund groups are consolidated to display budget totals, transactions that are outlays of one fund group for payment to the other fund group (i.e., interfund transactions) are deducted to avoid double counting. By law, budget authority and outlays of off-budget entities are excluded from the unified budget, but data relating to off-budget entities are displayed in the budget documents.

WARRANTS

The official documents issued pursuant to law by the Secretary of the Treasury that establish the amount of money authorized to be withdrawn from the Treasury.

WHOLLY-OWNED GOVERNMENT CORPORATION

A federally chartered enterprise or business activity designated by statute (31 U.S.C. 846) as a wholly-owned government corporation. Each such corporation is required to submit an annual business-type budget statement to the Office of Management and Budget and is subject to a financial audit by the General Accounting Office, pursuant to the Government Corporation Control Act of 1945, as amended (31 U.S.C. 846,847). An example of a wholly-owned Government corporation is the Pension Benefit Guaranty Corporation, which is an off-budget Federal entity whose fiscal activities are excluded from the budget totals under provisions of law. (*See also* Government-Sponsored Enterprises; Mixed-Ownership Government Corporation; Off-Budget Federal Entities.)

WITHDRAWAL

The transfer of unobligated balances of an appropriation to the surplus account of the general fund, or, if appropriate, to the special or trust fund from which derived, upon expiration of the period of availability for obligation. The surplus account of the general fund, or the Surplus Fund of the Treasury, does not represent a fund consisting of unappropriated surplus or other assets as the term would ordinarily imply in accounting terminology; nor does it have any relation to surplus income. It is merely an expression of the action to give effect to an act of Congress to withdraw or write-off balances of certain appropriations. The amount to be withdrawn is the difference between (1) the sum of orders placed but not received (undelivered orders) and payables applicable to the appropriation less amounts collectible as repayments to the appropriation, and (2) the undisbursed balance of the appropriation. (For distinction, *see* Write-Off. *See also* Merged Surplus Accounts; Undelivered Orders.)

WORKING CAPITAL FUND

A revolving fund operating as an accounting entity in which the assets are capitalized and in which all income is in the form of receipts derived from its operations and available in their entirety to finance the fund's continuing cycle of operations without fiscal year limitation. A working capital fund is a type of intragovernmental revolving fund. (*See also* Intragovernmental Revolving Fund Accounts *under* Appropriation (Expenditure), Receipt, and Fund Accounts.)

WRITE-OFF

The amount of no-year authority that is withdrawn from availability for obligation by administrative action, pursuant to 31 U.S.C. 706. A write-off excludes amounts withdrawn from expired accounts and amounts rescinded by Congress. (For distinction, *see* Withdrawal.)

YEAR-AHEAD REQUESTS

Any request for the enactment of legislation authorizing new budget authority to continue a program or activity for a fiscal year. Year-ahead requests must be submitted to Congress no later than May 15 of the year preceding the year in which such fiscal year begins. Any request for the enactment of legislation authorizing the enactment of new budget authority for a new program or activity which is to continue for *more than 1* fiscal year is required to be submitted for at least the first 2 fiscal years. (P.L. 93-344, 31 U.S.C. 11c.)

ZERO-BASE BUDGETING

A process emphasizing management's responsibility to plan, budget, and evaluate. Zero-base budgeting provides for analysis of alternative methods of operation and various levels of effort. It places new programs on an equal footing with existing programs by requiring that program priorities be ranked, thereby providing a systematic basis for allocating resources. (*See also* Consolidated Decision Packages; Cross Agency Ranking; Decision Package; Decision Package Set; Decision Unit; Decision Unit Overview; Ranking.)

Accounting Terms and Definitions _____

ACCOUNTING SYSTEMS

The total structure of records and procedures that record, classify, and report information on the financial position and operations of a governmental unit or any of its funds, balanced account groups, and organizational components.

Each executive agency is required to establish and maintain adequate systems of accounting to provide information on obligations, accrued expenditures, applied costs, and outlays, as needed for management purposes. Such systems must be consistent with the standards and principles prescribed by, and have the approval of, the Comptroller General of the United States. (*See also* Internal Control.)

ACCOUNTS PAYABLE

Amounts owed to others for goods and services received and assets acquired.

For reporting purposes under OMB Circular A-34, "accounts payable, net," consists of: (a) the amount owed by an account for goods received and services performed but not yet paid for; (b) the amount of income that has been received by an account but not yet earned; and, (c) as offsets, accounts receivable and the amount of advances made by the account for which goods have not yet been received or services performed. (*See also* Accounts Receivable.)

ACCOUNTS RECEIVABLE

Amounts due from others for goods furnished and services rendered. Such amounts include reimbursements earned and refunds receivable. (*See also* Accounts Payable.)

ACCRUAL BASIS OF ACCOUNTING

The basis of accounting under which revenues are recorded when earned and expenditures are recorded when goods are received and services performed even though the receipt of the revenue or the payment of the expenditure may take place, in whole or part, in another accounting period.

The accrual basis of accounting can contribute materially to effective financial control over resources and cost of operations, and it is essential to the development of adequate cost information. (*See also* Accrued Expenditures defined in the Budget Terms section of this glossary; Cash Basis of Accounting.)

ASSETS

Any item of economic value owned by a governmental unit. The item may be physical in nature (tangible) or a right to ownership (intangible) that is expressed in terms of cost or some other value. (*See also* Liabilities.)

CASH BASIS OF ACCOUNTING

The basis of accounting whereby revenues are recorded when received in cash and expenditures (outlays) are recorded when paid, without regard to the accounting period to which the transactions apply. (*See also* Accrual Basis of Accounting.)

CONTINGENT LIABILITY

An existing condition, situation, or set of circumstances involving uncertainty as to a possible loss to an agency that will ultimately be resolved when one or more future events occur or fail to occur.

For the purpose of Federal credit programs, a contingent liability is a conditional commitment that may become an actual liability because of a future event beyond the control of the Government. Contingent liabilities include such items as loan guarantees and bank deposit insurance. (*See also* Liabilities.)

COST ACCOUNTING STANDARD

A statement promulgated by the Cost Accounting Standards Board, which becomes effective unless disapproved by Congress. These statements are intended to achieve uniform and consistent standards in the cost accounting practices followed by Defense contractors.

DEPRECIATION

The systematic and rational allocation of the costs of equipment and buildings (having a life of more than 1 year) over their useful lives. To match costs with related revenues in measuring income or determining the costs of carrying out program activities, depreciation reflects the use of the asset(s) during specific operating periods.

FUND ACCOUNTING

The legal requirement for Federal agencies to establish accounts for segregating revenues and other resources, together with all related liabilities, obligations, and reserves, for the purpose of carrying on specific activities or attaining certain objectives in accordance with special regulations, restrictions, or limitations. Fund accounting, in a broad sense, is required in the Federal Government to demonstrate agency compliance with requirements of existing legislation for which Federal funds have been appropriated or otherwise authorized.

One of the most important laws requiring Federal agencies to adhere to fund accounting concepts is the Antideficiency Act. (*See also* Antideficiency Act defined in the Budget Terms section of this glossary.)

HOLDBACK

The amount of money withheld from periodic payments to contractors to assure compliance with contract terms. Usually the amount to be withheld is expressed as a percentage in the contract provisions. The amounts withheld are paid to the contractor after a designated official certifies that the contractor has completed work pursuant to the contract terms.

INDIRECT COST

Any cost incurred for common objectives and therefore cannot be directly charged to any single cost objective. These costs are allocated to the various classes of work in proportion to the benefit to each class. Indirect cost is also referred to as overhead or burden cost.

INTERNAL CONTROL

The plan of organization and all of the coordinate methods and measures adopted within a Federal agency to safeguard the agency's assets, check the accuracy and reliability of its accounting data, promote operational efficiency, and encourage adherence to prescribed managerial policies.

The system of internal control must be developed with appropriate regard to the size and nature of the particular agency or organizational unit that is to be served. (*See also* Accounting Systems.)

LIABILITIES

Amounts owed for items received, services rendered, expenses incurred, assets acquired, construction performed (regardless of whether invoices have been received), and amounts received but as yet unearned.

Included are amounts owed for goods in the hands of contractors under the constructive delivery concept (when the records of the agency provide such information), and amounts owed under grants, pensions, awards, and other indebtedness not involving the furnishing of goods and services. The two classifications occurring most frequently are the following:

Current Liabilities

Liabilities that will be due within a short time (usually 1 year or less) and that are to be paid out of current assets.

Includes all amounts owed on the basis of invoices or other evidence of receipt of goods and services, other amounts owed for the purchase of goods and services even if not "due and payable," and deferred income (received but not earned).

Long-term and Unfunded Liabilities

Liabilities that will not be due for a comparatively long time (usually more than 1 year). However, as they come within the 1-year range, and are to be paid, such liabilities become current.

Includes bonded debt, notes payable, and liabilities that will not become obligations until a later time (e.g., accrued annual leave in the case of appropriation accounts). (*See also* Accrued Expenditures defined in the Budget Terms section of this glossary; Assets; Contingent Liability.)

LIQUIDITY

The ease with which an asset can be converted to cash at prevailing prices. For example, demand deposits (checking accounts) are more liquid than time (savings) deposits, but both are more liquid than real estate or plant and equipment.

REVENUES

Revenues represent the increase in assets (or decrease in liabilities) that result from operations. Revenues result from (1) services performed by the Federal Government, (2) goods and other tangible property delivered to purchasers, and (3) amounts becoming owed to the Government for which no current performance by the Government is required.

Contingencies that might result in gains should not be recorded in the accounts since to do so would recognize revenue prior to its realization. Contingencies that might result in gains should be carefully explained in financial statements.

The term revenues is commonly used interchangeably with the term collections. (*See* Collections defined in the Budget Terms section of this glossary.)

Economic Terms and Definitions _____

ABILITY TO PAY

The principle that the tax burden should be distributed according to a person's income. It is based on the assumption that as a person's income increases, the person can and should contribute a larger percentage of his/her income to support government activities. The progressive Federal income tax is based on this principle.

AUTOMATIC STABILIZER (BUILT-IN STABILIZER)

A mechanism having a countercyclical effect that automatically moderates changes in incomes and outputs in the economy without specific decisions to change government policy. Unemployment insurance and the income tax are among the most important of the automatic stabilizers in the United States. (*See also* Countercyclical.)

BALANCE OF PAYMENTS

A statistical record of economic transactions between one country, for example, the United States, and the rest of the world. The balance of payments accounts normally distinguish among transactions involving goods, services, short-term capital, and long-term capital.

BUSINESS CYCLES

The recurrent phases of expansion and contraction in overall business activity, evidenced by fluctuations in measures of aggregate economic activity, notably real gross national product. Although business cycles are recurrent, both the duration and the magnitude of individual cycles vary greatly.

CAPITAL

The designation applied in economic theory to one of the three major factors of production, the others being land and labor. Capital can refer either to physical capital, such as plant and equipment, or to the financial resources required to purchase physical capital. (*See also* Capital Budget defined in the Budget Terms section of this glossary.)

CONSTANT DOLLAR

A dollar value adjusted for changes in prices. Constant dollars are derived by dividing current dollar amounts by an appropriate price index, a process generally known as deflating. The result is a constant dollar series as it would presumably exist if prices and transactions were the same in all subsequent years as in the base year. Any changes in such a series would reflect only changes in the real volume of goods and services. Constant dollar figures are commonly used for computing the gross national product and its components and for estimating total budget outlays. (*See also* Current Dollar.)

CONSUMER PRICE INDEX (CPI)

Either of two measures of the price change of a fixed "market basket" of goods and services customarily purchased by urban consumers. CPI-U is based on a market basket determined by expenditure patterns of *all urban households,* while the market basket for CPI-W is determined by expenditure patterns of *urban wage-earner and clerical-worker families.* The level of the CPI shows the relative cost of purchasing the specified market basket compared to the cost in a designated base year, while the current rate of change in the CPI measures how fast prices are currently rising or falling. Current rates of change can be expressed as either monthly or annual rates. Although the consumer price index is often called the "cost-of-living index," it measures only price changes, which is just one of the several important factors affecting living costs. Both CPI-U and CPI-W are published monthly by the Bureau of Labor Statistics.

COST-BENEFIT ANALYSIS

An analytical technique that compares the social costs and benefits of proposed programs or policy actions. All losses and gains experienced by society are included and measured in dollar terms. The net benefits created by an action are calculated by subtracting the losses incurred by some sectors of society from the gains that accrue to others. Alternative actions are compared to choose one or more that yield the greatest net benefits, or ratio of benefits to costs.

The inclusion of all gains and losses to society in cost-benefit analysis distinguishes it from cost-effectiveness analysis, which is a more limited view of costs and benefits. (For distinction, *see* Cost-Effectiveness Analysis.)

COST-EFFECTIVENESS ANALYSIS

An analytical technique used to choose the most efficient method for achieving a program or policy goal. The costs of alternatives are measured by their requisite estimated dollar expenditures. Effectiveness is defined by the degree of goal attainment, and may also (but not necessarily) be measured in dollars. Either the net effectiveness (effectiveness minus costs) or the cost-effectiveness ratios of alternatives are compared. The most cost-effective method chosen may involve one or more alternatives.

The limited view of costs and effectiveness distinguishes this technique from cost-benefit analysis, which encompasses society-wide impacts of alternatives. (For distinction, *see* Cost-Benefit Analysis.)

COUNTERCYCLICAL

Actions aimed at smoothing out swings in economic activity. Countercyclical actions may take the form of monetary and fiscal policy (such as countercyclical revenue sharing or jobs programs). Automatic (built-in) stabilizers have a countercyclical effect without necessitating changes in governmental policy. (*See also* Automatic Stabilizer; Stabilization.)

CROWDING OUT

Most commonly refers to the displacement of private investment expenditures by increases in public expenditures financed by sales of Federal Government securities. The extent of the displacement depends on such factors as the responsiveness of private saving and investment to changes in interest rates and the degree to which the Federal Reserve monetizes the increase in public debt.

CURRENT DOLLAR

The dollar value of a good or service in terms of prices current at the time the good or service was sold. This is in contrast to the value of the good or service in constant dollars. (*See also* Constant Dollar.)

DEFLATION

A decrease in the general price level, usually accompanied by declining levels of output, increasing unemployment, and a contraction of the supply of money and credit. A price level decline during the contraction phase of the business cycle has not occurred in the United States since the end of World War II. Some attribute this to institutional barriers that prevent downward adjustments in wages and prices. Declines in output with increases in unemployment, however, are themselves sometimes referred to as deflationary changes.

DEVALUATION

The lowering of the value of a nation's currency in relation to gold, or to the currency of other countries, when this value is set by government intervention in the exchange market. Devaluation normally refers to fixed exchange rates. In a system of flexible rates, if the value of the currency falls, it is referred to as depreciation; if the value of the currency rises, it is referred to as appreciation.

DISCOUNT RATE

The interest rate that a commercial bank pays when it borrows from a Federal Reserve Bank. The discount rate is one of the tools of monetary policy used by the Federal Reserve System. The Federal Reserve customarily raises or lowers the discount rate to signal a shift toward restraining or easing its money and credit policy. (*See also* Monetary Policy.)

DISPOSABLE PERSONAL INCOME

Personal income less personal taxes and nontax payments to the Federal Government. It is the income available to persons for consumption or saving.

ECONOMIC GROWTH

An increase in a nation's productive capacity leading to an increase in the production of goods and services. Economic growth usually is measured by the annual rate of increase in real (constant dollars) gross national product.

ECONOMIC INDICATORS

A set of statistical series that have had a systematic relationship to the business cycle. Each indicator is classified as leading, coincident, or lagging, depending on whether the indicator generally changes direction in advance of, coincident with, or subsequent to changes in the overall economy. Although no one indicator or set of indicators is a wholly satisfactory predictor of the business cycle, taken as a whole they are valuable tools for identifying and analyzing changes in business cycles.

EMPLOYMENT

In economic statistics, employment refers to all persons who, during the week when the employment survey was taken, did any work for pay or profit, or who worked for 15 hours or more without pay on a farm or in a business operated by a member of the person's family. Also included as employed are those who did not work or look for work, but had a job or business from which they were temporarily absent during the week. (*See also* Full Employment Budget defined in the .Budget Terms section of this glossary.)

GNP GAP

The difference between the economy's output of goods and services and its potential output at full employment—that is, the difference between actual GNP (gross national product) and potential GNP.

GROSS NATIONAL PRODUCT (GNP)

The market value of all final goods and services produced by labor and property supplied by residents of the United States in a given period of time. Depreciation charges and other allowances for business and institutional consumption of fixed capital goods are subtracted from GNP to derive net national product. GNP comprises the purchases of final goods and services by persons and governments, gross private domestic investment (including the change in business inventories), and net exports (exports less imports). The GNP can be expressed in current or constant dollars. (*See also* Net National Product; Potential Gross National Product.)

IMPLICIT PRICE DEFLATOR (GNP DEFLATOR)

A price index for all final goods and services produced in the economy, derived by calculating the ratio of the gross national product in current prices to the gross national product in constant prices. It is a weighted average of the price indexes used to deflate the components of current-dollar GNP, the implicit weights being expenditures in the current period.

INFLATION

A persistent rise in the general price level that results in a decline in the purchasing power of money.

LABOR FORCE

Those persons who are employed plus those who are seeking work but are unemployed. The total labor force consists of civilians and members of the U.S. armed forces stationed either in the United States or abroad. (*See also* Full Employment Budget defined in the Budget Terms section of this glossary.)

MACROECONOMICS

The branch of economics concerned with aggregate economic analysis in contrast to microeconomics, which is the analysis of individual economic units, markets, or industries. For example, macroeconomics includes the study of the general price level, national output or income, and total employment, rather than the prices of individual commodities or particular incomes and the employment of individual firms. (*See also* Microeconomics.)

MICROECONOMICS

The branch of economics concerned with analysis of individual economic units, markets, or industries as opposed to aggregates. For example, microeconomics deals with the division of total output among industries, products, and firms; with the allocation of resources among competing uses; and with the determination of relative prices of particular goods. (*See also* Macroeconomics.)

MONETARY POLICY

Policies, which affect the money supply, interest rates, and credit availability, that are intended to promote national macroeconomic goals—particularly with respect to employment, gross national product, price level stability, and equilibrium in balance of payments. Monetary policy is directed primarily by the Board of Governors of the Federal Reserve System and the Federal Open Market Committee. Monetary policy works by influencing the cost and availability of bank reserves. This is accomplished through open-market operations (the purchase and sale of securities, primarily Government securities), changes in the ratio of reserves to deposits that commercial banks are required to maintain, and changes in the discount rate. (*See also* Discount Rate; Fiscal Policy defined in the Budget Terms section of this glossary.)

MONEY SUPPLY

The amount of money in the economy variously defined.

M1-A consists of currency (coin and paper notes) plus demand deposits at commercial banks, exclusive of demand deposits held by other domestic banks, foreign banks, and official institutions, and the U.S. Government. M1-B consists of M1-A plus other checkable deposits, including negotiable orders of withdrawal and automatic transfers from savings accounts at commercial banks and thrift institutions, credit unions' share draft accounts, and demand deposits at mutual savings banks.

M-2 consists of M1-B plus savings and small denomination time deposits at all depository institutions, overnight repurchase agreements at commercial banks, overnight Euro-dollars held by U.S. residents other than Caribbean branches of member banks, and money market mutual fund shares.

M-3 consists of M-2 plus large denomination time deposits at all depository institutions and term repurchase agreements at commercial banks and savings and loan associations.

NATIONAL INCOME ACCOUNTS

Accounts prepared and published quarterly and annually by the Department of Commerce, providing a detailed statistical description of aggregate economic activity within the U.S. economy. These accounts depict in dollar terms the composition and use of the nation's output and the distribution of national income to different recipients. The accounts make it possible to trace trends and fluctuations in economic activity. The data that measure the nation's total output are estimated in two principal ways:

—The value of the goods and services produced by the economy—referred to as the product side of the account. This is divided into the major uses for the output of the economy: consumer purchases, business investment, exports, and government purchases.

—The costs incurred and types of income earned in producing those goods and services— referred to as the income side. This presents wages and salaries, profits, and other forms of income, indirect taxes, and capital consumption allowances generated in the production process.

Because the national income accounts offer a consistent picture of the economy, they are basic analytical tools used in quantifying past and current performance of the economy and also in forecasting future economic developments. Furthermore, this quantitative framework makes these accounts of great importance in the formulation of national economic policies. (*See also* Personal Income; Transfer Payments.)

NET NATIONAL PRODUCT (NNP)

The net market value of final goods and services produced by labor and property supplied by the residents of the United States. Net national product equals gross national product less capital consumption allowances, which are estimates of the value of the capital goods "used up" in producing the gross national product. (*See also* Gross National Product; Potential Gross National Product.)

OPEN-MARKET OPERATIONS

The purchase and sale of various securities, chiefly marketable Federal Government securities, by the Federal Reserve System in the open market for the purpose of implementing Federal Reserve monetary policy. Open-market operations, one of the most flexible instruments of monetary policy, affects the reserves of member banks, and thus the supply of money and the availability and cost of credit. (*See also* Reserve Requirements.)

PERSONAL INCOME

In the national income accounts, personal income is the income received by persons (i.e., individuals, nonprofit institutions, private noninsured welfare funds, and private trust funds) from all sources. These sources consist of participation in production transfer payments from government and business and government interest, which is treated like a transfer payment. Personal income is the sum of wage and salary disbursements, other labor income, proprietors' income, rental income of persons, dividends, personal interest income, and transfer payments, less personal contributions for social insurance. (*See also* National Income Accounts.)

POTENTIAL GROSS NATIONAL PRODUCT

An estimate of how much the economy could produce with full utilization of its productive resources and existing technology. Full utilization has conventionally been defined in terms of a benchmark unemployment rate. In 1979, the benchmark was an unemployment rate of 5.1 percent. (*See also* Gross National Product; Net National Product.)

PRIME RATE

The rate of interest charged by commercial banks for short-term loans to their most creditworthy customers.

PRODUCER PRICE INDEXES
(FORMERLY WHOLESALE PRICE INDEX)

A set of measures of average changes in prices received in all stages of processing by producers of commodities in the manufacturing, agriculture, forestry, fishing, mining, gas and electricity, and public utilities sectors. These indexes can be organized either by commodity or by stage-of-processing. Stage-of-processing indexes—finished goods, intermediate materials, and crude materials—are more useful for analyzing general price trends. These indexes are published monthly by the Bureau of Labor Statistics. Changes in these indexes from one month to another are usually expressed as percent changes representing either monthly or annualized rates of change.

RECESSION

A decline in overall business activity that is pervasive, substantial, and of at least several months duration. Historically, recessions have been identified by a decline in real gross national product for at least two consecutive quarters.

RESERVE REQUIREMENTS

The percentage of deposit liabilities that U.S. commercial banks are required to hold as a reserve at their Federal Reserve bank, as cash in their vaults, or as directed by State banking authorities. The reserve requirement is one of the tools of monetary policy. Federal Reserve authorities can control the lending capacity of the banks (thus influencing the money supply) by varying the ratio of reserves to deposits that commercial banks are required to maintain. (*See also* Open-Market Operations.)

STABILIZATION

The maintenance of high-level economic activity with an absence of severe cyclical fluctuations. Stability is usually measured by an absence of fluctuations in production, employment, and prices, three aspects of economic activity that tend to fluctuate in a cyclical fashion. (*See also* Countercyclical.)

STAGFLATION

The simultaneous existence of high unemployment and high inflation.

TRANSFER PAYMENTS

In the national income accounts, payments made by the Federal Government or business firms to individuals or organizations for which no current or future goods or services are required to be provided in return. Government transfer payments include social security benefits, unemployment insurance benefits, Government retirement and veterans benefits, and welfare payments. Transfer payments by business firms consist mainly of gifts to nonprofit institutions. It is also common to include as business transfer payments the debts of their customers that remain unpaid and are thus considered to be bad debts. While these debts were clearly not intended to be transfer payments when they were incurred, once they are written off the books of the business firm, the original transaction meets the definition of a transfer payment. (*See also* National Income Accounts.)

TREASURY BILLS

The shortest term Federal security. Treasury bills have maturity dates normally varying from 3 to 12 months and are sold at a discount from face value rather than carrying an explicit rate of interest.

UNEMPLOYMENT

Persons who, during a specified week, had no employment but were available for work and had sought employment within the past 4 weeks, were laid off from a job, or were waiting to report to a new job within 30 days.

UNEMPLOYMENT RATE

The number of unemployed persons expressed as a percentage of the civilian labor force.

UNEMPLOYMENT RATE, INSURED

The number of insured unemployed as a percentage of covered employment—that is, those persons who are eligible to receive unemployment compensation benefits.

WAGES AND SALARIES

Monetary remuneration of employees, including the compensation of corporate officers, commissions, tips, bonuses, and receipts in kind that represent income to the recipients. (*See also* Personal Services and Benefits defined in the Budget Terms section of this glossary.)

Tax Terms and Definitions _____

REFUNDABLE TAX CREDITS

Certain tax credits are refundable to the taxpayer. The tax credit is first to be applied against tax liability. If the amount of the credit is greater than the tax liability, the excess is treated as an overpayment of taxes and is refunded to the taxpayer. An example is the Earned Income Tax Credit payment in excess of tax liability. (*See also* Refunds defined in the Budget Terms section of this glossary; Tax Credits.)

TAX CREDITS

Tax credits include any special provision of law that results in a dollar-for-dollar reduction in tax liabilities that would otherwise be due. In some cases, tax credits may be carried forward or backward from one tax year to another, while other tax credits lapse if not used in the year earned. Tax credits may result in a reduction of tax collections or an increase in the value of tax refunds. (*See also* Refundable Tax Credits; Refunds defined in the Budget Terms section of this glossary; Tax Expenditures.)

TAX EXPENDITURES

Revenue losses attributable to provisions of the Federal income tax laws that allow a special exclusion, or deduction from gross income, or that provide a special credit, preferential tax rate, or deferral of tax liability.

Tax expenditures may be considered Federal Government subsidies provided through the tax system to encourage certain activities and to assist certain groups. For example, capital formation is encouraged by permitting businesses to claim some portion of the cost of an investment as a credit on their income taxes, and the unemployed are aided by excluding unemployment benefits from taxable income. Tax expenditures involve no transfer of funds from the Government to the private sector. Rather, the U.S. Treasury Department forgoes some of the receipts that it otherwise would have collected, and the beneficiary taxpayers pay lower taxes than they otherwise would have had to pay. (*See also* Subsidy defined in the Budget Terms section of this glossary; Tax Credits; Tax Expenditures Budget.)

TAX EXPENDITURES BUDGET

A list of legally sanctioned tax expenditures for each fiscal year which the 1974 Congressional Budget and Impoundment Control Act (P.L. 93-344, sec. 601(e)) requires be part of the President's budget submission to Congress. (*See also* President's Budget defined in the Budget Terms section of this glossary; Tax Expenditures.)

TAXES

Sums imposed by a government authority upon persons or property to pay for government services.

The power to impose and collect Federal taxes is given to Congress in Article I, Section 8 of the Constitution. As the collections arise from the sovereign and regulatory powers unique to the Federal Government, they are classified as governmental (budget) receipts, which are compared with budget outlays in calculating the budget surplus or deficit. Major tax legislation is contained in the United States Code, Title 26, Internal Revenue Code.

Appendix B
ACCOUNTING PRINCIPLES AND STANDARDS FOR
FEDERAL AGENCIES _____

INTRODUCTION

AUTHORITY AND PURPOSE

This appendix contains the Comptroller General's accounting
principles, standards, and related requirements that the head of
each executive agency shall observe as required by 31 U.S.C. 3511
and 3512. These principles have been developed in consultation
with the Secretary of the Treasury and the Director of the Office
of Management and Budget on their accounting, financial reporting,
and budgetary needs. The needs of the heads of other agencies have
also been systematically considered. This appendix updates and
supersedes the principles, standards, memoranda, and statements
issued in the prior edition of title 2.

Under 31 U.S.C. 3511, executive agency accounting systems must
conform to the accounting principles, standards, and related requirements prescribed by the Comptroller General. Under 31 U.S.C.
3512(c), agencies must report annually on whether their accounting
systems are operating in conformity with these accounting principles, standards, and related requirements. Agencies shall use the
accounting principles, standards, and related requirements contained in this and other titles when preparing their annual
statements.

31 U.S.C. 3511 also requires that the Comptroller General provide for integrated accounting as a method of complete disclosure
of the results of the financial operations of each agency and the
government, as well as provide for control needed by the President
and the Congress. These requirements are accomplished by coordinating accounting principles and standards with planning, budgeting, and auditing requirements; by establishing principles embrac-
ing an integrated combination of obligation and accrual accounting;
and by providing explicitly for the specific requirements levied by
the President and the Congress.

APPLICABILITY

The requirements contained in this statement apply to all federal departments, agencies, or instrumentalities in the executive
branch that fall within the definition of executive agency as defined in 31 U.S.C. 102 and 3501. These requirements may be cited

as "generally accepted accounting principles for the federal
government." Government corporations, which are excluded from the
definition, follow generally accepted accounting principles promulgated by the Financial Accounting Standards Board (FASB) and its
predecessors.

Any guidelines and instructions that the Treasury Department
may issue, setting forth policies of accounting and reporting
designed to implement the standards promulgated by the Comptroller
General herein, should be consistent with these standards. This
includes the Treasury Department's providing detailed requirements
for agencies to follow in accounting and reporting on collections,
budget authority, obligations, outlays and budgetary resources, as
well as assets, liabilities, revenues, and expenses.

Justification for material noncompliance with these principles
and standards needs to be disclosed in the financial statements.
These standards do not apply to immaterial items.

TERMINOLOGY

Terms used in these standards are defined consistently,
whether they are used in the budgetary, accounting, or legal
sense, except as specifically noted. The terms used in this
appendix are consistent with these terms as they are defined in the
third edition of A Glossary of Terms Used in the Federal Budget
Process, issued by GAO in March 1981 (PAD-81-27).

Unless otherwise indicated, the term "agency" is used throughout this title in a general sense to refer to the reporting entity.

ACCOUNTING INTERPRETATIONS

From time to time, interpretations will be issued to explain,
expand, and refine these accounting standards.

ORGANIZATION OF THIS APPENDIX

This appendix is organized into two parts, concepts and
standards. The concepts section describes the fundamentals that
underlie accounting standards. The standards are arranged
alphabetically by subject.

CONCEPTS

The accounting standards prescribed by the Comptroller General
are based on certain objectives and fundamental concepts. These
concepts, as discussed below, provide important assumptions in the
federal accounting environment and provide the foundation for a
consistent application of these accounting standards.

OBJECTIVES

Objectives, the goals or aims toward which agency accounting
and federal financial reporting is directed, are derived directly
from legal and regulatory requirements and the needs of intended
users. Two of the main objectives of federal government accounting
and financial reporting are to provide information which can be
useful in allocating resources and in assessing management's
performance and stewardship.

Resource allocation basically involves choosing among alternative uses of resources. It is the process of distributing budget
authority and deciding how resources will be used. Resource allocation is based on an assessment of national needs together with an

understanding of the accounting and reporting of currently controlled resources and on the prior uses of resources and
accomplishments. From these perspectives, management, legislators,
and the public decide how current and future resources will be
used, the extent to which additional resources should be obtained
and the source of these resources (primarily taxes, borrowing, and
other revenues).

Assessing management's performance and stewardship involves
determining whether allocation decisions implemented by management
are proper and whether congressional intent has been met. Making
this determination requires an analysis of information which
discloses

--the extent of legal compliance with applicable laws and
regulations;

--the nature and extent of activities within programs,
including the accomplishment of, spending for, and costs of
such activities; and

--the financial viability of the federal government.

By providing this type of information in federal accounting and
financial reporting, management's performance and stewardship can
be evaluated objectively, and sound decisions can be made.

THE REPORTING ENTITY

The reporting entity is the organization, component of the
organization, or activity for which financial statements are
prepared. In its broadest sense, the accounting and reporting
entity is the entire federal government. Financial statements of
the federal government are to be prepared at least annually (at the
end of the fiscal year).

At a lower level, the reporting entity is a department (or its
constituent agencies) or an independent agency. Financial
statements are to be prepared at least annually in accordance with
the Financial Reporting standard, section F20, by each of these
reporting entities.

If consolidated financial statements are not prepared at the
departmental level, a department may use agency-level statements.
If a department prepares financial statements of its constituent
agencies, it shall also include a statement on department-level
organizations, such as the Office of the Secretary, Office of
Inspector General, and other units which would not be included in
individual agency-level statements. Footnotes shall be included as
part of the financial reports when the reporting entity may be
unclear to the reader.

ELEMENTS OF FEDERAL ACCOUNTING AND FINANCIAL REPORTING

Federal accounting and financial reporting focuses on various
elements, covering budget and accrual concepts: assets,
liabilities, equity, expenses and losses, financing sources, and
results of operations, as well as collections, budget authority,
obligations, outlays, and budgetary resources. These are defined
below.

Assets

An asset is any item of economic value owned by a governmental
unit. The item may be physical in nature (tangible) or a right to
ownership (intangible) that is expressed in terms of cost or some
other value.

An asset has three essential characteristics:

--It embodies a probable future benefit that involves a capacity, singly or in combination with other assets, to contribute to future operations of the government.

--The entity can obtain the benefit from it and control access to it.

--The transaction or other events giving the agency the right to or control of the asset has already occurred.

Assets benefit the entity when they can be exchanged for goods or services of value, used to provide services, or used to liquidate or reduce liabilities. The entity's future benefit from the asset can include relief from having to expend cash in the future.

Assets commonly have other identifying features. For example, assets may be acquired at a cost, and they may be tangible, exchangeable, or legally enforceable. Assets also may be acquired without cost, they may be intangible, and, although not exchangeable, they may be used in the entity's operations or for distributing other goods or services. Similarly, although the entity's ability to benefit from an asset and to control others' access to it generally rests on legal rights, legal claim to the benefit is not necessary before it qualifies as an asset if its receipt by the entity is otherwise probable.

Budget Authority

Budget authority is the authority provided by law to enter into obligations that will result in immediate or future outlays involving federal funds, but it does not include authority to insure or guarantee the repayment of indebtedness incurred by another person or government. The basic forms of budget authority are appropriations, authority to borrow, and contract authority.

Budget Resources

In addition to budget authority, budgetary resources include, in the case of reimbursable work, (1) the value of entitlement to reimbursement based on goods and services furnished and as authorized by law, (2) the amount of orders received within the government that represents valid obligations of the ordering account, to the extent that reimbursements therefore, will be placed in the correct account when collected, and (3) the amount of unfilled customers' orders from the public for which advance payment has been made.

Collections

Collections are amounts received by the federal government during the fiscal year. Collections are classified into two major categories: budget receipts and offsetting collections. Budget receipts are collections from the public (based on the government's exercise of its sovereign powers) and from payments by participants in certain voluntary federal social insurance programs. Offsetting collections are collections from government accounts or from transactions with the public that are of a business-type or market-oriented nature.

Government Equity

Equity is the difference between assets and liabilities of an agency and consists of five components: (1) invested capital, (2) cumulative results of operations, (3) unexpended appropriations, (4) trust fund balances, and (5) donations and other items. The

Equity of the U.S. Government standard, section E20, further
explains each of these components. For budgetary purposes equity
also includes an additional item, unfinanced budget authority,
including unfiled customer orders, contract authority, and
borrowing authority.

Expenses and Losses and Transfers Out

Expenses and losses are outflows of assets or incurrences of
liabilities (or a combination of both) during a period. These can
result from rendering services, delivering or producing goods, or
carrying out other activities. Expenses relate to normal operating
activities, while losses generally relate to all other transactions. The distinction between expenses and losses is a matter
of classification in the statement of operations; expenses are
commonly displayed at their gross amount, and losses are usually
shown net of related revenue. Transfers out are assignments of
appropriations or contributions of other assets to another agency.

Financing Sources

Financing sources and gains are actual inflows and/or other
enhancements of assets, or certain settlements of liabilities, or a
combination of both. Financing sources is a term used in
statements of operations to include expended appropriations and
revenues. Revenues differ from gains only in that revenues
generally result from normal operations, while gains usually result
from nonoperating activities. The only practical difference
between gains and revenues is their presentation in statements of
operations; revenues are commonly shown at their gross amount, and
gains are usually shown net of related expenses. (Income is a
generic term which encompasses financing sources and gains.)

Liabilities

Liabilities are amounts owed for items received, services
rendered, expenses incurred, assets acquired, construction
performed (regardless of whether invoices have been received), and
amounts received but as yet unearned. Included are amounts owed
for goods in the hands of prime contractors under the constructive
delivery concept and amounts owed under grants, pensions, awards,
and other indebtedness not involving the furnishing of goods and
services.

A liability has three essential characteristics:

--It embodies a present obligation to others which will be
  settled by the probable future transfer or use of assets at
  (1) a specified or determinable date, (2) at the time of a
  specific event, or (3) on demand.

--Because of equitable or legal responsibility, the government
  has little or no discretion to avoid future sacrifice.

--The transaction or other event that created the liability
  has already happened.

Although liabilities rest generally on legal rights and
duties, a legal claim is not a prerequisite for qualification as a
liability if future cash or other transfer of assets in settlement
is otherwise probable and estimable. The decision to record liabilities is not always affected by whether funds for payment have
been provided or authorized, i.e., unfunded liabilities.

Obligations

Obligations are amounts of orders placed, contracts awarded,
services received, and similar transactions for bona fide needs

existing during a given period that will require payments during
the same or a future period and that comply with applicable laws
and regulations. 'Such amounts will include outlays for which
obligations had not been previously recorded and will reflect
adjustments for differences between obligations previously recorded
and actual outlays to liquidate those obligations.

Outlays

Obligations are generally liquidated when checks are issued or
cash disbursed. Such payments are called outlays. In lieu of
issuing checks, obligations may also be liquidated (and outlays
occur) by the maturing of interest coupons, in the case of some
bonds, or by the issuance of bonds or notes (or increases in the
redemption value of bonds outstanding).

Results of Operations

Results of operations are the net difference between (1)
expenses and losses of an agency or activity, and (2) financing
sources and gains of an agency or activity (whether financed from
appropriations, transfers in, revenues, reimbursements, or any
combination of the four) for the operating period reported. The
results of operations are sometimes referred to as "net income"or
"net loss" in revolving funds or business-like activities.

USEFULNESS OF ACCOUNTING INFORMATION

The overall goal of accounting and financial reporting in the
federal government is to provide information that is useful.
Accounting information is useful when it is timely, relevant, reliable, cost beneficial, material, comparable, and consistent. These
qualitites are described as follows:

Timeliness refers to the prompt reporting of financial information to its users when it will be of maximum benefit. Financial data should be recorded as soon as practicable after
the occurrence of a transaction.

Relevance is "the capacity of information to make a difference
in a decision by helping users to form predictions about the
outcomes of past, present, and future events or to confirm or
correct prior expectations." [1]

Reliability is "the quality of information that assures that
information is reasonably free from error and bias and
faithfully represents what it purports to represent." [2]

Cost Benefit refers to measuring the expense of obtaining
certain information against the benefits to be derived by
having the information. Information should not be provided if
the costs of providing it exceed the benefits to be derived,
unless it is required to meet legal or other specified purposes.

Materiality refers to whether the information is significant
enough to make a difference to a reasonable person relying on
the information. A decision not to disclose information in
the financial statements may be made because the amounts
involved are too small to make a difference or to affect

---

[1] Statement of Accounting Concepts No. 2, Financial Accounting
Standards Board.

[2] Ibid.

the reliability of the information. In addition to magnitude, the nature of the item must be considered when making a materiality judgment. Any information which is material shall be reported in financial statements.

Comparability relates to the similarity and consistency of information produced by an entity from period to period and by others operating in similar circumstances. The value and usefulness of information depends greatly on the degree to which it is comparable to information from prior periods and to similar information reported by others.

Consistency pertains primarily to information produced by one accounting entity using essentially the same methods over periods of time.

RECOGNITION

Periodic recognition of the effects of transactions in financial statements is fundamental to the accounting process. Recognition governs when the results of an event are to be included in the financial statements and ensures that the effects of similar events and transactions are accounted for similarly within the federal government. The three principles that form the basis of the recognition requirements in the federal government accounting standards are accrual accounting, matching, and allocation.

Accrual Accounting

The standards contained in this title are based on accrual accounting as prescribed by 31 U.S.C. 3512(d) and allow obligation accounting where required for budgetary purposes. That law states that the head of each executive agency shall cause the accounts of that agency to be maintained on an accrual basis while providing for suitable integration of agency accounting with the central accounting and reporting responsibility of the Secretary of the Treasury. Thus, the accrual basis is the prescribed basis of accounting to be used by federal agencies. When the differences between the results of cash and accrual accounting are insignificant, the cash basis of accounting can be followed.

The accrual basis of accounting recognizes the significance and accountable aspects of financial transactions, events, or allocations as they occur. Generally, accrual accounting can contribute materially to effective financial control over resources and costs of operations and is essential to develop adequate cost information. The reporting standards contained herein focus on accrual accounting. However, these standards also require complete financial information, including budgetary information to be captured and maintained in agency accounts.

Matching

In the typical appropriated fund activity, matching involves identifying and recording costs in the proper period, i.e., the period in which the cost is incurred rather than the period in which the disbursement is made. For commercial-type activities, matching is the simultaneous recognition of the revenues and expenses that result directly and jointly from the same transactions or other events.

Allocation

Allocation is a concept of distributing an amount between periods (interperiod) or to different elements within a period (intraperiod). Interperiod allocation is necessary because many assets yield their benefits to an entity over several periods. A common example of allocation is spreading the cost of a building or equipment to two or more accounting periods by depreciating it.

MEASUREMENT

Measurement principles are the bases for assigning numeric values to the elements of financial reports. The data reported in the financial statements required by these standards should be based on historical costs to maintain dollar compatibility with budget authority. Historical data are measured in terms of money agreed upon in transactions to which the entity was a party when the transactions first occurred. Thus, they are comparable to the dollar authorizations and limitations initially granted through budget authority. Therefore, financial reports must be based on historical costs.

COST

The standards contained in this statement are also based on the concept of cost. The term cost refers to the financial measurement of resources used in accomplishing a specified purpose, such as performing a service, carrying out an activity, acquiring an asset, or completing a unit of work or a specific project.

Reporting significant cost, obligation, and outlay information that is derived from an effective accounting system facilitates effective financial management. Such information must be available to agency management officials, the Office of Management and Budget (OMB), and the Congress for devising and approving realistic future financial plans (budgeting). It is needed in making meaningful comparisons and in keeping spending within limits established by law, regulation, or agency management policies. Finally, this information provides several common financial denominators for measuring and evaluating efficiency and economy in terms of the resources used in the various activities.

Accounting for activities on a cost basis means that all significant elements should be included in the amounts reported as total cost. Cost, in this context, is the value of goods and services used by a government agency within a given period, regardless of when they were ordered, received, or paid for. For example, cost may be the value of resources put into or removed from inventory. It may be the amount of depreciation or

amortization on an asset. It may be the amount of contractor or grantee performance under a contract or grant (accrued expenditure). It may be fully allocated or direct. Such factors as (a) differences in methods of financing the resources used, (b) prescribed requirements for reimbursement or setting prices for sales of goods or services, and (c) administrative policies relating to budgeting, accounting, and management reporting are not valid bases for excluding items of cost from agency financial reports.

In any given year, the obligations incurred may be less, equal to, or greater than the costs recognized for that period. The differences, which must be precisely tracked in the agency accounting system, are due to such things as increases or decreases in inventories, undelivered orders, depreciation, amortization, or other changes in certain resources. The difference in concept lies in the distribution of these different measures (costs and obligations) over a period of time. The following chart, using the purchases of inventory materials, illustrates these timing differences. These stages can occur in a different sequence; however, this example is typical.

FINANCIAL REPORTING

INTRODUCTION

.01 This standard prescribes the financial reporting standards for
agencies to follow.

ACCOUNTING STANDARD

Required Reports

.02 Financial statements are to be prepared and issued in
accordance with these standards to the Department of the Treasury
at the end of each fiscal year by each department or independent
agency. These statements shall be the culmination of the entity's
systematic accounting process. A full set of financial statements
of constituent agencies of a department shall be submitted when a
department does not prepare departmentwide consolidated financial
statements. When this occurs, the department must also provide a
full set of financial statements of department-level units which
are not a part of an individual agency, such as the Office of the
Secretary and the Office of Inspector General, and other units
which would not be included in individual agency-level statements.
The necessary financial statements are as follows:

    (1) Statement of Financial Position (Balance Sheet),
    (2) Statement of Operations,
    (3) Statement of Changes in Financial Position, and
    (4) Statement of Reconciliation to Budget Reports.

.03 The above financial statements shall result from an accounting
and budgeting system that is an integral part of its total
financial management system and one that contains sufficient
discipline, effective internal controls, and reliable data. The
financial statements and underlying financial system shall report
on the total operations of the reporting entity and shall comply
with the Comptroller General's principles, standards, and related
requirements. When comprehensive financial statements are prepared
by a reporting entity within a constituent agency of a department,
those financial statements shall also comply with the Comptroller
General's principles, standards, and related requirements.

Statement of Financial Position (Balance Sheet)

.04 All departments and independent agencies shall prepare a
Statement of Financial Position. Such a statement, including
footnotes thereto, shall disclose the bases on which major
categories of assets are accounted for and reported, the nature of
any significant restrictions on the use of assets, the amount and
nature of significant contingent liabilities, and such explanatory
information on the assets, liabilities, and equity as is necessary
to fully and clearly disclose the financial position of the
agency. Other standards in this document contain specific
requirements for various asset, liability, and equity accounts.

Statement of Operations

.05 Departments and independent agencies shall prepare a Statement
of Operations reporting expenses, losses, transfers out, and
financing sources (i.e., appropriations and revenues) and gains.
Other standards in this document discuss specific transactions that
flow through the Statement of Operations.

Statement of Changes in Financial Position

.06 A Statement of Changes in Financial Position shall be a part
of the financial statements. This statement shall show the changes
on a cash basis and shall present all significant sources and uses
of resources. Related sources and uses shall not be netted.

.07 The statement shall begin with the results of operations
before unusual and infrequent items, and add back (or deduct) items
recognized in determining operating results that did not use or
provide resources (depreciations, amortization on intangible
assets, etc.). The statement shall also include all significant
changes in the elements of financial position.

.08 Unusual and/or infrequent items affecting operations or
changes in elements of financial position shall be reported
separately.

.09 The totals of sources and uses of resources shall be shown
with the net change in "Funds with the U.S. Treasury and Cash" from
the beginning of the period to the end of the period.

Statement of Reconciliation to Budget Reports

.10 Department and independent agencies shall prepare a Statement
of Reconciliation to Budget Reports to ensure that the financial
information presented in the financial statements is consistent
with similar amounts presented in budget reports. This statement
shall reconcile the information presented in financial statements
to that reported in its Year-End Closing Statements (TFS Form
2108). Material items of reconciliation shall be disclosed in
either the financial statements or notes thereto.

Footnote Disclosures

.11 A description of all significant accounting policies of a
reporting entity shall be included in the footnotes of the financial statements as the Summary of Significant Accounting Policies.
Examples of accounting policies to be disclosed in this footnote
are recognition of revenue and other financing sources, depreciation methods, and related-party transactions.

.12 Significant transactions between federal entities that
materially impact the information presented in financial statements
shall be separately disclosed. Such disclosures will enable users
of the financial statements to assess the impact of related party
transactions on agency operations and compare the results obtained
to what would have resulted if the transactions had been conducted
as arm's-length transactions between unrelated parties. Disclosures about material related party transactions in the statements
or footnotes shall include the following:

  (a) the nature of the relationship(s) involved,

  (b) a general description of the transactions, including
       significant transactions to which no dollar amounts or
       nominal dollar amounts were ascribed and any other
       information necessary to understand the effects of the
       transactions on the financial statements,

  (c) the dollar amounts of transactions,

  (d) the effects of any changes in the terms of the related
       party transactions from those in the preceding year, and

  (e) amounts due from or to related parties and the terms and
       manner of settlement, if not otherwise apparent.

.13 All significant changes in their equity accounts during the period for which the Statement of Operations is prepared shall be disclosed in the footnotes to the financial statements.

.14 Additionally, the following standards contained in this appendix also discuss disclosures to be made in footnotes to the financial statements.

--Advances and Prepayments, section A30, paragraphs .05 and .06.

--Capitalization of Interest, section C10, paragraph .08.

--Comparative Financial Statements, section C20, paragraphs .03 and .04.

--Consolidated Financial Statements of the U.S. Government, section C40, paragraphs .04 and .09.

--Contingencies, section C50, paragraphs .03 and .06 through .11.

--Debt Agreement Modification, section D10, paragraph .13.

--Depreciation and Amortization, section D20, paragraph .09.

--Equity of the U.S. Government, section E20, paragraph .05.

--Foreign Currency, section F30, paragraphs .07 and .09.

--Fund Control, section F50, paragraph .09.

--Funds With the Treasury and Cash, section F60, paragraphs .06. and .07.

--Grants and Cooperative Agreements, section G10, paragraph .07.

--Inventory, section I30, paragraphs .05, .07, and .08.

--Investment, section I40, paragraph .06.

--Leases, section L10, paragraphs .09 through .12.

--Liabilities Based on Actuarial Calculations, section L20, paragraphs .16 and .18.

--Loan Guarantees and Commitments, section L30, paragraphs .03 and .04.

--Payroll, section P10, paragraph .02.

--Pensions, section P20, paragraph .03.

--Prior-Period Adjustments of Financial Statements, section P30, paragraphs .06, .07, and .09.

--Property, Plant, and Equipment, section P40, paragraphs .19 and .21.

--Receivables, section R10, paragraphs .04, .05, .06, .07, .08, and .11

--Unusual and Infrequent Items: Statement of Operations, section U10, paragraphs .02 and .04.

Presentation of Statements

.15 The above statements are to be prepared on a consolidated
basis, reflecting all activities at each federal department or
independent agency. In addition, each agency having more than one
significant fund type (e.g., general fund, special fund, revolving
fund, etc.) shall prepare financial statements reflecting the
activities for each major fund type. If an agency has numerous
funds, it shall group related or similar funds into the major fund
types. Information by individual fund within fund types, however,
may be necessary for complete disclosure.

.16 The financial statements of each department or independent
agency shall include all funds and appropriations for which the
agency is responsible, as well as all funds and appropriations
transferred in from another department or independent agency.
Appropriations for reimbursements or transfers to other federal
departments or independent agencies shall include the offsetting
expenses or transfers out in financial statements. Reimbursements
or transfers from other federal departments or independent agencies
shall be included with appropriations in the financial statements,
and the reimbursement shall be recorded to offset expenses
incurred. Transfers of organizational units between departments or
independent agencies shall be reflected as transferred in the year
in which the transfer takes place for budget purposes.

.17 In the preparation of consolidated statements, all intra-
department or intra-agency balances for independent agencies and
transactions, such as receivables, payables, sales, purchases,
reimbursements, and transfers, and material intra-departmental and
(for independent agencies) intra-agency profits or losses remaining
in assets (such as inventory, fixed assets, etc.) that were transferred between revolving funds and other components shall be eliminated in consolidation. Appropriate accounting records must be
maintained to determine these eliminations. The eliminations are
made to avoid duplication when adding such items. Such eliminations neither carry nor imply legal status.

.18 Financial information for federal retirement plans shall be
included in the financial statements of the administering department or independent agency in accordance with this standard even
though a different reporting format may be used by the plans to
meet other reporting requirements. (See the Pensions standard,
section P20.) The differences in the required reports reflect
differences in format but not in accounting theory.

FUND ACCOUNTING

INTRODUCTION

.01 Fund accounting is a fundamental requirement for federal
agencies to demonstrate compliance with legislation. This standard
contains the fund accounting requirements that agencies must
follow.

ACCOUNTING STANDARD

.02 Agencies shall establish the following two fund types as required by their operations and in accordance with those funds
established by the Treasury: (1) funds derived from general taxation and revenue powers and from business operations and (2) funds
held by the government in the capacity of custodian or trustee.

.03 Funds derived from general taxation and revenue powers and
from business operations include the following:

--<u>General fund accounts</u>. These consist of (1) receipt
accounts used to account for collections not dedi-
cated to specific purposes and (2) expenditure accounts used to record financial transactions arising
under congressional appropriations or other authorizations to spend general revenues.

--<u>Special fund accounts</u>. These consist of separate receipt and expenditure accounts established to account
for receipts of the government that are ear-marked by
law for a specific purpose but are not generated by a
cycle of operations for which there is continuing
authority to reuse such receipts.

--<u>Revolving fund accounts</u>. These are combined receipt
and expenditure accounts established by law to finance a continuing cycle of operations, with receipts
derived from such operations usually available in
their entirety for use by the fund without further
action by the Congress. Consolidated working funds
under 31 U.S.C. 1536 are not revolving funds. See
title 7, subsections 3.8 and 5.6, of the <u>General Accounting Office Policy and Procedures Manual for
Guidance of Federal Agencies</u>.

--<u>Management fund accounts</u>. These are combined receipt
and expenditure accounts established by law to facilitate accounting for and administration of intragovernmental operations of an agency. Working funds,
which are a type of management fund, may be established in connection with each of the foregoing account types to account for advances from other
agencies.

.04 Funds held by the government in the capacity of custodian or
trustee include the following:

--<u>Trust fund accounts</u>. These are accounts established
to account for receipts that are held in trust for
use in carrying out specific purposes and programs
in accordance with an agreement or statute. The
assets of trust funds are frequently held over a
period of time and may involve such transactions as
investments in revenue-producing assets and the
collection of revenue therefrom. Generally, trust
fund accounts consist of separate receipt and expenditure accounts, but when the trust corpus is dedica-
ted to a business-like operation, the fund entity is
called a trust-revolving fund, and a combined receipt
and expenditure account is used.

--<u>Deposit fund accounts</u>. These are expenditure
accounts established to account for receipts (1)
held in suspense temporarily and later refunded or
paid into some other fund of the government or
other entity or (2) held by the government as
banker or agent for others and paid out at the
direction of the owner. Such funds are not
available for paying salaries, grants, or other
expenses of the government. Expenditures are
often offset by receipts within this fund.

.05 Agencies shall establish, for each reporting entity, general
ledger accounts for all

--assets,
--liabilities,

--equity of the U.S. government,
--expenses, losses, and transfers out, and
--financing sources and gains.

Agencies shall also establish budgetary general ledger accounts for
each appropriation fund account for selected assets, liabilities,
and equities.

.06 For financial statements, agencies shall report information
from their fund accounts established as required above in accordance with the Financial Reporting standard, section F20, paragraphs
.05 through .10. In addition, agencies shall report information
from their fund accounts as required by the Treasury and OMB.
Differences between an agency's financial statements and budgetary
reports shall be explained in the Statement of Reconciliation to
Budget Reports as required by the Financial Reporting standard,
section F20.

FUND CONTROL

INTRODUCTION

.01 The term "fund control" refers to control over use and
management of fund appropriations to ensure that (1) funds are used
only for authorized purposes, (2) they are economically and
efficiently used, (3) obligations and expenditures do not exceed
the amounts authorized and available, and (4) the obligation or
disbursement of funds is not reserved or otherwise withheld without
congressional knowledge and approval. Each accounting system shall
incorporate appropriate techniques to assist in achieving fund
control objectives.

ACCOUNTING STANDARD

.02 Every agency is required by 31 U.S.C. 1514 to have a system of
administrative control of funds, approved by the President, that
will restrict obligations or expenditures to the amounts
appropriated to applicable fund balances and to the amounts of
apportionments or reapportionments made for the current fiscal
period. Reserves established by the Director of OMB or other
authorized officials are also to be controlled. In addition, the
system of administrative control of funds must fix responsibility
for the creation of any obligation, the making of any expenditure,
or the making of any disbursement in excess of an apportionment,
reapportionment, or other subdivision of authority. The requirements for these systems are prescribed by OMB in its Circular A-34,
and the related guidelines.

.03 Agency systems must also control funds in accordance with 2
U.S.C. 681, et seq., which prescribes limitations on the establishment of reserves or other withholdings (title 7, section 23.4) of
budget authority. Restraints on obligations or expenditures must
be reported by the President to the Congress as proposed
rescissions or deferrals. The Comptroller General is required
under 2 U.S.C. 685 and 686 to report to the Congress on proposed
rescissions or deferrals of budget authority, including those
reported by the President and those which should have been but were
not reported by the President.

.04 To control funds adequately, there must be an effective veri-
fication of available funds (positive knowledge) before creating an
obligation, and obligation information must be accumulated and
reported promptly and accurately. Specific criteria governing the
recording and reporting of financial transactions as obligations
are prescribed in 31 U.S.C. 1501. (See also title 7, section 16.5
of this manual.) That law provides that no amount shall be

recorded as an obligation unless it meets the specified criteria
and that statements of obligations furnished to the Congress or to
any of its committees shall include only amounts representing valid
obligations, as so defined.

.05 For purposes of effective financial planning, including fund
management, data on proposed expenditures must be systematically
accumulated in accounting records in advance of becoming valid obligations, but only valid obligations as defined by law or regulation (and disbursements, in the case of advances and prepayments)
are to be reported as obligations incurred.

.06 Agency accounting procedures shall provide for appropriate
recognition of apportionments made pursuant to law and for divisions of fund authorizations made to facilitate their management
and compliance with applicable limitations. In accordance with 31
U.S.C. 1514(b), divisions of fund authorizations for budgetary
control purposes shall be established at the highest practical
level, consistent with assignments of responsibility, and shall be
limited to those essential for effective control. For example, a
single allotment of funds to the head of an agency within the
amounts apportioned for each appropriation or fund affecting such
agency can usually provide an appropriate basis for fund control
without making further subdivisions by object classes of
expenditure or other categories.

.07 The accounting system must effectively provide for compliance
with dollar limitations imposed by law within the scope of an
appropriation. Such limitations ordinarily require the use of
separate allotments or agency limitations.

Relation of Fund Control to
Financial Reporting

.08 As discussed above, administrative control of funds is required by law. The status of funds and related transactions must
be reported to the Department of the Treasury and OMB in accordance
with laws and regulations, and as required by these standards. For
further details on the requirements of these standards, see the Financial Reporting standard, section F20 (paragraph .10) and the
Reporting Appropriations in the Statements of Financial Position,
Operation, and Changes in Financial Position standard, section R30.

.09 In addition, any violations of appropriations or other fund
limitations shall be disclosed in the notes to the financial statements required by these standards. Any major restrictions or limitations on the use of funds (such as limitations on amounts which
can be spent for certain types of expenditures, e.g., travel) contained in the appropriation acts shall also be disclosed, as well
as any violations of such restrictions.

INDEX

Nonfund assets *cont.*
87; disposition of, 84; General
Fund and, 84; list of, 86; management standards, 85; origin of, 85,
152; supplementary cost accounts
and, 152. *See also* Equipment; Materials and supplies
Nonfund entities, 83, 102, 103
Nonfund liabilities (Public Debt):
accountability for, 90, 91, 92, 93;
balance sheet for, 92; General
Fund and, 84, 94; origin of, 84;
redemption of, 84, 93, 96; refunding, 84, 87, 93, 96
Nonrevenue receipts, 71
No-year (multi-year) appropriation,
74

Obligation(s): authority, basis of, 75,
78, 116, 133; incurred with appropriations, 136, 137; ledger, 161,
176, 177
Off-budget items, 23–24, 50–52
Office of Management and Budget
(OMB): budgetary controls, 10, 59,
126, 127, 129; functions of, 10, 11,
12; reports, 129
Operating federal deficit, planned,
26, 37
Operating expenses, agency: allocation of, 81; as cost of performance,
145; measurement of, 143; by program, 139; by program and object,
73, 183
Operating statement, agency: depreciation provision and, 144;
multi-concept statement, model of,
138, 140–143. *See also* Agency financial statements
Outstanding contracts and orders:
changes in, 131, 136, 150, 182; in
statement of financial position,
77, 104, 148, 184
Overappropriated condition of the
General Fund, 79–80
Overobligation: and Anti-deficiency
Act, 34; condition of a fund, 134;
preventing, 114

Overseas operations, financing of,
58, 59

Paper money, 17, 59, 106
Pay as you go concept for federal
pension plans, 100
Payroll taxes, 24, 100
Percentage of contract completion
method, 54
Permanent appropriation, 124, 127
Permanently unbalanced federal
budget, proposal for, 24
Perpetuity of federal debt, concept
of, 28
Physical facilities, nonfund, 85, 155
Postal Service Fund, 52
President's budget, 10, 22, 43
President's Task Force on Joint Eco-
nomic Outlook, 123
Pricing system, for internal agency
transactions, 117
Private sector, and the government,
26, 28, 37, 44, 100
Procurement contracts, 12, 164
Program(s), 111; accounts, 161; al-
lotment for, 114; apportionment
for, 113; appropriation for, 112;
authorization of, 112; budgeting
for, 111, 122, 123; justification of,
7, 10, 112, 122; preserving identi-
ty of, 145; reach of, 3
Progress payments on contracted
work, 155
Property taxes, 24
Proprietary receipts, 47
Public enterprise revolving funds,
35, 47, 50

Quarterly financial statements,
agency, 130, 131, 139, 148

Receipts, 25, 46, 53
Recession: federal budget and, 24;
federal intervention and, 37
Reimbursement(s): definition of, 67;
obligational authority and, 78,
131, 134, 182; principle of, 134,
148, 166; transactions entries, 135

About the Authors

JOSEPH F. MORAGLIO, CPA, is Director of the Federal Government Division of the American Institute of Certified Public Accountants (AICPA), the division responsible for serving as a liaison between the accounting profession and governmental bodies. Before joining AICPA, Mr. Moraglio was a self-employed management consultant and also worked for Peat, Marwick, Mitchell & Co. as a senior auditor and staff consultant. He has taught accounting and auditing part-time at American University; has co-authored two articles published in the *Journal of Accountancy;* and frequently speaks at accounting seminars.

HARRY D. KERRIGAN is currently a member of the management and accounting faculty of San Diego State University. He has had extensive tours of duty as a professor in a number of universities, including the University of Connecticut, Northwestern University, and Columbia University, and as a consultant, Office of the Deputy Comptroller, Department of Defense. He is author or co-author of six published books, including the pioneering work, *Fund Accounting,* and has contributed numerous articles to well-known periodicals.